EDINBURGH'S CONTRIBUTION TO MEDICAL MICROBIOLOGY

Charles J. Smith

Edited by J.G. Collee

With contributions from
Professor Sir John Crofton
Professor J.P. Duguid
Dr J.C. Gould
Dr J.M. Inglis
Dr L. J.R. Milne
Dr K.C. Watson

Wellcome Unit for the History of Medicine
University of Glasgow

Charles John Smith F.I.M.L.S. was formerly Senior Chief Medical Laboratory Scientific Officer in the Department of Bacteriology at Edinburgh University Medical School. He is the author of several books on the history of South Edinburgh, and he is locally well known as a lecturer on historical aspects of the city.

J. Gerald Collee C.B.E., M.D., F.R.C.Path., F.R.C.P.(Edin.), F.R.S.E. was formerly Professor and Head of the Department of Bacteriology (subsequently Medical Microbiology) at Edinburgh University Medical School, and Chief Bacteriologist to the Royal Infirmary, Edinburgh.

This publication has been made possible by the financial support of the following bodies to whom we wish to record our thanks:

The Wellcome Trust

Mackay and Lynn, Edinburgh

Sterilin Ltd, Middlesex

Department of Medical Microbiology,
University of Edinburgh

Margaret Ross Fund,
Faculty of Medicine,
University of Edinburgh

Lothian Health Board

The Carnegie Trust for the Universities of Scotland

Scottish Society for the History of Medicine

Published by the Wellcome Unit for the History of Medicine
5 University Gardens
University of Glasgow
Glasgow, G12 8QQ

Printed by Alna Limited, Broxburn, West Lothian

ISBN 0 9511765 6 0

CONTENTS

ILLUSTRATIONS

Portaits to accompany the entries in the biographical section (Appendix D2) are ordered alphabetically and grouped together following page 282.

Other figures and tables are interspersed throughout the volume. They are referred to by superscript numbers in the text and will be found on pages adjacent to the relevant number.

FOREWORD

by Professor J.G. Collee

Charles J. Smith, our departmental archivist, undertook the huge task of researching and creating this historical account. He brings to it all the affection and commitment to the Department that were so typical of his years of service here. When he retired from the Department in 1982 he was already developing his skill as a historical commentator and he went on to make his mark as a recorder. Author of the successful *Historic South Edinburgh* books (Smith 1978, 1979, 1986, 1988), he has been hailed as a natural and gifted observer of so much that would otherwise drift from our own observation and memory. In *South Edinburgh in Pictures* (Smith 1989), he "traces the story of the places and the people" . . . and he prompts "questions about a way of life which has passed forever but a short time ago".

It is typical of Charles that he has made no mention of his extracurricular talents and activities in the manuscript of our text, but the omission must be corrected. He is much sought after as a lecturer in Edinburgh, and his genius for unearthing detail and interesting anecdotes on historical associations is widely acknowledged. A very practical churchman, an introspective and caring person, he nurtured and helped very many of our junior technical staff through the difficulties of their early training years. And he gradually and inexorably emerged as a raconteur who loved the people around him as he warmed to the characters in his stories. He flourished as an extraordinary conversationalist – in the staffroom, at social occasions, at street corners and even in the middle of pedestrian crossings. In all of this, he was noting and recording impressions, as our departmental archives now show.

These several years, he has been carrying sections of the manuscript of this work across Edinburgh in all sorts of weather; I see him slightly stooped into the wind, clutching a large collection of papers and a bulging briefcase. The whole seems to merge amorphously into his thick baggy coat, a muffler, and a nonchalant hairstyle. The glasses glint and the cheery greeting is there, with all the enthusiasm of a school pal on the terracing at Easter Road. "Nice to see you. This won't take a moment. Did you know that Dr Isabella Purdie at Bangour knew Miss Jean Brodie . . . ?" I listen intently to the unfolding tale. Charles is the Ancient Mariner. He develops the theme with wonderful associations of ideas, a flowing motility, and some dreadful puns in which he finds a puckish delight.

In more serious vein, I must pay tribute to the industry and dedication that Charles has brought to this task. He has taken great care to find and to check his facts. His meticulous acknowledgements of help from so many quarters will give the reader some insight into the breadth and depth of the assignment that he undertook on our behalf. He has worked tirelessly and most unselfishly and always with courtesy and consideration. A note on the professional (bacteriological) contributions of CJS appears elsewhere in these records. Let us here applaud his skill in developing this archive for us, and in turn record our great debt and our gratitude to a remarkable colleague.

J.G.C.
November 1993.

PREFACE AND ACKNOWLEDGEMENTS

This account of the beginnings and development of bacteriology (now known as medical microbiology) in Edinburgh originated in an illustrated talk I gave to the University Department of Medical Microbiology staff in 1982. The presentation was confined primarily to a short historical account of the University department as such, with rather brief reference to other (then) bacteriology laboratories in Edinburgh, and this mainly as regards the relationship of these to the University department. It was suggested by a number of staff members who attended the talk, especially those who had joined the department some time ago and who personally recalled much of what was described, but also by people from other city laboratories, that what I had presented should be "written up" and possibly published. When, after my retiral in August 1982, Professor J.G. Collee, Head of the University department, honoured me with the appointment of departmental archivist, this was an added incentive to carry out further research and attempt to produce a publication.

A history of bacteriology, or medical microbiology, in Edinburgh can be presented in various ways. It could consist of the bacteriological work as carried out in chronological order by successive workers in teaching, research or diagnostic methods in the city's several laboratories, as the subject developed from the pioneering efforts of Lister and Watson Cheyne in the old Royal Infirmary in 1876 to the most advanced work of the present day. This would mean collating summaries of published papers from a cumulative index. It would be a complex task with the anxiety of ensuring that all significant developments were known and recorded. In this approach, the people involved would be secondary to the work itself. Another alternative would be to deal primarily with the people concerned, their background, their achievements. Yet again, one could concentrate on the opening of the various laboratories. Finally, there could be a combination of all of the above aspects. This is what has been attempted here and it is hoped that it is an acceptable and balanced survey.

As I proceeded it seemed that, while the original intention was to present a historical account principally of the University department, the significant importance of the latter's establishment and development would best be understood and appreciated in the wider context. Thus, I have made frequent reference to the general state of the "public health" in the city in the late nineteenth century and the earliest attempts to apply the historic discoveries of the pioneer bacteriologists Pasteur, Koch and Ehrlich to the understanding, laboratory diagnosis, prevention and treatment of infectious diseases, many of which were endemic and of high incidence. I fear that in undertaking this wide-ranging study, I was eventually to present Professor Collee with a much longer and more complex script than he had bargained for and that I set him a considerable task for his editorial pen. Nevertheless I do hope that these annals may be more interesting on the wider canvas and that our readers can accept that this perspective has been essential.

I am indebted to so many people for their ready and patient assistance that the problem in expressing my deep appreciation is to avoid a long litany of formal acknowledgements. At the outset I have to thank most sincerely Professor J.G. Collee. Before his retiral from the Robert Irvine Chair of Bacteriology in the University, and indeed after doing so, he has shown constant interest and encouragement. After having laid down the burden of departmental responsibility and before taking up his own many personal interests, he has completed the task of editing and shaping a rather large and ungainly manuscript into a relevant and readable account. This is a further measure, if one were required, of his long-standing dedication and affection for the University department and for medical microbiology to which he has contributed so substantially and significantly. I am grateful for the kind words in his Foreword, and I suppose I must just settle for the image he presents!

From the earliest preparation of the manuscript, with much information to be gathered, untangled and more clearly expressed, I had the invaluable guidance and assistance of my former colleague and successor in the Department, Bill Marr. For his attention to many enquiries and great patience, I am very grateful. Likewise, Norma Marr exercised ungrudging patience as she typed several successive and yet further revised versions of the manuscript. From the initial stages, I was greatly assisted by Professor J.P. Duguid, former member of staff of the University department, who read the entire manuscript, providing additional information which I could not trace and suggesting corrections and alterations, much of this drawn from his relatively early and long service in the University department. Many of the brief biographies could not have been completed without his personal recollections and notes on former staff. His various notes of historic interest are also greatly appreciated.

Professor Sydney Selwyn of the Chair of Medical Microbiology at Charing Cross and Westminster Medical School, and a former member of the University departmental staff, kindly drew my attention in the early stages of my researches to the pioneers in the study of hospital cross-infection in Scotland. He called my attention to papers on matters of hygiene, disinfection and epidemiology, all based on a vague and evolving awareness of the "germ theory" of disease by pioneers from the early eighteenth century onwards until the discoveries of Pasteur and others vindicated their efforts, and the first bacteriology proper carried out by Lister and Watson Cheyne in Edinburgh.

Of the present University departmental staff, Professor Donald Weir expressed much interest and encouragement and Dr Isabel Smith provided helpful guidance in my necessarily brief and sporadic references to the early days of the Virology laboratory. Dr Andrew Fraser drew my attention to several passages in my manuscript that required correction and further research and Dr Hugh Young assisted me on historical aspects of his own special field, sexually transmitted diseases. Mrs Joan Collins, Professor Collee's secretary, was of much assistance, not least in making access possible to her extremely busy boss.

Outwith the Department, I received invaluable assistance from my former senior colleague, the late Robert K. Farmer, in his provision of information; his long service in the Department enabled him to draw upon recollections of people and the development of the University department as regards early premises, the training of technical staff and many other aspects. The late Duncan B. Colquhoun, one of the department's earliest "lab. boys", who had produced written historical notes and taped these, was a most valuable source of information. I am particularly grateful to Dr Alison Ritchie and Dr Joan Mackie for kindly supplying notes, information and photographs of their fathers, successive holders of the University Chair.

In presenting something of the annals of the other Edinburgh bacteriological and microbiological laboratories, I have to record my sincere appreciation to very many people who assisted me with basic data or an elusive name or date. Space prevents my doing more than simply recording names, but this is no mere formal acknowledgement. I do so in the chronological order of the establishment of the various laboratories.

While the Royal College of Physicians' Laboratory (1887) was opened "long before his time", nevertheless Stanley Hay, for long the senior pathology technician there, was able to provide helpful information; so too did Mrs J. Ferguson, whose late husband John was one of the earliest bacteriology technicians. Dr Una McLean and Mrs Elizabeth Angell of the University Department of Community Medicine, formerly the Usher Institute of Public Health, assisted me in tracing the early bacteriologists in the Institute's laboratory (1902); and Mrs Evelyn McGuigan, daughter of well-known senior technician, Henry Bott, at the Usher, was very helpful. Although the City Hospital laboratory (1903) was opened considerably before their time, I was able to trace early information through the kind assistance of the late Dr Archie Wallace and Bill Webber, whose knowledge and experience of the beginnings of the more modern laboratory were invaluable. Dr Margaret Calder, Miss Edith Wallace and Mike Croughan kept me right as regards more recent times.

As regards the Royal Infirmary Bacteriology Department (1914) I have to express my sincere thanks to Dr Tom Durie, James Robertson, Ian Samuel and Gerald McInnes for their considerable assistance in constructing an account of their very important laboratory. While it would appear that some bacteriological work was carried out in the Royal Hospital for Sick Children as early as 1909, the subsequent more systematic laboratory work began with Dr Agnes McGregor in 1922. In piecing together the RHSC laboratory annals, I am indebted to Allan Smith of the University Pathology department for kindly supplying information about his father James, the technician who first worked with Dr McGregor. John Dow, who succeeded James Smith and gave many years of service to the laboratory, also helped me.

The Astley Ainslie Hospital laboratory (1931), established by Lt. Colonel John Cunningham, was, in the years before its incorporation in the Central Microbiology Laboratories, under the charge of the late Dr Pat Edmunds and John Ferguson. I am much indebted to Mrs Edmunds and Mrs Ferguson for kind assistance. An important development in the city in relatively recent times was the establishment of the Central Microbiological Laboratories at the Western General Hospital in 1961. I am grateful to the CML's former Director, Dr J.C. Gould, for kindly contributing the historical note on this laboratory and for much other assistance. In tracing the laboratory opened a few years previously at the Northern General Hospital and then recording the transfer of its work and staff to the CML, I am greatly obliged to Miss Sarah McFadyen and Miss Sheila Holgate. Mrs E.J. Boyle, Dr Gould's secretary at the laboratories and still in post, was a constant source of information. Eric Kerr, the former Senior Chief MLSO at the CML, was also of much assistance. For a valuable supplementation of the necessarily brief historical accounts of various other Edinburgh laboratories, I am most grateful for the papers contributed by Professor Sir John Crofton, Dr K.C. Watson and Dr J.M. Inglis.

The sources of information essential in compiling this historical account were almost innumerable and highly varied. The late Dr J.D. Allan Gray, an early member of the University department staff who served under Professor T.J. Mackie, was one of the first to whom I turned and who gave generously of his time and factual assistance. James Waugh, former Principal MLSO in the University Pathology department, responded most helpfully to my many enquiries as regards the period and people involved when his department "gave birth" to the original Bacteriology Department and the early days of bacteriology in the Royal Infirmary. John MacPherson, former University Assistant Secretary, kindly dealt with many enquiries drawing upon his own personal experience and close association with the University department. Noel Anderson, former University Building Officer, kept me right as regards the development of premises. Dr Andrew Doig, an authority on the history of medicine in Edinburgh, kindly answered many queries. The late Dr Haldane P. Tait, former Principal Medical Officer, Edinburgh Child Health Service, generously and personally put his unrivalled knowledge and experience in the development of the city's Public Health Department and various hospitals at my disposal. His book, cited in the bibliography, is an invaluable record. Mrs H.P. Tait also gave valuable assistance. Miss Sheila D. Fletcher, former secretary to the late Charles Stewart, Edinburgh University Secretary, solved an important photographic captioning problem.

In constructing any piece of medical history, libraries and the professional guidance of their staff are essential. Thus I must record sincere appreciation to Miss Joan Ferguson, Librarian to the Royal College of Physicians, Edinburgh, who was of very considerable and patient assistance. Miss Alison Stevenson of the Royal College of Surgeons library was most helpful in my research on the early Lister-Watson Cheyne bacteriological work "in a little passage behind the operating theatre in the Old Edinburgh Infirmary". In the University Library, Mrs Jo Currie of the Special Collections section and Dr Mike Barfoot, Archivist of the Medical Archive Centre, kindly answered my many queries. The use of data from the Edinburgh Room, Edinburgh City Public Library at George IV Bridge, is gratefully acknowledged. The very many photographs published were professionally processed by Dave Dirom of the University's Medical Illustration Department. I am most grateful to him and the department's receptionist, Sandra Conner; and we thank Ian Lennox for his help with the cover design. The photograph of Joan MacDonald with her father Ramsay MacDonald (Appendix D5) is reproduced by permission of the Hulton Deutsch Collection.

I have to record my thanks to Dr Malcolm Nicolson and the staff of the Wellcome Unit for the History of Medicine, University of Glasgow, who have provided splendid support and made the production of this book possible. And I am indebted to Mr Bert Brown and his colleagues of Alna Limited for their patience and their technical skill.

Finally, and not simply last at the end of a long list of acknowledgements but rather to draw special attention, I am deeply appreciative of the very great and indispensable assistance and co-operation of past members of staff in the various departments and laboratories; the wives and other relatives of late members of staff who so kindly sent me *curricula vitae* and photographs and who answered my telephone enquiries. This aspect of my researches has given the account a valued human dimension. I have been privileged to record the contributions, distinguished or humble, of those who have played their part in the foundation and development of medical microbiology in Edinburgh. To them, my many colleagues and friends, I present these annals by way of tribute to their labours.

Charles J. Smith
November 1993.

CHAPTER ONE

EARLY HISTORY
(including Pre-Microbiology)

W ho was the first to practise bacteriology in Edinburgh? Where was the first such laboratory? A preliminary considered study of the most readily available published records suggests that Joseph Lister qualifies for this historic distinction shortly after the illustrious pioneer of antiseptic surgery was appointed to the Chair of Clinical Surgery in 1870 and worked in the early Edinburgh Royal Infirmary in Infirmary Street, in the former High School Building. Lister's clinical and other teaching responsibilities greatly reduced his time available for laboratory work, in which he was certainly deeply interested. Accordingly, his house surgeon, William Watson Cheyne, to whom he delegated such investigations in 1876, was perhaps the first to carry out significant bacteriological work in the city.

To appreciate the work of Lister and Cheyne in a wider context and to highlight its importance, it is necessary to note the important observations of Professors Sydney Selwyn and Alastair C. Wardlaw in their substantial and informative paper published in the *Proceedings of the Royal Society of Edinburgh* in 1983: "Microbiology, including Virology", within the theme "Two Hundred Years of the Biological Sciences in Scotland". The paper deals first with the era of "premicrobiology". Here the authors make the point that most textbooks on the history of science or medicine tend to trace the origins of microbiology no further back than the latter quarter of the nineteenth century with the discoveries of Pasteur and Koch. Although many books refer to Anton van Leeuwenhoek's (1632-1723) first simple microscopes which, with their adequate resolving power, enabled him to see and study his little "animalcules" – and while these objects had no medical implications – many medical historians have overlooked or have been unaware of the relatively early, albeit rudimentary, efforts of numerous British workers, many of whom were Scots.

Selwyn and Wardlaw note that when the principles of microbiology were not yet understood, they were nevertheless unknowingly applied from quite early times, for example, in the fermentation processes of brewing and distilling, the leavening of bread with yeast, the preservation of fish and animal meat by salting and smoking and the production of cheese. Even during devastating and recurrent epidemics of plague and the less widespread occurrence of leprosy, the authorities enforced measures of isolation and quarantine for victims, and imposed severe penalties on any relatives who concealed such infected people in their houses. The vacated houses of plague victims were fumigated by the burning of heather.

Amongst very many early scientists and others who indulged in a primitive kind of microbiology and related investigations, Selwyn and Wardlaw draw particular attention to various pioneers in the preparation and use of antiseptics, notably John Pringle[1], a native of Roxburghshire and subsequently Professor of Pneumatical and Ethical Philosophy in Edinburgh. Pringle qualified as a physician in Edinburgh University in 1733, and his references to "hospital infection" and the use of antiseptics – as he actually named them (Pringle, 1750) – and other medical practices, anticipated the discoveries and methods of Pasteur, Koch and Lister more than a century later. John Francis Home, Professor of Materia Medica at Edinburgh University circa 1759, produced a vaccine effective against measles (Selwyn & Wardlaw, 1983). James Lind[2], circa 1757, an Edinburgh medical graduate, better known for his pioneering treatment of scurvy, also introduced separate hospital wards for different infections and produced filtered drinking water. A group of Edinburgh doctors were the first to recognise the infectious nature of puerperal fever and to relate its occurrence to the particular midwives attending various

1. *Sir John Pringle* (1707-82)

2. *Dr James Lind* (1716-94)

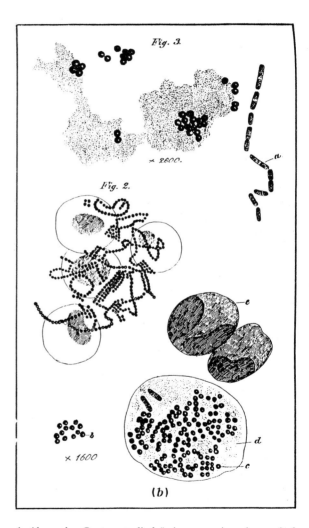

Ueber Abscesse.

Von

Dr. Alexander Ogston,

Docent der klinischen Chirurgie zu Aberdeen*).

(Hierzu Taf. VIII.)

3. *Sir Alexander Ogston*
(1844-1929)

4. Alexander Ogston studied "micro-organisms in surgical diseases" (*British Medical Journal* 1881: 1, 369-375) and in abscesses (*Archiv für Klinische Chirurgie* 1880: 25, 589-600). He identified and named *Staphylococcus pyogenes* (now *aureus*) as an important pathogen, and he distinguished between staphylococci and streptococci (see Selwyn & Wardlaw, 1983).

women. It was not until the following century that Semmelweiss developed this theme in the 1860s in Vienna. In 1797 another two Edinburgh medicals were using a type of phenol for disinfecting ships' hospitals. John Goodsir, Professor of Anatomy at Edinburgh, reported upon his microscopic observations of coccal bacteria (Goodsir, 1842) although his speculations on their pathogenicity were incorrect. In due course, in the 1880s, Ogston in Aberdeen was to show the association between wound infection and the pathogenic staphylococci and streptococci (Ogston, 1880)[3,4].

This selection from many may give some indication of the early "microbiological work" that was to be of practical medical importance. Impressive as it was, throughout it all there was naturally a missing dimension, a degree of incompleteness. Many workers were noting interesting phenomena and were attempting to explain and act upon their findings. There was a groping towards an enlightenment which was yet to come. An authentic scientific basis was awaited for so much that had been noted and acted upon empirically. The powerful and revealing illumination was at last to come with the discoveries of Louis Pasteur and Robert Koch, the fruits of whose researches were to be harvested and brought to bear upon medical understanding and practice by Joseph Lister[5] and so many others.

The Lister Era

Much effort was directed in quite early times in trying to understand the cause of infections and to introduce the isolation of cases in hospital wards and elsewhere, and to prevent the spread of infection by the use of antiseptics. The first recorded reference to the practice of bacteriology in Edinburgh, based on the discoveries of Pasteur and Koch occurs in *Lister and His Achievement* by Sir William Watson Cheyne, FRCS (Cheyne, 1925). The author was Lister's house surgeon for a year (1876) in the old Edinburgh Royal Infirmary before Lister returned to London. Watson Cheyne[6] records the scene:

> When I began bacteriological work in a little passage behind the operating theatre in the old Edinburgh Infirmary in 1876 there was no staining of bacteria, no oil-immersion lenses, no solid cultivating media, no proper incubators; in fact everything was in its infancy and I had to carry out my observations by the aid of fluid cultivating media, though it was not long before I was able to go over all the work again with a proper microscope and other appliances. I used various media: at first milk, which was soon discarded, and I finally did most of the work with a vegetable (cucumber) infusion or meat infusion.

Watson Cheyne provides further details of his primitive laboratory facilities and techniques. He describes his main efforts to correlate his laboratory findings, in consultation with Lister, with the clinical condition of the patients. He recounts how his distinguished "Chief" based his surgical procedures and patient aftercare on the then relatively recent and quite revolutionary findings of Louis Pasteur, first published in 1864, followed by the important and systematic laboratory investigations of Robert Koch. During his first period in Edinburgh, while acting as Professor James Syme's assistant, Lister had done several bacteriological studies, but the pressure of his clinical duties forced him to curtail these. Watson Cheyne summarised the various theories propounded at the time by surgeons on the cause of the putrefaction of a wound following an injury or subsequent surgery (Cheyne, 1889). Such theories were based on the widely held belief that suppuration or putrefaction

5. *Joseph Lister*

6. *William Watson Cheyne*
Reproduced by kind permission of the
Royal College of Surgeons, Edinburgh (R.C.S.E.)

was due to "indefinite substances" in the atmosphere that were called "miasmas". Watson Cheyne comments that such an explanation was of little value since no one could define a miasma although it was thought to be gaseous in nature. While the precise reasons for doing so were unknown, many surgeons were concerned to exclude air from wounds and thus for the reasons subsequently discovered by Pasteur, infection of wounds was reduced.

In March 1860, by a commission from Queen Victoria, Joseph Lister had been appointed Professor of Surgery at Glasgow University. It was while occupying this post and from 1861, operating on patients in Glasgow Royal Infirmary, that Lister achieved quite spectacular results from his antiseptic surgical techniques involving the use of his carbolic spray. In 1870, Lister returned to Edinburgh to succeed his former chief and father-in-law, James Syme, as Professor of Clinical Surgery. Six years later, Watson Cheyne continued Lister's earlier bacteriological work. Lister and Watson Cheyne were intent on correlating the clinical situations that they encountered with their laboratory microscopical findings and the results of their primitive fluid cultures. Watson Cheyne provides much detail of his laboratory findings, for example of "micrococci" which occurred frequently in cultures made from pieces of wound dressing or drainage tubes. Lister himself made well-defined drawings of the various types of organisms seen microscopically. In Edinburgh, Lister insisted on handwashing by his surgical staff before operating, and he stressed the importance of the boiling of instruments and, of course, the constant use of his famous carbolic atomiser or spray. Watson Cheyne notes that when he and Lister joined the staff of the University College Hospital in London in 1877, a year after their early laboratory work in Edinburgh, they found that the surgeons there had little regard for the application of Pasteur's findings to their surgical technique. Lister had a difficult period when he insisted that his aseptic procedures must be adopted.

Professor John Chiene

When Lister and Watson Cheyne had gone, their early work to relate the new science of bacteriology to surgery at Edinburgh Royal Infirmary did not fall into abeyance. Indeed, their pioneering efforts were soon afterwards continued and adopted with strong conviction by Professor John Chiene who was appointed to the Chair of Surgery in 1882. This has been documented by Dr John Ritchie in his valuable history of the laboratory of the Edinburgh Royal College of Physicians (Ritchie, 1955). He confirms that the city's first laboratory devoted to bacteriological research and teaching, primarily in relation to surgery, was established and sustained by John Chiene. Ritchie endorsed Chiene's claim that this was the first bacteriology teaching laboratory in the United Kingdom. Chiene was greatly inspired in his interest in bacteriology not only by Lister, whose colleague he had been at the old Royal Infirmary[7,8], but also by Robert Koch and his work on tuberculosis.

The location of Chiene's bacteriological laboratory has been debated. Ritchie, Sir Harold Stiles in his obituary of Chiene, and later Professor T.J. Mackie, all state that it was situated in the Department of Surgery in the Medical School in Teviot Place and was opened in 1884. It was entered by the doorway on the south side of the Medical School quadrangle above which is inscribed "Anatomy" with "Surgery" and "Practice of Physic" above and below. In due course the Department of Surgery, on an upper floor, was linked to the Sir David Wilkie Research laboratory by a

7. *Old Royal Infirmary, Infirmary Street, early Surgical Hospital*

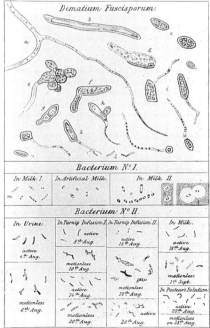

8. *Lister's drawings of microscopic observations
with acknowledgement to R.C.S.E.*

9. *Professor John Chiene*

10. *Dr John B. Buist*

wooden catwalk which still remains. Stiles was for several years assistant to Chiene and worked in his laboratory, introducing many important new techniques in surgical pathology. He was appointed to the Regius Chair of Clinical Surgery in 1919. Stiles and Sir John Fraser incidentally differed from Robert Koch with regard to the significance of bovine tuberculosis in man, especially children. Stiles had treated many cases during his twenty-one years as principal surgeon to the Royal Hospital for Sick Children.

In 1884, at the 52nd Annual General Meeting of the British Medical Association, Chiene read a paper on "The Desirability of Establishing Bacteriological Laboratories in Connection with Hospital Wards" (Chiene, 1884). His principal theme was that: "The laboratories, to be most efficient, should be placed where the micro-organisms occur – namely in the hospitals". Chiene[9] was deeply concerned that, in his view, Britain was lagging far behind other European countries in the establishment of such laboratories.

In 1894, Edinburgh University established its first lectureship in "Pathological Bacteriology" in the Department of Pathology, and Dr Robert Muir was appointed. Robert Muir, subsequently appointed to the Chair of Pathology in St Andrews and later in Glasgow, was to become very distinguished in his field. When Muir was appointed to the Edinburgh lectureship, Professor Chiene observed that "the teaching of bacteriology has now passed very properly into the hands of my friend, the Professor of Pathology." This was the noted William Smith Greenfield, who assigned the task to Dr Robert Muir. Although the teaching and practice of bacteriology were to develop steadily in the Pathology Department until the foundation of the first chair in the subject in 1913, Chiene kept his own laboratory in operation until his retirement in 1909. Chiene's conviction that bacteriology laboratories should be established in hospitals was to be honoured in Edinburgh Royal Infirmary at Lauriston Place from about 1900 and in other Edinburgh hospitals in later years.

Dr John Brown Buist[10], an Edinburgh medical graduate, contributed a paper to the *Transactions of the Royal Society of Edinburgh* in 1886 in which he described his studies on vaccinia (cowpox) and variola (smallpox). Here was a virologist ahead of his time. He went on to publish his book *Vaccinia and Variola* in 1887 with accurate (light microscope) observations of the so-called elementary bodies of these infections and with fine coloured plates to illustrate the structures that he identified. Buist was a Fifer, born at Abdie in 1846. He graduated MB at Edinburgh in 1867, and MD in 1870. He was accepted as a Lecturer in General Pathology in the School of Medicine of the Royal Colleges in 1879, having gained membership (1878) and subsequently fellowship (1879) of the Royal College of Physicians of Edinburgh.

In the preface to his book Dr Buist acknowledged his indebtedness to Professor Chiene for facilities afforded him in Chiene's bacteriological laboratory in the University of Edinburgh. Here, then, it seems that the first discovery of the virus bodies of variola was made. Buist died in 1915 and his obituary sadly recounts that his work "on the bacteriology [*sic*] of vaccinia and variola hardly received the attention it deserves". In due course, T.J. Mackie and C.E. van Rooyen published an outline of Dr Buist's life and work in the *Edinburgh Medical Journal* (1937), as a tribute to a former research worker, to complement an article in the same issue of the *Journal* by Dr Mervyn Gordon who recorded the sequence of discoveries that identified the agents of vaccinia and variola (Gordon, 1937). It was Gordon who first established Buist's priority in this difficult field.

CHAPTER TWO

EDINBURGH AND PUBLIC HEALTH

Chiene's observation that "microbiological laboratories should be established in hospitals since that is where micro-organisms occur" was no doubt valid, but micro-organisms were certainly not entirely confined to hospitals. Infections were just as prevalent outside the hospitals and in the country at large – especially in cities – as they had always been, though this was not appreciated until the discoveries of Pasteur and Koch. Virulent strains were (and are) commonest in hospitals, and Professor James Y. Simpson showed that surgical infection was commonest in the largest hospitals and less frequent when operations were carried out in the patients' own homes (see Selwyn, 1965).

Dr Haldane Tait, a former Principal Medical Officer in the City of Edinburgh's Child Health Service, wrote a most interesting book – *A Doctor and Two Policemen* – on the history of the Edinburgh Public Health Department from 1862 to 1974 (Tait, 1974). This includes a graphic and valuable account of the incidence of the various infectious diseases prevalent in the city from early centuries. Bubonic and pneumonic plague – the dreaded "Black Death" – which killed millions throughout Europe and on several occasions decimated the population of Edinburgh and Leith, and cholera, typhoid fever, typhus, influenza, poliomyelitis, anthrax, scarlet fever, diphtheria and tuberculosis were the principal diseases that took their toll. Outbreaks of smallpox were common, until relatively recent times. The virtually endemic occurrence of this much-feared disease led to widespread agitation in the city for the appointment of a Medical Officer of Health in 1862.

The state of the city's public health in the early nineteenth century was quite appalling and several notable visitors to Edinburgh around that time have left records of their observations. In the late eighteenth century the tall tenements or "lands" towering above the narrow closes and cramped congested streets became honeycombs of small, subdivided houses, devoid of sunlight and overcrowded. The cobbled streets were covered with horse and cattle excreta. The unpleasant stench was supplemented by the regular discarding from the windows of human excreta to the accompanying warning cry of "Gardy-loo" – "*Gardez l'eau*". Pigs and poultry were commonly kept on the ground floors of houses. Drinking water was brought in buckets from the stagnant Burgh Loch or South Loch (near the Meadows) and the Nor' Loch (beneath the Castle, eventually drained to make way for Princes Street Gardens) or from open streams frequented by cattle. Houses were rat-infested. The sources of plague, typhoid, cholera and airborne density-dependent infections were not far to seek.

Appointment of the City's First Medical Officer of Health –
Dr Henry Littlejohn

Towards the end of the eighteenth century when Edinburgh's better-off citizens had left the congested closes and streets of the Old Town to establish themselves in the elegant New Town across the North Bridge or later to move southwards to the villas of Newington, the Grange and Morningside, the tenements of the High Street and adjoining closes became grossly overcrowded as labourers and poor people occupied subdivided flats. Health problems steadily increased. Efforts had been made by William Pulteney Alison, Professor of Medicine in the 1850s, to call attention to the undoubted link between poverty, overcrowding and ill health. He called for planned social change by the civic authorities. The threat of cholera added urgency to his appeals. In 1861 a two-hundred-year-old seven-storey tenement at No. 101 High Street collapsed. The very large number of those killed and injured dramatically drew attention to the serious overcrowding. The disaster persuaded the Town Council to take action against the problems of inadequate housing and ill health. They decided to appoint a Medical Officer of Health (MOH). The man appointed was Dr Henry Littlejohn[11] who took up his duties in 1862. While several English cities, influenced by such pioneers as Edwin Chadwick, the distinguished sanitarian, had appointed medical officers many years earlier, Edinburgh's appointment was the first such in Scotland. Dr Littlejohn was to serve the city for 46 years, and was to witness and to play a vitally important part in vast reforms to improve the state of the city's health.

Henry Littlejohn was born in Leith Street of a well-known family of bakers. After attending the High School he studied medicine, graduating MD in 1847. He became Police Surgeon in 1856. When he was appointed Medical Officer of Health in 1862, Edinburgh's population totalled 170,000. By his retiral in 1908, it had doubled. Confronted with serious and urgent problems, Littlejohn lost little time in taking up the challenge. First, he instituted a wide and detailed study of the city's social conditions and incidence of disease. This resulted in his classical *Report on the Sanitary Conditions of the People of Edinburgh* (Littlejohn, 1865). It ran to 120 pages, with a further 77 pages of appendices and statistics. This was a graphic and revealing document, statistically relating disease to social conditions, districts of the city, type of employment, and so on. It drew attention to such serious features as the number of open sewers, notably the Foul Burn that flowed through the Abbeyhill area where there was the highest death rate from infectious diseases. The report also drew urgent attention to (1) the insanitary shops of butchers and their mode of storing and handling meat; (2) the health dangers to the workers employed in, and the customers of, underground bakehouses; (3) the menace of the many byres housing large numbers of cows never let out to pasture or daylight; and (4) the unhygienic milking methods and containers for milk related to incidence of tuberculosis and other infections.

Littlejohn drew attention to the problems and campaigned unceasingly for reforms. He observed that "disease spreads like wildfire". In this campaign he had as his strong supporter for improvement Lord Provost W. Chambers, the publisher, who personally surveyed the slum areas and who is commemorated by Chambers Street. In 1879 the ever active Dr Littlejohn gained one of his most important achievements – the compulsory notification of all cases of serious infectious disease to his office by the city's general practitioners. At first, many practitioners and others criticised such local legislation as an interference with confidentiality between doctor and patient. However, Dr Littlejohn's proposal to the Town Council was adopted and an incentive to general practitioners to co-operate was given in the form of 2/6d for each case notified when their diagnosis was confirmed as correct by the Medical Officer of Health's department! With the great prevalence of infectious diseases such as smallpox, cholera, typhus, diphtheria and scarlet fever, compulsory notification brought general practitioners an added source of income and the system worked. In the introduction of such legislation, Edinburgh was eighteen years ahead of other Scottish cities, anticipating the Public Health (Scotland) Act of 1897.

As an indication of the prevalence of serious infectious diseases, so often fatal, it may be noted that the Registrar General's report for 1855-1865 recorded 10,548 cases of smallpox, very many of these being children. In turn, this prompted Henry Littlejohn in 1862 to campaign for the compulsory smallpox vaccination of infants. With the many improvements in social conditions and public health measures introduced by Dr Littlejohn's persuasion, a gradual but significant improvement in the health of the city took place, as indicated by a substantial reduction in the crude death rate and the disappearance of cholera and typhus from Edinburgh sooner than from any other large town in Britain.

Early Fever Hospitals

It might be suggested that Edinburgh's first infectious diseases hospital and isolation unit consisted of a group of primitive wooden huts built for the compulsory quarantining of plague victims in the Middle Ages. The principal area assigned for this was on the Burgh Muir, now the pleasant grounds of the Astley Ainslie Hospital in Canaan Lane ... but we digress into sparsely documented times.

One of the great advantages of the compulsory notification of infectious diseases was the ability to isolate such cases in the city's early fever hospitals. Not until 1887 at the earliest with the opening of the Edinburgh Royal College of Physicians' Laboratory in Lauriston Lane and then more systematically with the establishment of the city's first diagnostic bacteriology laboratory in the Usher Institute in 1902, was it possible to confirm the clinical diagnosis of infections with laboratory reports. The development of these fever hospital facilities is described later, as a wide range of infectious diseases now known to be bacterial in origin but then diagnosed on clinical grounds came to be recognised. In the pre-Pasteur/Koch era, very many illnesses not known to be of bacterial aetiology were simply labelled "fevers" and as such appear in the records and statistics of the old Royal Infirmary in Infirmary Street.

Soon after its opening in Infirmary Street in 1748, the Royal Infirmary provided beds for cases of infectious diseases in its "fever block". From 1817 to 1848 there were repeated outbreaks of relapsing fever and typhus fever. The latter flourished amidst widespread poverty and malnutrition. During severe epidemics the Royal Infirmary was unable to admit all requiring treatment and the civic authorities were compelled to provide additional accommodation. Thus in 1817 the Government was approached for the use of the former military barracks which had been established in the vacated Queensberry House in the Canongate. This became a hospital of 150 beds for cases of typhus fever. As the lease of these premises ended in 1837, additional beds were made available in the main Infirmary building in Drummond Street, many surgical cases being transferred to the small surgical hospital established in the nearby former High School at the foot of Infirmary Street purchased in 1829. In addition, a house previously used as a Lock Hospital (see references later) in Surgeons Square was also made available. Indeed from the mid-nineteenth century onwards, very many premises were pressed into use for fever cases, though the exact date of their usage is not always on record. At one period, infectious disease cases were accommodated at Portobello and Fountainbridge. On another occasion, tents were borrowed from Edinburgh Castle and the Archers' Hall and set up in the Infirmary precincts. During a cholera outbreak in 1866, the City Poorhouse near Forrest Road was used. At another period the former George Watson's Hospital (College), vacated to make way for the building of the new Royal Infirmary on its site in Lauriston Place, provided fever beds. The original Sick Children's Hospital in

11. *Sir Henry Duncan Littlejohn*
Edinburgh's first Medical Officer of Health

12. *Edinburgh's Second City Fever Hospital, Drummond Street (David Bryce, Architect)*

TABLE 2.1

An illustrative example of the nature and range of infectious diseases recognised in Edinburgh at the end of the 19th century.

Table showing the number of Cases of the undermentioned diseases admitted to Hospital since the year 1890. The percentage of cases admitted to total notifications in each year, together with the averages for the last thirteen years.

Years.	Typhus. Admissions	Typhus. Rate per cent. to Total Cases Notified.	Typhoid, Relapsing, and Continued Fever. Admissions	Typhoid, Relapsing, and Continued Fever. Rate per cent. to Total Cases Notified.	Puerperal Fever. Admissions	Puerperal Fever. Rate per cent. to Total Cases Notified.	Diphtheria, Membranous Croup. Admissions	Diphtheria, Membranous Croup. Rate per cent. to Total Cases Notified.	Smallpox. Admissions	Smallpox. Rate per cent. to Total Cases Notified.	Scarlet Fever. Admissions	Scarlet Fever. Rate per cent. to Total Cases Notified.	Erysipelas. Admissions	Erysipelas. Rate per cent. to Total Cases Notified.
1890	9	100·00	241	48·02			122	29·59	...	...	480	40·10		
1891	1	100·00	227	51·01			82	39·61	...	...	433	44·12		
1892	16	88·88	115	48·31			66	32·51	8	100·00	862	46·44		
1893	5	83·33	144	52·55			85	33·86	51	100·00	780	47·88		
1894	3	100·00	176	56·77			122	33·70	533	99·25	958	52·60		
1895	...	...	288	69·06	Not Notified.		146	46·49	109	100·00	1519	53·63	Not Notified.	
1896	10	100·00	233	71·03			108	43·02	...	...	1381	63·20		
1897	3	100·00	175	68·89			109	50·93	...	...	1658	63·84		
1898	78	98·73	143	51·03			111	41·26	7	100·00	1350	56·55		
1899	11	91·66	207	71·62			136	48·74	...	...	816	68·86		
1900	35	100·00	181	72·69			309	63·97	5	100·00	676	68·21		
1901	14	100·00	166	76·85			364	67·15	6	100·00	601	67·37		
1902	10	100·00	153	79·68	5	19·23	297	72·79	7	100·00	605	74·50	207	40·35
Average	195	98·48	2449	61·96	5	19·23	2057	49·63	726	99·45	12119	56·72	207	40·35

Lauriston Lane admitted children with diphtheria and scarlet fever.

Some degree of rationalisation and greater stability was reached in 1870 when the Canongate Poorhouse, which had been established in the former Queensberry House, was purchased by Edinburgh Town Council and became Edinburgh's first City Fever Hospital. Again, Littlejohn's special plea was a crucial factor. A statistic from the preceding half-century, when cases of infectious disease were treated in so many different places, is revealing. During the period 1841-48, 17,542 patients with various types of "fevers" were recorded as admitted to the many "sick houses" or the Royal Infirmary.

When around 1880 the City Fever Hospital in the Canongate was proving quite inadequate, the city's ever campaigning Medical Officer of Health urged the civic authorities to purchase the vacated Royal Infirmary in Infirmary Street. This was not possible, but the Drummond Street Surgical Hospital, built as an addition to the Royal Infirmary by David Bryce in 1853, was purchased by the city. This building had 260 beds with good reception and isolation facilities and was very suitable; and it was supplemented by the little surgical hospital in the former High School. This new complex became Edinburgh's second City Fever Hospital[12] in 1885. Here Dr Henry Littlejohn established the first training school in fevers nursing, and here the hospital was to remain until the opening of the impressive purpose-built third City Fever Hospital at Colinton Mains by Greenbank Drive in 1903. This marked the realisation of another dream and campaign of Littlejohn and it is described in a later chapter. Table 2.1 shows numbers of cases of various infections admitted to the City Hospital in Drummond Street for the period 1890-1902.

The Lock Hospitals

Historical accounts of the old Royal Infirmary in Infirmary Street and maps of the hospital's environment make reference to the "Lock Wards" and "Lock Hospital". The meaning of these designations, to be found in other hospitals in Britain about the same period, remained something of a mystery – so much so that in 1960, Dr Robert Lees, venereologist at the new Royal Infirmary at Lauriston, was invited to contribute a paper on the subject. This was published a year later in the *British Journal of Venereal Diseases* (Lees, 1961). Lees noted that some writers described the "Lock wards" as "lock ups" for the forceful segregation of patients, while others suggested that "Lock" was derived from *"les lacques"* the French name for the dressings or rags with which leprous and syphilitic patients were obliged to cover their sores and were required to deposit in a special receptacle when entering a church. The *Oxford English Dictionary* describes a "lock hospital" as that used for the treatment of venereal diseases (VD) and refers to the "Lock lazar house" in Southwark, on record in 1452 as an isolation hospital for lepers and later becoming used for patients with venereal diseases. Certainly, whatever its earliest origins, a "Lock ward" or "Lock hospital" became generally the name for a venereal diseases hospital and so it was in Edinburgh.

Syphilis was first recorded in Edinburgh in 1497. It was known as "the seiknis of Napilis", due to its having first been recognised in epidemic form during the siege of Naples in 1495. The disease was said to have been brought back by Christopher Columbus' sailors from America about 1492 and to have gradually spread throughout Europe. Edinburgh's earliest infirmary, the tiny "hospital" of six beds in Robertson's Close in Infirmary Street, did not admit VD cases but did have a "salivation room" and, according to Dr Lees, was clearly used for the mercurial treatment of syphilitic outpatients. In the first proper infirmary opened in Infirmary Street in 1748, a small VD ward was opened in 1750 and another a year later, providing accommodation for both sexes. These wards became known as the "Lock wards". In 1833 they were closed and the city magistrates offered the infirmary managers VD hospital facilities in a house in the old Surgeons Square, a little eastwards of the main hospital. In 1863 a new "Lock Hospital" was opened in a building in Surgeons Square formerly occupied by John Bell, surgeon, and used as a lecture theatre. A plan of the Royal Infirmary precincts of this period shows the "Lock Hospital" as situated near the Burn Hospital, just within the Flodden Wall at the Pleasance. The very strict regulations binding upon patients in the "Lock Hospital" and their visitors remain on record. Dr Lees concludes his paper with an account of the successive facilities established for the treatment of venereal diseases, progressing from the old and dingy ward 5A in the new Royal Infirmary at Lauriston to the large pavilion of five floors at first shared with the Department of Dermatology and, when opened in 1934, amongst the best such accommodation in Britain.

CHAPTER THREE

EARLIEST BACTERIOLOGICAL DIAGNOSTIC LABORATORIES

Great progress was made in the diagnosis and treatment of infectious diseases in Edinburgh's second City Fever Hospital in Drummond Street, established in 1885 in the Infirmary's former surgical hospital. With the publication of the work of Pasteur, Koch and others, it became increasingly necessary to obtain accurate laboratory confirmation of the clinical diagnosis in cases of infectious disease. This also had an important bearing on the study of the epidemiology of infections. While Lister had lost no time in attempting to bring the findings of Pasteur to bear upon the problems of surgical infections, with Dr Watson Cheyne and later Professor John Chiene as active disciples in the cause, events were to occur that spurred on the setting up of the city's first public health diagnostic bacteriological laboratory. This initiative was coupled with the more systematic teaching of public health or community medicine. The occasion was the celebration of the University's Tercentenary in 1884 (see Report, 1885).

Louis Pasteur's Visit

The official record of the celebrations reveals that the number and varied background and calibre of the distinguished guests, who included delegates from many countries, created a uniquely distinguished assembly of widely ranging scholarship and international renown, never to be equalled by any such gathering in the city since. As regards the future development of bacteriology in the city and the application of laboratory research and diagnosis to the city's very many problems of public health, the presence of one particular visitor was not only of historic importance, but also of far-reaching practical significance. The visitor was the representative of the French Academy of Sciences, "the father of bacteriology", the illustrious Louis Pasteur. His attendance at the opening of the new Medical School at Teviot Place[13,14] was of special importance.

The impact of Pasteur's presence must have been felt not only during the official formal occasions such as the great banquet in the Drill Hall in Forrest Road on 17 April, 1884, and the lively students' gathering during which the distinguished French scientist spoke, but also in the informal meetings that Pasteur had with those attempting to develop bacteriology in the city. At the luncheon given in the then recently opened large Anatomy Department Museum in the new Medical School in Teviot Place on Wednesday, 16 April, there were over 400 guests, including all the professors of the Medical Faculty. Pasteur was at the top table and Lister at another. At other tables were Professor William Smith Greenfield, his assistant Dr German Sims Woodhead, and Dr Henry Littlejohn, all key men for the further development of bacteriology and public health in Edinburgh. It is reasonable to assume that in private conversations, many problems must have been discussed and much encouragement given by Pasteur and Lister to the new Edinburgh developments. During the luncheon it was stated that the new Medical School could expect to be teaching 1500 students and was the largest school of medicine not only in Great Britain but in the world. It was Lister who replied for the guests with the toast to the University Principal, Sir Alexander Grant.

Royal College of Physicians' Laboratory

Soon after Pasteur's visit and the private meetings that almost certainly took place with those pioneering the development of bacteriology in Edinburgh, Dr (later Sir) John Batty Tuke made a formal proposal at a meeting of the Royal College of

20

13. *New University Medical School, Teviot Place (Inset: Sir Robert Rowand Anderson, Architect)*

14. *New Medical School under construction*

Physicians of Edinburgh on 4 February, 1885, "that a committee be appointed to take into consideration the expediency of establishing a laboratory for original research in connection with the Royal College of Physicians". After remission to a committee for consideration Tuke's proposal was adopted and this led to the establishment of Edinburgh's first independent purpose-built laboratory for research in pathology and other branches of medicine, and in due course, bacteriology. This was the Edinburgh Royal College of Physicians' Laboratory, opened at Lauriston Lane, immediately west of the new Royal Infirmary in Lauriston Place, in 1887 and subsequently transferred to larger premises in 1896, adjacent to and including part of the former City Charity Workhouse at the corner of Forrest Road and Bristo Place[15,16,17,18].

The purpose of the Royal College of Physicians' Laboratory then was primarily to promote physiological and pathological investigations and the examination of specimens encountered in practice "in a manner not possible or practicable at home" (i.e. the general practitioner's home). At first, less than three-quarters of the Fellows supported or used the College laboratory. Many argued that the expense incurred would be better devoted to clinical medicine and therapeutics rather than scientific research. In due course, however, the laboratory's work became increasingly appreciated and in February 1887 its first Annual Report was the charter of the first laboratory established in Britain for medical research. Although its function was primarily to conduct research, the laboratory reported upon submitted specimens from the outset.

The first possible premises considered were part of the former City Charity Workhouse, in the Bedlam section, the primitive mental hospital at the corner of Forrest Road and Bristo Port then used by the Queen's Edinburgh Rifle Volunteer Brigade. These were considered too large. Instead, more suitable accommodation was obtained from the directors of the new Royal Infirmary at Lauriston, in Lauriston Lane. Structural alterations created quite a number of small laboratories. The first superintendent appointed was Dr G. Sims Woodhead, from 1887 to 1890, who was later to have a distinguished career in pathology. The first laboratory assistant appointed was Willie Watson who was to serve the College laboratory for 54 years. There were 130 applications for this post. Watson, with Richard Muir, was one of the earliest laboratory assistants in Edinburgh. Later he was to be joined by Robert Barr who subsequently became the first chief technician at the Bacteriology Laboratory of the Edinburgh Royal Infirmary at Westgate. Watson lived on the premises at Lauriston Lane. By 1889 the staff consisted of eleven Fellows of the College, two Members and eighteen others.

About this time, 1894, work was carried out after the publication by Klebs and Loeffler of the discovery of the bacillus which caused diphtheria, then a widespread and frequently fatal infection of children. Staff at the Lauriston Lane laboratory began to produce diphtheria antitoxin, following upon the successful preparations by Behring and Wernicke and latterly Roux, Martin and Chaillon in Paris. The Edinburgh workers used two horses and produced a relatively effective antitoxin, until increased commercial production rendered their work uneconomic. The other work of the laboratory increased steadily in scope and volume. Larger premises were soon required and it was decided to move to the old Charity Workhouse accommodation at Forrest Road. The move to the new laboratories was completed in 1896, at a cost of £7,350. A house above the laboratories was provided

15. *Early Royal College of Physicians Laboratory Staff c.1894*

16. *Early Royal College of Physicians Laboratory Staff, Forrest Road,*
the then Dr James Ritchie, Superintendent, (white coat) in centre

17. *Former Royal College of Physicians Laboratory, Forrest Road, c.1982*

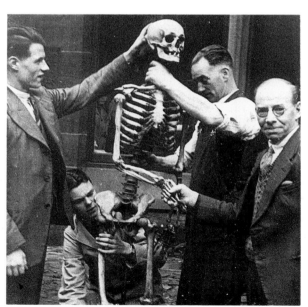

18. *R.C.P. Laboratory Technical Staff, Forrest Road*
John Ferguson (left) and Willie Watson (right)

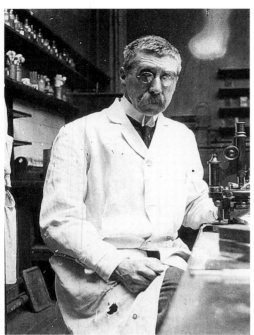

19. *Dr James Ritchie in R.C.P. Laboratory*

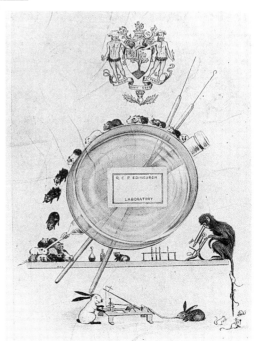

20. *Culture Plate, R.C.P. Laboratory*

for the senior technician Willie Watson and his family. By 1901, there were thirty-five members of laboratory staff, one group working on bacteriological topics as diverse as scarlet fever, diphtheria, typhoid fever, and *E. coli cystitis.* James Ritchie[19, 20] was in charge of the laboratory from 1907 until 1913.

The College of Physicians' Laboratory, set up originally as a research laboratory, was to continue as such until 1950. Its laboratory diagnostic service extended outwith Edinburgh to other local authority public health authorities and practitioners. However, the inauguration of the National Health Service in 1948 saw new arrangements introduced by the various Edinburgh health authorities. The laboratory closed in 1950 and the Medical Research Council's Clinical Endocrinology Research Unit was established in the premises leased to the University. The closure of the Royal College of Physicians' Laboratory was reluctantly accepted by its administrators with great regret.

The Usher Institute and its Bacteriological Diagnostic Laboratory

Just prior to 1902 concern was expressed, within the administration of the Royal College of Physicians' Laboratory, that of the average of 1500 histological and bacteriological specimens being reported upon annually, very many were submitted by general practitioners who were not members of the College and the financial burden of this open diagnostic service was increasingly worrying. Dr J. Ritchie, in his history of the laboratory (Ritchie, 1953), states for 1902:

> In the meantime, however, a change had occurred in the attitude of the municipality of Edinburgh in regard to the arrangements for reporting that they had made with the College little more than a year before. An offer by the Trustees of the Usher Institute to undertake all bacteriological examinations required by the Medical Officer of Health, the Fever Hospital and the medical practitioners of Edinburgh was received by the Town Council and referred to the Public Health Committee for consideration and report. That Committee decided that the offer should not be accepted, mainly it appears because they hoped that it would shortly be possible to have all bacteriological work for the city done at the new Isolation Hospital then in course of erection [at Colinton Mains].

Negotiations for the transfer of specimens from the College laboratory to the Usher Institute (then newly opened in 1902) continued. Both the Colleges of Physicians and Surgeons opposed the proposed change and their views were conveyed to the Town Council. Later a well attended meeting of the medical profession in Edinburgh unanimously voted in favour of retaining the College of Physicians' diagnostic laboratory. The Town Council, however, adhered to its policy and arrangements with the College laboratory were terminated as from 15 May, 1902. Ritchie comments that the reaction of the College was dignified and generous. Strangely, as the College laboratory continued to provide a service for its Members and Fellows, the number of specimens received in 1902 exceeded that for 1901 by over 400. Many of the specimens were sent for examination for diphtheria, typhoid or tuberculosis. In addition, the substantial research programme of the laboratory continued.

Bacteriological Examinations for the Diagnosis of Tuberculosis, Typhoid Fever and Diphtheria

The following table (Table 3.1) affords information from the City of Edinburgh Public Health Department for 1901 on the bacteriological diagnosis of phthisis,

TABLE 3.1

Examinations by the Royal College of Physicians Laboratory, 1901

Months.	For Tubercle. Total Specimens Examined.	Negative.	Positive.	For Typhoid Fever. Total Specimens Examined.	Negative.	Positive.	For Diphtheria. Total Specimens Examined.	Negative.	Positive.	Cost per Month. £ s. d.
January . . .	21	11	10	11	8	3	28	16	12	12 7 6
February . .	18	9	9	6	6	...	20	15	5	8 15 0
March . . .	21	15	6	8	6	2	25	16	9	10 17 6
April . . .	30	22	8	14	12	2	19	16	3	12 0 0
May . . .	22	16	6	9	7	2	14	11	3	8 10 0
June . . .	19	11	8	9	9	...	48	30	18	16 12 6
July . . .	15	11	4	9	5	4	23	18	5	9 17 6
August . . .	5	3	2	5	3	2	19	13	6	6 12 6
September . .	24	15	9	16	10	6	16	10	6	11 0 0
October . . .	24	14	10	13	8	5	16	12	4	10 5 0
November . .	15	9	6	15	9	6	19	16	3	10 7 6
December . .	24	13	11	9	9	...	21	17	4	10 10 0
TOTALS .	238	149	89	124	92	32	268	190	78	127 15 0

Total number of specimens examined for Tubercle,   238   £29 15 0
        „   Typhoid Fever,   124   31 0 0
        „   Diphtheria, .   268   67 0 0
                                     630   £127 15 0

TABLE 3.2: *Examinations by the Usher Institute Laboratory,* 1902

Months.	For Tubercle.			For Typhoid Fever.			For Diphtheria.		
	Total Specimens Examined.	Negative.	Positive.	Total Specimens Examined.	Negative.	Positive.	Total Specimens Examined.	Negative.	Positive.
January .	23	16	7	9	6	3	18	15	3
February .	37	29	8	7	6	1	18	15	3
March . .	41	28	13	8	8	...	19	17	2
April . .	36	29	7	6	5	1	18	14	4
May . .	10	5	5	2	1	1	11	10	1
June . .	4	3	1	1	1	...	3	3	\(^.\)
July . .	3	1	2	2	1	1	1	1	...
August .	4	2	2	2	1	1	20	8	12
September .	4	2	2	2	1	1	6	5	1
October .	13	5	8	5	3	2	7	6	1
November .	9	5	4	1	1	...	7	7	...
December .	13	8	5	4	4	...	9	7	2
Totals .	197	133	64	49	38	11	137	108	29

Total number of specimens examined for Tubercle, . . 197
,, ,, Typhoid and Relapsing or Continued Fever, 49
,, ,, Diphtheria and Membranous Croup, . . 137

383

TABLE 3.3: *Notifications of Infectious Diseases in Edinburgh,* 1902

Disease.	Jan.	Feb.	Mar.	Apr.	May.	June.	July.	Aug.	Sept.	Oct.	Nov.	Dec.	Total.
Typhus	5	1	...	2	...	1	1	...	...	...	...	...	10
Typhoid, Relapsing, and Continued Fever .	9	13	8	15	21	20	21	15	24	14	19	13	192
Puerperal Fever . .	3	1	6	2	4	1	3	2	1	2	...	1	26
Diphtheria, Membranous Croup . . .	44	39	34	29	26	23	28	53	22	26	43	41	408
Smallpox . . .	...	1	...	1	...	1	...	...	2	1	...	1	7
Scarlet Fever . .	53	71	63	44	56	64	52	50	87	113	84	75	812
Erysipelas . . .	67	38	36	37	35	37	28	31	45	58	49	52	513
Total . . .	181	164	147	130	142	147	133	151	181	214	195	183	1968

typhoid fever and diphtheria, carried out on behalf of Edinburgh Corporation in the Laboratory of the Royal College of Physicians during the above year. The City Medical Officer of Health commented:

> It will be seen that the total cost to the City of this important work has only amounted to £127.15s.0d., and I cannot too highly commend the efficiency and promptness with which, upon all occasions, it has been carried out by the able Director of the Laboratory, Dr Noel Paton. There can be little doubt that the institution of this means of determining the true nature of suspicious cases of illness is of the greatest benefit. It will be noticed that in no fewer than 92 out of 124 suspected cases of Typhoid Fever, and in 190 out of 268 suspected cases of Diphtheria, the examination negatived the existence of these diseases. Had such a means of diagnosis not been at our disposal, there is no question that many of these patients would have been removed to the Fever Hospital, thus entailing considerable expense in removal, disinfection, etc., and at the same time, no small inconvenience to the families concerned.

Nevertheless, despite the Royal College of Physicians' Laboratory's valuable diagnostic service, Edinburgh Corporation had decided "to take its business elsewhere". The Public Health Department Report for 1902 stated: "The Corporation decided towards the end of the year 1902 that this work [i.e. as carried out by the RCP Laboratory] should be transferred to the Usher Institute of Public Health and the sum of £300 per year should be paid for its performance" (Report, 1902). The Report gives the following statistics as regards the specimens examined at the Usher Institute during that year (Table 3.2). Table 3.3 shows the incidence of infectious diseases in Edinburgh for that year.

A note in the Annual Report stated that "these figures did not represent the extent to which Bacteriology is employed in the diagnosis of the above diseases since a large number of medical men still continue to send their specimens to the College of Physicians' Laboratory whose work is performed gratuitously".

Foundation of the Usher Institute

While the establishment in 1887 of the Royal College of Physicians' Laboratory may have been promoted by Pasteur's visit to Edinburgh and the positive encouragement that this gave to the new science of bacteriology in Edinburgh, certainly the opening of the Usher Institute in 1902 with its diagnostic bacteriology and other laboratories was a direct consequence of the visit and the effect it had on one particular Edinburgh businessman, Alastair Low Bruce, a director of William Younger's brewery at Holyrood[21,22].

William Younger & Co. Ltd., one of Scotland's most famous brewing companies, was established in Leith in 1749 and then at Holyrood Road in 1778 (see Keir, 1951). Production and prosperity steadily increased. Around 1880, however, the firm was encountering problems. The quality of the beer had deteriorated. Even Henry Younger, senior partner, is on record as being reluctant to drink his own firm's product. Sales remained unaffected but there were fears for loss of the market. Low Bruce[23], a man of great initiative and competence, much involved in the brewing process, considered that there was something seriously wrong with the fermentation technique.

In 1883, Henry Younger and Low Bruce learned that Edinburgh might be honoured by the visit of a very distinguished French chemist whose special field, in which he had made some historic discoveries, was fermentation. This was Louis

Pasteur. At the last moment, however, it seemed that Pasteur might not attend after all, on account of the death of his close friend and mentor, the distinguished chemist Dumas. It would appear that possibly Henry Younger and Low Bruce persuaded Pasteur to attend so that they might seek his advice on their fermentation problems.

On their arrival in London, Pasteur and his French colleagues were pleasantly surprised to find a private railway coach awaiting them provided by Henry Younger who, with his family and Low Bruce, were waiting to greet them at Edinburgh. While attending the various University Tercentenary events, Pasteur resided with Younger at his home in Grange Loan. On 17 April, Pasteur visited the Holyrood brewery and spent much time there at the microscope. Apparently his technical advice proved most valuable and the brewery's production techniques were greatly improved. Pasteur also paid a visit to the home of Low Bruce in Regent Terrace. Bruce's wife was the daughter of the famous African missionary and explorer, Dr David Livingstone, and the French visitor, who had a great admiration for the latter, wished to pay his respects to his daughter. In appreciation of Pasteur's beneficial advice, Henry Younger donated £500 to the University's Medical School building fund.

Another generous expression of appreciation was to be made that had important and lasting consequences. A. Low Bruce, who had already been following the course of Pasteur's researches in bacteriology with deep interest, was greatly impressed by the famous scientist's visit. As a result he decided to contribute towards the foundation of a Chair of Public Health in the University. Sadly, Bruce died before seeing this executed but on his deathbed he instructed his solicitor to allocate a substantial bequest to the University. This was supplemented by members of his family and by Sir John Usher[24] of Norton and Wells, of the notable brewers and distillers family. A total of £15,000 was raised. The Bruce and John Usher Chair of Public Health was established in 1898 and was the first of its kind in Britain. The first incumbent was Charles Hunter Stewart, close colleague of Dr Henry Littlejohn, who had been much involved in the setting up of the Chair – another milestone in his labours for the health of the city – and who himself became Professor of Medical Jurisprudence in the University.

As a consequence of Pasteur's visit, the subject of public health and epidemiology, for long taught at postgraduate level, was given a new importance. Later, Sir John Usher, commenting that a Chair without an institute was incomplete, provided substantial funds for the building of the Usher Institute[25] opened in 1902 in Warrender Park Road, and, at the time of writing, recently closed with the transference of the Department of Community Medicine to the Medical School in Teviot Place. Not only were important new courses inaugurated at the Usher, but the Institute had good facilities including a very large lecture theatre, teaching laboratories and a large bacteriological laboratory which, as referred to above, in 1902, the Edinburgh Public Health Department chose to designate as the city's first official municipal public health laboratory for diagnostic bacteriology.

We have found it difficult to obtain much significant or detailed information concerning the earliest lecturers on bacteriology at the Usher Institute when the subject was an important one in the Public Health Diploma Course. When Professor Charles Hunter Stewart was appointed the first Professor of Public Health in the Bruce and John Usher Chair in 1898, according to his obituary, he continued to

21. *Louis Pasteur*

22. *Younger's Brewery, Holyrood Road*

23. *Alastair Low Bruce*

24. *Sir John Usher*

432. *University of Edinburgh, The John Usher Institute of Public Health*, LEADBETTER AND FAIRLEY, Architects.

25. Usher Institute, Warrender Park Road

26. *Professor John Brotherston makes the retiral presentation to Henry amd Mrs Bott*

work in the University's Department of Medical Jurisprudence which, until the establishment of the new Chair, had taught public health. It appears that Professor Hunter Stewart also had a public health laboratory within Medical Jurisprudence, in the then relatively New Medical School Building in Teviot Place. He was assisted in the running of the laboratory by Dr James B. Young who from 1892 had also been assistant to Dr Douglas Maclagan and later Dr Henry Littlejohn, the successive Professors of Medical Jurisprudence (later re-named Forensic Medicine).

In 1902 the Department of Public Health moved to the newly opened Usher Institute in Warrender Park Road. Dr Young also transferred to the new department. While Professor Hunter Stewart was responsible for the teaching of bacteriology, Dr Young was the principal teacher and he was in charge of the bacteriological diagnostic laboratory established in the Usher Institute in 1902. Dr Young contributed several papers to the *Proceedings of the Royal Society of Edinburgh* of which he was a Fellow. He remained in charge of the diagnostic laboratory until it was transferred to the University Bacteriology Department in 1926. Dr C.J. Lewis, who was described as of the "Public Health Laboratory, University of Edinburgh" – presumably at the Usher Institute – published a number of papers on bacteriological studies carried out between 1902 and 1907 at the Royal College of Physicians' Laboratory at Forrest Road.

Certainly one of the Institute's earliest technicians is more clearly on record. This was Henry Bott[26] who had been in the RAMC before joining the Institute in 1929. He played an important part in the preparation of teaching material for Professor P.S. Lelean, appointed to the Chair of Public Health in 1926. Mr Bott tutored students for examinations and at times these were referred to as "Bott's swots". He retired in 1968.

By the early 1900s then, considerable progress had been made in the development of bacteriology in Edinburgh, in research and in the diagnosis of infections. Alongside the work already described at the College of Physicians' Laboratory and the Usher Institute, much bacteriological research and teaching was being done by Dr Robert Muir of the University Pathology Department. Muir collaborated with Dr James Ritchie, then of the Pathology Department in Oxford, in the joint authorship of a *Manual of Bacteriology* (Muir and Ritchie, 1897)[27,28] which was the first textbook of its kind in Britain and was to become a classic work. Ritchie then came to Edinburgh as the University's first Professor of Bacteriology in 1913 (see below).

City Fever Hospital Laboratory

In addition to the various centres of bacteriological work that we have described, a significant and important further development was the establishment of a bacteriology laboratory in the city's impressive purpose-built City Fever Hospital opened at Colinton Mains in 1903 at a cost of £350,000. Dr Claude Buchanan Ker, who had been Medical Superintendent of the City Fever Hospital in Drummond Street, was involved in the planning of the new hospital and was its first Medical Superintendent. In 1904, a year after the hospital had been opened, he wrote:

> The bacteriological laboratory in the hospital was opened in October and a systematic examination has been made of all cases of diphtheria, scarlet fever and typhoid in which diagnosis has been doubtful. This departure, it is hoped, will tend to prevent the risk of cross-infection in scarlet fever and diphtheria and also enable the discharge of patients who have suffered from the latter disease to be regulated on a scientific basis.

34

27. *Professor Sir Robert Muir*

OXFORD MEDICAL PUBLICATIONS

MANUAL OF
BACTERIOLOGY

BY

ROBERT MUIR, M.A., M.D., Sc.D., LL.D., F.R.S.
PROFESSOR OF PATHOLOGY, UNIVERSITY OF GLASGOW

AND

THE LATE JAMES RITCHIE, M.A., M.D., F.R.C.P.(Ed.)
LATE IRVINE PROFESSOR OF BACTERIOLOGY, UNIVERSITY OF EDINBURGH
FORMERLY FELLOW OF NEW COLLEGE, OXFORD

REVISED WITH THE CO-OPERATION OF

CARL H. BROWNING, M.D., D.P.H.
GARDINER PROFESSOR OF BACTERIOLOGY, UNIVERSITY OF GLASGOW

AND

THOMAS J. MACKIE, M.D., D.P.H.
IRVINE PROFESSOR OF BACTERIOLOGY, UNIVERSITY OF EDINBURGH

EIGHTH EDITION

*WITH 211 ILLUSTRATIONS IN THE TEXT
AND 6 COLOURED PLATES*

HUMPHREY MILFORD
OXFORD UNIVERSITY PRESS

London   Edinburgh   Glasgow   Copenhagen   New York   Toronto
Melbourne   Cape Town   Bombay   Calcutta   Madras   Shanghai
1927

28. *Title page, Muir & Ritchie's
"Manual of Bacteriology"*

In 1905 there were 3,000 such laboratory examinations and by 1914, 10,639. The laboratory work at the City Hospital contributed greatly to related epidemiological studies. Some years after its opening, the laboratory was to work in close association with the then newly established Department of Bacteriology in the Medical School. The City Hospital laboratory has survived (see later), but its days now seem to be numbered.

From a relatively early date bacteriology was also done in the Royal Infirmary; apart from the very early work of Dr Watson Cheyne in the Drummond Street hospital, this was at the new Lauriston hospital initially under the aegis of the University Pathology Department. The development of the Royal Infirmary's separate bacteriology laboratory is the subject of a later chapter. Moreover, after the opening of the new Royal Hospital for Sick Children (RHSC) at Sciennes in 1895, the pathology laboratory there began to assume importance and was responsible for a small amount of bacteriology until a separate bacteriology unit was set up at the hospital. Reference to the bacteriological work done at the Municipal Hospitals in Edinburgh is made later.

CHAPTER FOUR

THE
ROBERT IRVINE CHAIR
OF BACTERIOLOGY

By 1912 a considerable amount of bacteriology was being done in various laboratories in Edinburgh, with some teaching of the subject notably in the University Pathology Department and the Usher Institute. However, there was a growing and urgent need for a more systematic teaching of the subject. Moreover a focal point for its further development and for the co-ordination of the valuable work being carried out in various places was required. With the consolidation of the early work of Pasteur, Koch, Ehrlich and others and a steady flow of new discoveries about the causative organisms of infectious diseases, it was essential to incorporate systematic teaching of bacteriology into the medical school curriculum.

On the retiral of Professor Greenfield in 1912 from the Chair of Pathology, the University Senate decided that the combined duties of the Professor of Pathology with responsibility for beds in the Royal Infirmary were incompatible, since each tended to detract from the other. The hospital beds associated with the Pathology Chair were therefore transferred to form the basis for the creation of the new Moncrieff Arnot Chair of Medicine. The Professor of Pathology was further relieved of his responsibility for the teaching of bacteriology and the opportunity was taken to institute the Robert Irvine Chair of Bacteriology in 1913. As the University record of the time relates "three separate Chairs therefore stemmed from what had originally been one".

While the need for a Chair in Bacteriology was urgent, its creation had become possible sooner than might have been the case through the availability of the necessary funding in a manner to which, as the University account of the events records, "a certain amount of romance attaches" (Logan Turner, 1933). This was indeed the case and merits a little relevant digression into the origins of the funding with some detail of the man whose generosity is commemorated by the name of the Chair.

Mr Robert Irvine

Robert Irvine[29] was born in Edinburgh in 1839. He was educated at the Royal High School where he developed a deep and lasting interest in chemistry. After leaving school he was trained as a chemist in the extensive paper-making firm of Messrs Cowan at Penicuik, later moving to a chemical works at Musselburgh. Eventually, he transferred to the ink manufacturing firm of A.B. Fleming & Co. whose premises were in the very impressive late seventeenth-century villa Caroline Park House, off West Granton Road. He became Director and Consultant Chemist. The house was in the estate of Royston and in the records is frequently referred to simply as Royston or Royston House. Caroline Park House, still extant, has attracted considerable attention and praise from writers on architecture and is of great interest.

At his home, Royston House at Granton, Irvine gathered round him a group of Edinburgh's leading scientists. One of these was John Murray, born in Canada, who at Edinburgh University pursued courses in various scientific subjects such as chemistry, physics, mathematics and engineering, but "showed no respect for the tedious discipline of examinations nor a wish to acquire the decoration of degrees". He had also begun to study medicine at Edinburgh, but discontinued this after only a few weeks while readily conceding that he was known to his companions as "the chronic student" (Boog-Watson, 1967). These early meanderings and seeming lack of direction are well documented by Boog-Watson who paid tribute to the perspicacity of Professor P. Guthrie Tait of the Chair of Natural Philosophy who admired

29. *Robert Irvine*

30. *Christmas Island (with acknowledgement to the Mansell Collection)*

31. *Sir John Murray*

Murray's strength of character and resourcefulness, and to the judgement of Lord Kelvin. These sponsors secured a senior place for Murray on *HMS Challenger* which was being fitted out by the Admiralty in 1872 for a scientific voyage, largely initiated by Edinburgh University. Murray's significant contributions to the success of the Challenger Expedition, his personal financial support, the usefulness of his scientific reports and the value of his other scientific services to the government were to earn him a knighthood in 1898.

The ship set sail in December 1872 on a voyage that proved to be long and arduous. The link between the Challenger Expedition and the foundation of the Robert Irvine Chair of Bacteriology in 1913 is a rather indirect one. Contrary to some accounts, the *Challenger* did not visit Christmas Island[30] in the Indian Ocean. Fourteen years after this expedition however, the desolate island was in fact visited by a British Surveying Vessel, *HMS Flying Fish.* On his return to Britain, the commanding officer of this ship, who had served on *Challenger,* discussed his visit with his friend Sir John Murray[31] and drew attention to the island's coral reefs and especially its volcanic rock and limestone formations. Murray was greatly interested and when a year later another ship was due to visit Christmas Island, Murray asked its commander, also a former *Challenger* shipmate, to bring back samples of the soil and rock.

The Christmas Island material was duly given to Murray and Robert Irvine who examined it in the *Challenger* office in Frederick Street in Edinburgh. They were startled to find that the samples consisted almost entirely of pure phosphate of lime. They immediately recognised the great economic value of the material as a fertiliser and for other purposes. Murray and certain influential friends privately approached the then Prime Minister, Lord Salisbury, and in June 1888 a party from *HMS Imperieuse* landed and took possession of Christmas Island. Murray then arranged a proper survey. His original findings were confirmed and in due course the Christmas Island Phosphate Company was set up with Murray and Irvine as directors.

The enormously valuable beds of phosphate of lime were quarried and the precious cargo brought back to Britain. It is said that from this enterprise Sir John Murray and Robert Irvine "made a fortune". Sir John Murray resided in Challenger Lodge, originally Wardie House, in Boswall Road. This house was to become St Columba's Hospice. Murray died in 1914, a year after the Robert Irvine Chair in Bacteriology was inaugurated.

Robert Irvine died on 20 March, 1902. As a result of his deep interest in the then relatively new science of bacteriology his will decreed that his trustees invest "the whole rest and remainder of his means and estate. for the purpose of accumulating the income till it reached the sum of £25,000 or £30,000, to be devoted to the founding of a Professorship of Bacteriology in the University of Edinburgh and the equipment of a classroom and laboratory for the teaching of the same and for conducting original investigations". Thus Irvine's generous interest in bacteriology founded a Chair that was to become internationally renowned. It has been claimed that this was the first Chair of Bacteriology to be established in Great Britain but this is now difficult to verify.

Amongst Irvine's trustees was his close friend Professor G. Sims Woodhead, who, after serving on the staff of Edinburgh University Pathology Department, and as Superintendent of the Royal College of Physicians' Laboratory in Forrest Road, became Professor of Pathology in Cambridge. Details of the conditions specified in

Irvine's will included one requiring the University to charge students attending classes in bacteriology a nominal fee only. Other information concerning the Chair's foundation is to be found in the Ordinance of the University Court No. 14, 18 November, 1912.

Robert Irvine himself had a fairly notable academic career. He had acted at one time as assistant to Professor George Wilson of the Chair of Technology in Edinburgh University and pioneer of the Scottish Industrial Museum (now the Royal Museum of Scotland) in Chambers Street. He was a Fellow of the Chemical Society. In 1886, he was elected a Fellow of the Royal Society of Edinburgh and later became a member of its Council. With Sir John Murray he contributed many papers to the *Transactions and Proceedings of the Royal Society of Edinburgh,* concerned with important aspects of oceanography. For his own individual papers he was awarded the Society's Neill Prize for 1892-95. He was also awarded medals by the Society and the Royal Scottish Society of Arts. Irvine and Murray carried out much biological experimentation in a laboratory set up on an old barge in Granton harbour, established by Murray in 1884. Other buildings on shore became the Granton Marine Station, subsequently incorporated in the Marine Biology Station at Millport.

CHAPTER FIVE

PROFESSOR JAMES RITCHIE

The University, acting upon Robert Irvine's generous endowment, sought to appoint its first Professor of Bacteriology in 1913. The man chosen was Dr James Ritchie, an Edinburgh graduate. After a sojourn in Oxford, where he was appointed Professor of Pathology in 1902, Ritchie had returned to the city in 1906 as Superintendent of the Royal College of Physicians' Laboratory. It is believed that Ritchie had met Robert Irvine, founder of the Chair, on at least one occasion. Certainly the new professor was a close friend of Dr G. Sims Woodhead who was one of Irvine's friends and was the first superintendent of the RCP Laboratory in Edinburgh. Ritchie's experience in Oxford and at the RCP Laboratory made him an ideal candidate for the Chair.

James Ritchie was born in Duns on 5 August, 1864, the only son of the Rev. William Ritchie, DD, minister of the United Presbyterian Church in this Border town. After attending the Royal High School in Edinburgh, Ritchie proceeded to take an arts degree in the University in 1884. This broadening of his education was later to be a valuable asset as a background to his medical studies and in his dealings with people and situations. In 1888 Ritchie graduated in Medicine with Honours, aged 24. His popularity with his fellow students was enhanced by his ability to take lecture notes in shorthand, to his own and their advantage! Early in his studies, his contemporaries regarded him as someone "who would make his mark".

During his appointment as a Resident in the Royal Infirmary in 1889, Dr James Ritchie also acted as house surgeon to Professor John Chiene, of the Chair of Surgery. Chiene had set up an early bacteriology laboratory in his department in the Medical School and it is believed that Ritchie thus acquired a special interest in bacteriology and also obtained considerable experience in working with infectious diseases. Ritchie was President of the Royal Medical Society from 1889 to 1900. By this time he had also obtained a BSc degree in Public Health.

Through the suggestion of Professor Chiene and at the invitation of Dr Horatio Symonds, James Ritchie went to Oxford in 1890 where he became a close friend of Sir Henry Ackland. Ackland was the Regius Professor of Medicine at Oxford and, with Ritchie, saw the increasing importance of bacteriology in relation to medicine. They sought the advice of Robert Koch on various problems and the famous German bacteriologist sent over his colleague, Dr Menge, to supervise the equipping of an Oxford bacteriology laboratory. Here Ritchie began work initiating research on the action of germicides on bacteria. This work was the subject of his MD thesis, presented to Edinburgh University in 1895, for which he was awarded a gold medal.

In 1896 Sir Henry Ackland invited Ritchie to establish a course in bacteriology at Oxford and although attendance was optional, very many medical students were attracted. Ritchie was next asked to undertake the teaching of pathology and when Dr John Burdon Sanderson, one of Britain's earliest bacteriologists, succeeded Ackland in the Oxford Chair of Medicine, he was influential in Ritchie's appointment as a lecturer in pathology at Oxford in 1897. Ritchie was promoted Reader in the subject in 1901 and then Professor a year later. Shortly after his appointment, Ritchie was elected a Fellow of New College. He worked on bacterial toxins, especially those of tetanus, and attempted to modify these in order to create an immune response in animals. Oxford University awarded him its BSc degree in 1901.

During his lectureship in Pathology at Oxford, with special involvement in the teaching of bacteriology, James Ritchie collaborated with his close friend and fellow student of Edinburgh Medical School days, Robert Muir, to produce Britain's first

32. *Professor James Ritchie*

UNIVERSITY OF EDINBURGH

₵he Robert Irvine ₵hair of Bacteriology

Professor JAMES RITCHIE, M.D., F.R.C.P.E.

will deliver his INAUGURAL LECTURE

IN THE

M'EWAN HALL

On TUESDAY, 7th inst. ʾ - - at 3 p.m.

Subject - "₵he Place of Bacteriology among the Sciences"

THIS LECTURE IS OPEN TO THE PUBLIC

3rd OCTOBER 1913

L. J. GRANT, Sec. Sen. Acad.

33. *Notice of Inaugural Lecture*

systematic textbook on the subject, *A Manual of Bacteriology* (Muir and Ritchie, 1897). This eventually ran to nine editions, six of these before his death. When the Pathological Society of Great Britain was founded in 1906, James Ritchie was one of its first secretaries and later assistant editor of its Journal under Dr G. Sims Woodhead. After the latter's death, Ritchie assumed the editorship and held this position for many years.

James Ritchie might well have continued and enhanced his distinguished career at Oxford and would probably have been appointed first Professor of Bacteriology there. However, to the great regret of his Oxford colleagues, he accepted the appointment as Superintendent of the Royal College of Physicians' Laboratory in Forrest Road. It has been said that in returning to Scotland he was motivated by a strong sense of patriotism. When James Ritchie took charge of the RCP Laboratory in 1907 it was in its twentieth year, well-established and expanding in importance. In the bacteriological field, much work had been done on the relationship between diet amongst the poorer classes and their susceptibility to infectious disease. Ritchie's own research interests were in the field of bacterial toxins and their action in relation to their chemical constitution and the nature of the immune response – on which he wrote a major article in the *Journal of Hygiene* in 1902. The action of antiseptics was another of his interests.

Shortly after his appointment to the RCP Laboratory, Ritchie introduced a popular course there on bacteriology. At times the research programme had to be modified to take account of urgent, contemporary problems, such as the prevalence of diphtheria and scarlet fever in the city. It was wrongly believed that the two diseases were closely related and Ritchie initiated research on this. Further work included experimentation with the Widal reaction; in relation to typhoid, the infection of the gall bladder from the bowel; the bacteriological efficacy of the city's water supply filters; the bacteriological examination of milk, with special reference to the incidence of bovine tuberculosis in children; and the preparation of autogenous vaccines. Between 1906 and 1914, 98 papers had been published – by a relatively small research staff, many greatly encouraged by Dr Ritchie. With the outbreak of the First World War in 1914, the RCP Laboratory was to play an important part in providing much-needed medical laboratory services. By this time its superintendent was directing its work along with his duties as the newly appointed Professor of Bacteriology in the University Medical School, as first occupant of the Robert Irvine Chair established in 1913.

Inaugural Address

Professor James Ritchie[32] took up his appointment in the University on 1 October, 1913. His Inaugural Address[33], delivered on 7 October, 1913, provides a valuable insight into the interests and aims of the first incumbent of the new Chair and his view on priorities for the further development of the science of bacteriology and of his new department.* Ritchie paid tribute to Mr Robert Irvine. He went on to trace the origins of bacteriology, praising the pioneering discoveries of Pasteur, Koch and the consequent work of Lister, who had been much inspired by Burdon Sanderson, one of Britain's first disciples of these great pioneers. By 1886, within his own lifetime, Ritchie noted that tuberculosis, diphtheria, typhoid fever, septicaemia,

---

* The Inaugural Addresses of the successive professors at Edinburgh are listed in Appendix D.

cholera and pneumonia had all been shown to have bacterial causes. He then outlined the principles of the isolation of organisms in relation to diagnosis, and he emphasised that infections were responsible for half of the country's total death rate.

Professor Ritchie then dealt with some of his own particular interests: immunisation, the use of antitoxin against "the scourge of diphtheria", the action and neutralisation of other toxins, hypersensitivity and chemotherapy. He observed that not all infectious diseases were due to "ordinary bacteria" and he went on to refer to viruses and their association with smallpox, measles and poliomyelitis, but these organisms were, so far, invisible by the highest microscopic power available. He offered "comfort" to the already overworked medical students in his audience by assuring them that bacteriological teaching in their currently heavy syllabus would be kept to the essential minimum. The subject, he believed, was essentially for postgraduate study.

In conclusion, Professor Ritchie stated that in accordance with Robert Irvine's wishes and with the University's agreement, the function of the Chair would be primarily to foster inquiry but also to initiate instruction in bacteriology. He appealed for even greater financial support for the advancement of his subject. The old motto of the *Edinburgh Review,* Professor Ritchie stressed, namely, "we cultivate learning on a little oatmeal" was for science now a dead letter. In appealing again for the support of other wealthy benefactors, the new professor pledged the ready response of a band of talented research workers – "who will carry on the traditions which have in the past placed the Edinburgh Medical School in the foremost rank".

Development of the New Department

As the echoes of the newly appointed professor's inaugural address and the vigorous applause faded, he turned to the practicalities of his new task. Facilities, working conditions and circumstances were not the most conducive to immediate progress. The clouds were already gathering to foreshadow the outbreak of the First World War when ideal schemes for academic and other developments had to be laid aside. Urgent and emergency calls were being made upon the medical services by the military authorities, demanding the use of all available resources and personnel.

The Edinburgh University Calendar for the academic year 1913-14, the time of Professor Ritchie's appointment, indicates that the Professor and his small staff had to work within whatever space was available in the Pathology Department. The Calendar does not indicate a separate Bacteriology Department but, as it did for the previous academic year, lists a number of courses in bacteriology. Presumably these were those conducted by Dr Robert Muir until his appointment to the Chair of Pathology in St. Andrews University. While from the records it is not very clear, Professor Ritchie would have had responsibility for the courses and the assistance of some of the Pathology Department academic staff until he was able to recruit his own for the new department.

At the time of Professor Ritchie's appointment, large numbers of medical students appear in the University Calendar's statistics. While these came under the aegis of the Faculty of Medicine, very many, it is believed, were probably attending lectures outwith the Medical School, i.e. in the Royal Colleges of Physicians and Surgeons with courses leading to the Colleges' own qualifications in medicine. Professor Ritchie's first academic staff, listed separately for the Bacteriology Department, were Dr W.E. Carnegie Dickson and Dr Alfred Vincent Dill.

34. *Richard Muir*

35. *Miss Netta Muir*

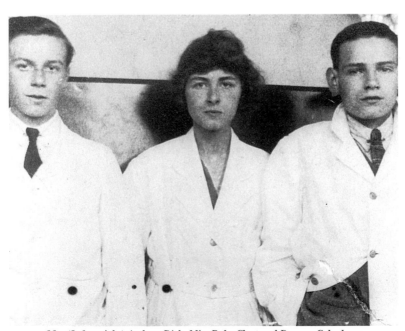

36. *(Left to right) Andrew Dick, Miss Ruby Cleat and Duncan Colquhoun*

Technical Staff

From the outset, Professor Ritchie had the services of a distinguished laboratory assistant in his new University Department. This was Richard Muir[34] who had joined the University Pathology Department as a "lab. boy" in about 1880, being possibly the first of such to be employed in Edinburgh medical circles. He was followed closely in time by Willie Watson who began in the same lowly capacity in the Royal College of Physicians' Laboratory then in Lauriston Lane in 1887. Richard Muir was to earn a high reputation throughout Britain and indeed beyond as a well-informed and highly skilled technician to whom many pathologists came or wrote seeking his expert opinion on a wide variety of pathological conditions and particularly his comments on stained tissue preparations from patients. In Richard Muir's earliest days in the pre-microtome era, sections were skilfully cut manually. So high indeed was Richard Muir's reputation that the University eventually designated him a Demonstrator in Pathological and Bacteriological Methods.

Muir was a very good artist and in 1927 published his Muir's Bacteriological Atlas (Muir, 1927), presenting his fine drawings of bacteria, cells and other selected microscopic material which he had produced originally as classroom wall charts. Richard Muir, with Professor David Hamilton of Aberdeen, contributed the chapter on "Pathology" in the 11th Edition of the Encyclopaedia Britannica (Muir and Hamilton, 1910-11). Encouraged by his Pathology Department colleague, Dr German Sims Woodhead, Richard Muir was co-founder in 1912 of the Pathological and Bacteriological Laboratory Assistants' Association (PBLAA) and was its first vice-president. The PBLAA organised local evening classes in pathological and bacteriological technique (and later other subjects) in various cities and initiated the steady if slow progress of the "lab. boy" to the highly skilled professional Medical Laboratory Scientific Officer (MLSO) of today. Richard Muir, who was attached primarily to the Pathology Department, withdrew his services from the Bacteriology Department some years after Professor T.J. Mackie had been appointed to the Chair in 1923. Richard Muir retired in 1931.

Professor Ritchie's other early technical staff[35,36] included Miss Ruby Cleat who was appointed at the outbreak of the First World War in 1914, and who was in charge of the preparation of culture media, and sterilisation, a post which she held until her resignation in 1936. Miss Cleat's junior colleagues were Duncan B. Colquhoun, Andrew Dick and Robert Hunter. Miss Netta Muir, Richard Muir's daughter, a laboratory assistant in the Pathology Department, also served for some time in the Bacteriology Department. The department's earliest animal attendant was Mrs Weir. A "lab. boy" recruited to the Pathology Department in 1912, Alexander Cheyne, would have been known to Professor Ritchie when he was appointed to the Bacteriology Chair a year later. Sandy Cheyne (as he was always familiarly known) was to return after military service to join the staff of the Bacteriology Department in 1923 under Professor Mackie and as the Department's first senior laboratory assistant (see later).

Continued Development

While the embryonic Bacteriology Department shared accommodation with the Pathology Department on the second top floor of the west wing of the Medical School in Teviot Place, research facilities were quite inadequate. By arrangement between the University and the Royal College of Physicians' Laboratory – of which Professor Ritchie remained Superintendent until 1920 – research workers were able to work in the Forrest Road laboratory. The University paid the College for such facilities, Professor Ritchie's continued services in the College Laboratory forming part of the financial arrangements made. From 1913, the University Calendar directed anyone wishing to carry out research in bacteriology to apply to Professor Ritchie for permission to work in the Forrest Road laboratory.

During the First World War, Professor Ritchie's duties increased very considerably when the College Laboratory was called upon to provide much assistance to the Forces. In September 1914, there was an urgent appeal for anti-typhoid and "anti-sepsis" vaccines, along with anti-tetanus, anti-dysentery and anti-meningococcal sera for soldiers in the front line and the College laboratory did a substantial amount of work along these lines. The income obtained by the College of Physicians' Laboratory for its considerable services to the War Office was put aside in the "Lister Memorial Fund". While the facilities of his Medical School department were so clearly inadequate and a source of great frustration to Ritchie in his new professorship, he had great hopes of a new department with purpose-built facilities, not in the Medical School but in the projected "Lister Institute of Pathology" which would be built near the Royal Infirmary and would house both the Pathology and Bacteriology Departments. The envisaged Institute had first been proposed by the Royal College of Surgeons as Edinburgh's great memorial to the illustrious Lord Lister who, having done much of his early work in Edinburgh, had died in 1912. Professor Ritchie had been involved in discussions about the future Institute and his enthusiasm for the project and the opportunities which it would present probably enabled him to tolerate the inadequate Medical School facilities until the end of the War and the advancement of the scheme. However, the projected Lister Institute was never to materialise. A brief account of the re-direction of its funds into other institutions is presented below.

Numerous Tributes

A year after the end of the First World War, the University Calendar for the academic year 1919-20 lists the staff of the Bacteriology Department as the professor and two academics. Dr W.E. Carnegie Dickson appears to have resigned and Dr A.V. Dill is joined by a new colleague whose name was to become internationally known in the annals of bacteriology – Dr J.E. McCartney. The three, including Professor Ritchie, were to work together until Ritchie's death in January 1923. On account of his dual commitment to the University and the Royal College of Physicians' Laboratory, and with the outbreak of the First World War soon after his appointment, Professor Ritchie's development of the department was frustrated. With further constraints imposed by periods of illness before his death, he was able to lay only the preliminary foundations of the Department of Bacteriology. Nevertheless, through his distinguished career in Oxford and his valuable work at the RCP Laboratory, Ritchie's death on 28 January, 1923, brought a deep sense of loss to the world of laboratory medicine, in Edinburgh and far beyond. Certainly, as one of his early teachers had forecast, Ritchie had made his mark.

The many tributes paid to this pioneer in pathology and bacteriology provide an impressive picture of the man who was first to occupy Edinburgh's new Chair of Bacteriology. He was a fine teacher and many of his students subsequently enjoyed distinguished careers. With his wide commitments to the Royal College of Physicians, the University Chair, his service on the Royal Infirmary Board of Managers and his authorship and editorial duties, Professor Ritchie was an extremely busy man; yet he never seemed to be in a hurry. He made time for colleagues and students who sought his counsel. He enjoyed a happy family life; it has been said that a strong reason for Ritchie leaving the attractive career possibilities of Oxford was his eagerness that his three daughters should be educated in Scotland. One of them, Alison, was to follow her father into medicine, becoming a general practitioner and later an anaesthetist. She provided valuable assistance in the compilation of this brief biography of her father. Ritchie enjoyed the company of his colleagues and was a prime mover in forming a dinner club. He was seen, all too occasionally, on the golf course. His wit and lively sense of humour enlivened many a social function. A former Oxford colleague wrote: "Of Ritchie, I never heard anyone say an ill word – a tribute few can claim". Another colleague wrote: "He not only taught pathology and bacteriology: he also taught accuracy and dependability". Another distinguished colleague said: "While ever in favour of progress and reform, he was no revolutionary. He would rather that improvements came slowly with the co-operation of those concerned rather than be forced upon them against honest although perhaps unintelligible opposition."

CHAPTER SIX

PROFESSOR
THOMAS JONES MACKIE

In 1917, four years after Professor Ritchie had taken up the newly created Chair of Bacteriology in the University, a Glasgow medical graduate of considerable distinction was appointed to another new chair, the Wernher-Beit Professorship of Bacteriology in the University of Cape Town at the relatively early age of 29. This was Thomas Jones Mackie who, only six years later, was to return to Scotland to succeed Ritchie in the Edinburgh chair.

"T.J." as he was to become familiarly known, was born in Hamilton, Lanarkshire, on 5 June, 1888, where his father and grandfather had both successively held the post of Town Chamberlain. Mackie's performance at Hamilton Academy was apparently quite unspectacular but he did qualify for entrance to study medicine at Glasgow University. He graduated MBChB with Honours in 1910, gaining the Brunton Memorial Prize as the most distinguished student of his year. After completing an appointment as a surgeon in the Glasgow Western Royal Infirmary he was for two years on the research staff of the Pathology Department there which was under the joint aegis of the Infirmary and the University. The director was Professor Robert Muir, the former pioneer lecturer in bacteriology in the Edinburgh University Pathology Department and a close friend of Professor James Ritchie.

Although built on a solid grounding in pathology, T.J.'s interests turned to bacteriology, perhaps under the influence of Professor Robert Muir and his lecturer Carl Browning. In 1914, Mackie joined the Bland-Sutton Institute of the Middlesex Hospital as an assistant bacteriologist. The outbreak of the First World War cut this experience short and he maintained a family tradition by joining the Cameronians (Scottish Rifles); the tradition was continued by his son in the 1939-45 war. As a medical officer experienced in pathology and bacteriology, T.J. served in laboratories in Gallipoli and Alexandria. He was released from military service to take up the chair at Cape Town. En route by sea to South Africa his ships were twice torpedoed.

Shortly after Mackie took up the appointment at Cape Town, the Professor of Pathology there died and Mackie took charge of both departments. He played an important part in designing the university's general medical studies curriculum, an interest which duly proved of great value when he came to Edinburgh. While occupying the Chair of Bacteriology at Cape Town, Mackie produced his first little practical handbook of bacteriology – essentially notes on laboratory methods and the forerunner of the renowned Mackie and McCartney's *Introduction to Practical Bacteriology*, first published in Edinburgh in 1925. In October 1923, Professor T.J. Mackie[37] succeeded Professor James Ritchie in the Robert Irvine Chair of Bacteriology at Edinburgh.

Development of the Department

In his inaugural address (see appendix D1) delivered on 11 October 1923, entitled "The Present Position of Medical Bacteriology", Professor Mackie paid more than simply formal tribute to his predecessor and he stressed the important achievements of Professor James Ritchie as a pioneer in the subject. Mackie commented upon the remarkable scientific progress made in his own lifetime, and he said that he was in favour of the word "microbiology" as against "bacteriology", in view of the wider and widening scope of the subject. He urged the need for a new classification of micro-organisms. Pure research was not to be neglected even though bacteriology must make itself more widely relevant to disease and the problems of industrial infections. He stressed the importance of research on "filterable viruses", citing influenza as a

37. *Professor T.J. Mackie*

38. *Professor Mackie lecturing*

case in point. Many "territories" had already been won. There were signs that immunology would become an independent science. The mechanisms of infection and the study of toxicology demanded close attention. It was time to separate the teaching of pathology and bacteriology. Finally, there was a great need for specialised courses, treating bacteriology as a science and meeting the needs of postgraduate students.

The task confronting Professor Mackie had to be approached on a wide variety of fronts. Professor Ritchie's attempts to establish the teaching of bacteriology in the medical curriculum, to initiate research, and to build up the department's laboratory facilities and staff had been limited by the war and other circumstances. Nevertheless, significant foundations had been laid. Mackie's task was to build upon these, rapidly and substantially. His immediate priorities were clear and he set them down as such. From a valuable handwritten record which Mackie kept in three "sixpenny" hard-backed notebooks headed: "Record of Department of Bacteriology, University of Edinburgh from date of Professor Mackie's assumption of duties of Chair on 1 October 1923", many of the department's principal areas of development can be traced, in relation to each academic year. Even a quick glance through this log book strikingly reveals the tremendous surge of development that he began and sustained for so long. This progress was in very many directions: it may be summarised thus: The early acquisition of additional teaching and research laboratories, with the necessary equipment; increased financial resources to permit the recruitment of additional academic staff, most of whom were specially selected young medical graduates of high calibre and very many of whom were eventually to gain professorial chairs or other posts of importance throughout the United Kingdom and beyond and to achieve distinction in bacteriology and other branches of medicine; the expansion of teaching within the medical curriculum and the introduction of a bacteriology BSc Honours course for both medical and science students; the strong thrust of research in many directions, much of it concerned with the prevalent infectious diseases of the period, and thus yielding a steady output of published papers; the forging of valuable relations with general practitioners, hospital clinicians and the city public health and government health authorities.

So wide was the spectrum of development that to relate all of it in detail is not feasible; accordingly, the progress is recorded here in summary. The steady succession of staff who contributed to the department's development under Mackie's direction and inspiration, and who in due course left for other posts, is referred to in relation to the phases of the department's development and to the research priorities that were linked to current health problems in the city.

World Progress of Bacteriology

In relation to the impressive and spectacular importance of the new science of bacteriology established in the 1880s, two comments may be apposite. Dr Una Maclean in her invaluable history of the Usher Institute (Maclean, 1975) wrote: "The impetus which bacteriology gave to medicine at that time was infinitely exhilarating, prompting confidence in the ultimate defeat of disease. The sense of medical progress was pristine and undimmed, and evidence of the vital importance of public health and preventive medicine could confidently be offered not only to members of the profession but to intelligent laymen". And Professor Topley, the distinguished bacteriologist, wrote of the riotous growth of the eighteen-eighties. This great vision

39. *Dr James E. McCartney*

40. *Professor Sir Stanley Davidson*

41. *Dr Alexander Joe*

42. *Alexander Bremner Cheyne (1896-1979)*

of possibilities and progress was still bright when Professor Mackie took the chair.

Professor Mackie died in post in 1955. Looking back at so much progress recorded in Professor Mackie's notebooks, it might seem that the period in the department's development was quite unique and unlikely to be equalled again in range and quality. The impressive advances must be seen in context. Under the direction of Mackie, and not least through his qualities for the task, the department was caught up and driven on by the nationwide momentum of an increasingly wider appreciation of the importance and relevance of bacteriology by general practitioners, hospital clinicians and various public health authorities. The development and achievements of the discipline increased steadily since the principles of approach to diagnosis, therapy and prevention evolved by Pasteur, Koch, Ehrlich and others seemed to provide almost limitless possibilities. As the aetiologies of more and more of the infectious diseases were discovered, dramatic progress was being made in chemotherapy and the use of antibiotics. For workers in bacteriology throughout the world, it was a spectacular period. By the time of Mackie's death in 1955, the problems and challenges confronting the bacteriologist, virologist and immunologist had become rather different and of new complexity. Who was to know that the lull was to be followed by another dauntingly rapid succession of discoveries of new diseases and transmissible agents!

Staff

Professor Mackie's "log book" records that when he took over the chair in 1923 he was assisted by three medical staff:

> Lecturer: Dr James E. McCartney[39], who had been appointed during Professor Ritchie's term.
> Assistants: Dr Laybourne S.P. Davidson, Dr Alexander Joe[40,41].

All of these three original members of Mackie's staff were to achieve distinction in their subsequent careers. The original research workers were:

> Miss Muriel Thomson – Vans Dunlop and BMA Scholar
> Miss Jessie Sells – Freeland Buchan Scholar
> Dr H.F. Watson – Research Student
> Dr T. Sprint – Carnegie Fellow.

Technical Staff: Sandy Cheyne

When Professor Mackie took up his post, he inherited a number of technical staff from Professor Ritchie's period. Richard Muir, already referred to, although primarily on the staff of the Pathology Department, continued to assist Professor Mackie for a short time. It is said that through his good laboratory housekeeping during Professor Ritchie's years, Muir was able to present Professor Mackie with a sum of around £1,000 (a considerable amount at that time). In addition to Richard Muir, the technical staff in the Bacteriology Department included Miss Ruby Cleat, Miss Netta Muir, Duncan Colquhoun and Andrew Dick. In November 1923, a month after his own arrival in the department, Professor Mackie appointed Alexander Cheyne[42] as the department's first senior laboratory assistant. Sandy Cheyne had first begun as a "lab. boy" in the Pathology Department in 1912, but after the outbreak of the First World War had joined the RAMC. Following his demobilisation at the end of the war, he had worked for a few years in a military hospital at Bellahouston in Glasgow. Then he came to the Edinburgh department taking up his new appointment in 1923.

Apart from the training of his junior technical staff, Sandy Cheyne's primary responsibility was the provision of demonstration and other material for the large classes of medical students who, at that period and for long afterwards, did quite comprehensive practical exercises with clinical material such as specimens of pus and strongly positive tuberculous sputum. The present-day requirements of the Health and Safety Act, especially regarding dangerous pathogens, had not been visualised! The unfailing provision of good practical material was to constitute a major part of Sandy Cheyne's work and to be his forte for most of the forty-one years of his career. Professor Mackie believed in the value of visual aids in teaching. These took the form of the large wall diagrams produced by Richard Muir (some of which still remain in the Department) and the writing up on the practical classroom or lecture theatre blackboards of Professor Mackie's copious notes before each session. This was for very many years Sandy Cheyne's task and his prerogative.

In 1926, when the Department took over the Edinburgh Corporation Public Health diagnostic bacteriological service from the Usher Institute, this work was done in one of three rooms acquired from the then Medical Chemistry Department situated on the first floor. Dr Alexander Grierson, who later became Assistant Medical Officer of Health in Edinburgh – and one technician – were for some time the sole staff of the original diagnostic laboratory which had a considerable workload as the statistics of the time indicate. Robert Farmer, who joined the technical staff in 1929, and who later became technician in charge of the diagnostic laboratory, played an important part in the designing and operating of a training scheme for the Department's considerable succession of junior technical staff. He also took over much of the technical administration of the Department. In 1946, Farmer joined the research staff of Boots of Nottingham. Passing reference only is made at this point to a number of other technical staff of the early 1930s, namely J.L. Herrick, Andrew Baillie, Sydney Barlow, J.S. Keppie and Robert Weir, some of whom, where information was available, are referred to in Appendix D2.

New Premises

When part of the Chemistry Department moved out to King's Buildings in 1923, three rooms vacated on the first floor on the west side of the Medical Buildings became available as laboratories. Professor Mackie occupied the room facing the clock across the quadrangle (today Room 350). These rooms were probably the first additional separate accommodation allocated to the Bacteriology Department since the provision of the top floor classrooms A and B on the south-west corner of the original medical buildings during Professor James Ritchie's period in office. Originally Classroom A was for undergraduate teaching and B for postgraduate work. They remain in use having been modified successively by Professors Cruickshank and Marmion. The large lecture theatre with its gallery, entered from the Pathology Department, was shared with that department. There was a small door leading into the gallery from near the two top floor classrooms. In more recent times this lecture theatre was laminated to provide the Bacteriology Department with a third classroom which was ultimately converted into the main area of the present preparation suite.

With such new accommodation, four new research workers were engaged and £1,000 was allocated by the University Court for equipment. One of the additional research workers engaged was Dr J. Maxwell Alston. Dr Alston graduated in medicine at Edinburgh University in 1924 and then worked on in the department as a Vans Dunlop Scholar. Shortly afterwards, he was appointed as an Assistant. His research included studies on the filterability of the tubercle bacillus. After two years' research work in the department, Alston was appointed head of the Archway Group Laboratory, London. His special studies of leptospirosis began in 1930 and he was joint author with J.C. Broom of a book on this subject in 1959. In 1967 he published a book on infectious diseases.

By 1924, the department's teaching load was also reorganised: the instruction of medical undergraduates was extended and new courses were introduced for the Diploma in Public Health, the Diploma in Tropical Medicine, Bachelor of Science (Honours) in Bacteriology, and a course for veterinary students studying for a BSc. By 1925, accommodation problems were again acute and four additional research laboratories were provided in rooms vacated by the Chemistry Department on the second floor.

In an undated typescript memorandum probably produced in 1935, Mackie summarised the progress of the department from his appointment in 1923. In 1931 a complete reconstruction of accommodation had been made providing laboratories on the top floor of the west side of the building, including the Tower Landing. In the same year a new staircase was built leading from what was known as the Physiology Department corridor to the Bacteriology Department on the top floor. A lift encased in wire mesh was installed in the well of this staircase. The staircase remains but the lift was eventually removed and replaced nearby. The provision of the new and greatly increased laboratory accommodation in 1931 provided facilities for fifteen research workers, including teaching staff. The technical staff at this time numbered about a dozen.

Professor Mackie, at the conclusion of his memorandum, noted that facilities for the keeping of experimental animals were still unsatisfactory. The department's animal house was in rather primitive accommodation adjacent to the Surgery Department's Wilkie Research Laboratories, and backing on to Charles Street Lane. It was not until Professor Robert Cruickshank's appointment that better animal facilities were provided on the top floor of the new south block, completed in 1960.

Teaching and Research

Even before he had acquired adequate laboratory accommodation, Mackie lost no time in initiating research work. The grant of £1,000 voted for apparatus, plus the investment income from the Irvine Fund, were to be used for maintenance of the laboratories and equipment.

In November 1923 Dr J.E. McCartney was awarded a research grant by the Medical Research Council for work on "The question of the viruses of scarlatina and measles". For his thesis on "Encephalitis lethargica and herpes febrilis" McCartney was awarded a Doctor of Science degree in the following year. In 1924, Mackie published a paper on a subject which was to remain a life-long interest: "The specificity of acquired immunity and non-specific factors in immunisation" (Mackie, 1924a). He also contributed a chapter to a new edition of a textbook on his other great interest: "Recent Methods in the Diagnosis and Treatment of Syphilis" (Mackie, 1924b).

In 1924, one of Mackie's assistant lecturers, Dr L.S.P. Davidson, read a paper to the BMA. conference in Bradford on "The effects of chemical and physical agencies on bacterial vaccines". At the end of the 1924 summer session Dr Stanley Davidson, as he was familiarly known, resigned to work part time as a physician in the Royal Infirmary and to continue part-time research in the Bacteriology Department. Davidson was unpaid in both these posts and drew upon his private income. In 1924, he was awarded a Doctorate of Medicine with Gold Medal for his thesis: "Immunisation and Antibody Reactions: A Series of Experimental Studies". In due course he was to become Regius Professor of Medicine in Aberdeen and ultimately returned to Edinburgh in 1938 to the Chair of Medicine.

Soon after Dr Stanley Davidson's resignation from full-time work in the Bacteriology Department, Dr Alexander Joe resigned to become Assistant Physician Superintendent and Bacteriologist of the Edinburgh City Fever Hospital where he later became Physician Superintendent. The City Hospital had a small bacteriology laboratory since its opening in 1903 and is described in more detail later.

1925 was a notable year, being the occasion of the publication in January of the first edition of what was to become a famous textbook *An Introduction to Bacteriology: A Practical Text Book* by T.J. Mackie and J.E. McCartney. Just as the "Muir and Ritchie" *Manual of Bacteriology* published in 1897 had rapidly become a classic, so too "Mackie and McCartney" became essential reading for all bacteriology workers, research, teaching or technical staff, and undergraduate and postgraduate students. The book was to go through nine editions under Mackie's and McCartney's editorship.

Dr J.E. McCartney's co-authorship of the new textbook with Professor Mackie was to mark the end of his six years' service in the department. In March 1925 he took up the appointment of Director of Research and Pathology Services for the Metropolitan Asylums Board in London. Amongst his work in this newly established post, McCartney included the development of a centralised service for the supply of culture medium, various reagents and certain types of equipment such as screw-capped glass containers for transport of culture medium. When the Metropolitan Asylums Board was dissolved in 1930 and its functions taken over by London County Council, McCartney was confirmed in his directorship of the culture medium supply service then extended widely in London. From 1931 onwards McCartney introduced a wide range of various sizes of screw-capped bottles, notably the 6 oz. "medical flat" used extensively for blood culture and distributed with culture media ready for use. The 1 oz. "Universal container" came to be known as a "McCartney bottle".

During 1923 and 1924 much research had been carried out in the department on the role of streptococci in puerperal fever and scarlet fever. In 1926 Dr J. Buchanan was working on *Leptospira icterohaemorrhagiae*. By the end of 1926, research had been extended to syphilis serology, tubercle bacilli in milk, diphtheria, sarcoma in mice and *Bacillus salmonicida* in fish. Professor Mackie then and for many years afterwards acted as a consultant to the Fishery Board for Scotland.

Establishment of a Bacteriological Diagnostic Laboratory for the Local Authorities

By the end of 1925, the practical importance of the department's research and its interest to various public health authorities was recognised when Edinburgh Corporation Public Health Department completed arrangements to transfer their diagnostic work from the Usher Institute to the University Bacteriology Department, with effect from October 1926. This was the beginning of an important new era for the department. Mackie noted that, in addition to providing a diagnostic service for the City of Edinburgh, "certain neighbouring counties" were also included. For this new development in the department's work a special assistantship was added to the staff.

Table 6.1 shows the number of specimens examined in the Usher Institute Bacteriology Laboratory in 1925. Table 6.2 shows the number of specimens examined in the University Bacteriology Department after the transfer of the diagnostic work there in 1926. Table 6.3 lists the number of cases of various infectious diseases in the city in 1926.

Professor Mackie recognised that the new laboratory provided valuable material for investigative studies and established an active connection with Public Health practice which would be of increasing advantage to the department's teaching and research. The diagnostic laboratory was also to provide valuable training to medical academic staff and technical staff over the years. It was especially valuable to the very many technical staff who were given an all-round training in the laboratory to prepare them for the qualifying examinations of the Pathological and Bacteriological Laboratory Assistants' Association and later the Institute of Medical Laboratory Technology. As a result of the experience gained in diagnostic bacteriology, very many academic and technical staff eventually acquired posts of responsibility in laboratories in the United Kingdom and abroad. Professor Mackie also commented that, in many instances, members of the department's research staff were able to bring their specialised expertise to bear upon the problems encountered by the diagnostic laboratory. A summary of the work of the department's diagnostic laboratory: "Bacteriological Services: The First Fifty Years" was contributed to the city Public Health Department's Annual Report for 1950 by Dr Helen A. Wright and extracts from this are provided in an appendix to this general historical account.

Continuing Development

From 1925, Mackie began to implement the responsibilities conferred by his appointment to the charge of the then newly created Royal Infirmary Department of Bacteriology. This important added dimension to the University department's work, culminating just over fifty years later in the transference of the Royal Infirmary laboratory to the Medical School in Teviot Place, is the subject of a separate section.

With the establishment of the Public Health laboratory within the department, and with such a range of infections requiring laboratory investigation, the department's research was significantly related to the prevalent infectious diseases. Work was also done on associated problems such as the occurrence and transmission of tubercle bacilli in milk, the monitoring of the city's water supply, and other collaborative studies with the public health authorities. Other research was linked with cases of bacterial infection admitted to or discovered in the Royal Infirmary, where Dr Stanley Davidson preserved his links with the department and worked on *Clostridium welchii (C. perfringens)* in relation to pernicious anaemia.

In 1927 Professor Mackie was appointed a special commissioner to the Board of Health in connection with the Therapeutic Substances Act of the same year, and had a special interest for many years in the bacteriological monitoring of the manufacture of "catgut" or surgical sutures in Edinburgh then carried out by

TABLE 6.1

Examinations by Usher Institute Laboratory, 1925

	Jan.	Feb.	Mar.	April.	May.	June.	July.	Aug.	Sept.	Oct.	Nov.	Dec.	Total.
For Tubercle:—													
Number of Examinations	85	84	79	87	101	66	60	62	62	65	77	64	892
Positive	13	14	12	14	9	14	15	7	14	9	12	7	140
Negative	72	70	67	73	92	52	45	55	48	56	65	57	752
For Enteric:—													
Number of Examinations	3	9	8	5	3	11	3	8	5	7	1	1	64
Positive	...	1	...	1	...	...	...	...	...	1	...	...	3
Negative	3	6	5	4	3	10	3	8	4	5	1	1	53
Suspicious	...	2	3	...	...	1	...	...	1	1	...	...	8
For Diphtheria:—													
Number of Examinations	500	532	720	408	406	413	456	391	352	555	569	510	5812
Positive	61	59	70	52	35	40	57	38	33	42	65	49	601
Negative	439	473	650	356	371	373	399	353	319	513	504	461	5211
Other Specimens:—													
Negative	6	8	...	...	...	3	2	...	...	1	1	2	23

Total 6791

TABLE 6.2

Examinations by University Bacteriology Department
after transfer of Laboratory Work there in 1926

	Jan.	Feb.	Mar.	Apr.	May.	June.	July.	Aug.	Sept.	Oct.	Nov.	Dec.	Total.
For Tubercle:—													
Number of Examinations	78	86	94	73	85	57	56	50	40	54	54	45	772
Positive	12	9	15	19	17	8	10	7	5	17	3	5	127
Negative	66	77	79	54	68	49	46	43	35	37	51	40	645
For Enteric:—													
Number of Examinations	3	10	6	2	1	4	6	4	6	4	3	4	53
Positive	...	1	1	...	...	...	...	...	...	...	...	...	2
Negative	3	9	5	2	1	4	6	4	6	4	3	4	51
For Diphtheria:—													
Number of Examinations	650	652	422	265	292	293	262	236	320	390	369	460	4611
Positive	54	49	48	38	31	24	29	16	14	55	35	66	459
Negative	596	603	374	227	261	269	233	220	306	335	334	394	4152
Other Specimens:—													
Negative	1	...	...	...	1	1	...	1	1	1	2	...	8
TOTAL													5444

TABLE 6.3

Occurrence of Infectious Diseases in Edinburgh, 1926

Disease.	Jan.	Feb.	Mar.	Apr.	May.	June.	July.	Aug.	Sept.	Oct.	Nov.	Dec.	Total.
Smallpox	...	...	...	...	...	...	...	...	...	...	...	...	...
Cholera	...	...	...	...	...	...	...	...	...	...	...	...	...
Diphtheria and Membranous Croup	64	63	56	42	40	41	27	23	38	45	52	61	552
Erysipelas	25	21	20	15	13	11	8	15	16	27	39	31	241
Scarlet Fever	258	167	139	123	98	76	94	92	148	191	239	227	1,852
Typhus	...	...	...	...	...	...	...	...	...	...	...	...	...
Typhoid Fever	3	3	2	3	3	...	2	1	9	4	...	3	33
Relapsing Fever	...	...	...	...	...	...	...	...	...	...	...	...	...
Continued Fever	...	...	...	...	...	...	...	...	...	...	...	...	...
Puerperal Fever	3	2	7	2	2	4	...	5	3	5	3	4	40
Cerebro-spinal Fever	...	1	5	3	...	2	1	3	1	3	1	5	25
Infective Jaundice	...	...	...	...	...	...	...	...	...	...	...	...	...
Tuberculosis, Pulmonary	66	71	65	77	57	59	53	49	36	36	40	47	656
Tuberculosis, other forms	34	48	52	50	44	34	42	30	26	20	25	28	433
Ophthalmia Neonatorum	3	2	3	5	2	2	4	2	5	2	1	3	34
Malaria	...	...	...	2	...	...	1	...	...	...	...	1	4
Dysentery	...	1	...	...	...	4	...	...	...	2	1	1	9
Trench Fever	...	...	...	...	...	...	...	...	...	...	...	...	...
Acute Primary Pneumonia	38	40	51	27	24	16	11	20	17	25	65	34	368
Acute Influenzal Pneumonia	8	15	41	23	10	1	...	4	...	5	10	12	129
Measles	15	95	99	217	505	809	717	199	88	78	108	416	3,346
Whooping Cough	23	32	12	9	14	22	34	39	37	19	9	30	280
Poliomyelitis	...	...	...	...	1	...	...	...	...	...	1	...	2
Polio-encephalitis	...	...	...	...	...	...	...	...	...	...	...	...	...
Encephalitis Lethargica	9	3	11	3	2	1	2	3	...	1	2	1	38
Totals	549	564	563	601	815	1082	996	485	424	463	596	904	8,042

Messrs. Merson in St. John's Hill. Mackie did useful work on post-operative tetanus in relation to the sterilisation of catgut and he remained closely involved in this until his death. Possibly on account of the important economic aspects, research on fish infections received considerable attention. Significantly, in view of her experience of this work in the department, Miss May Williamson, a science graduate, was appointed to the Ministry of Agriculture and Fisheries in 1928. For many years the department had experimental fish tanks in a little yard behind the McEwan Hall.

In 1929 Dr J.D. Allan Gray, who had joined the staff in 1926 and had done important work on food poisoning and paratyphoid B, including a comparative study of selective media for isolating food-poisoning bacteria, was appointed Assistant Bacteriologist to the City of Liverpool. In 1930, Dr Gow Brown joined the department. After a few years, he was appointed County Bacteriologist to Lanarkshire in Hamilton. Dr Gow Brown's distinctions in the world of sport are noted later.

Haemolytic streptococci in relation to the then ever-prevalent scarlatina – averaging at least 2,000 cases annually – received continuing considerable attention. Much research was also devoted to pneumococcal infections and cholera. In April 1930, Professor Mackie read a paper to the Tuberculosis Society on behalf of Dr R.S. Begbie on the desiccation of BCG, based on studies carried out very much in advance of the general introduction of this vaccine as a means of conferring immunity to tuberculosis. During the 1930-31 academic year, Dr Alexander Haddow joined the department. Over many years Haddow did important pioneering work on the inducement of carcinomas in mice and rats, and studies on the blood of cancer patients. While on the staff he was awarded a Doctorate of Science for his thesis on "The Biology of Cancer". Haddow was eventually appointed Director of the Chester-Beattie Cancer Research Institute in London and was awarded a knighthood for his important contributions to cancer research.

In 1931, Dr Colin P. Beattie joined the staff. His special field of research was *Brucella abortus*, work which he pursued further in the United States as a Rockefeller Fellow. He returned to the department and for some years was in charge of the Public Health Laboratory. In 1931, Professor Mackie was appointed a member of the Agriculture Research Council. In the same year, Miss May Christison was appointed a research worker and began studies of diphtheroid bacilli, to be continued with Dr Helen Wright who also joined the staff at this time having worked with Dr Agnes McGregor in the laboratory of the Royal Hospital for Sick Children at Sciennes. Dr Wright was to become an authority on the diphtheria bacillus. She carried out much work on diphtheria in collaboration with the clinicians at the City Fever Hospital. During her long service to the department "Nell" Wright was, for many years and until her retiral in 1960, in charge of the Public Health Laboratory. Further reference to her work is made later.

Early Virologists

In the summer of 1931, a final year medical student began working part time in the department on a number of research projects. He was later to bring an important new dimension to the work of the department. When C.E. Van Rooyen began his virological studies under the direction of Professor Mackie he was to become Edinburgh's first medical virologist and one of the world's earliest workers in this new field. Mackie's initial encouragement of Dr Van Rooyen to commence virological studies reflected T.J.'s characteristic sense of new developments that merited support.

In 1933 Professor Mackie was appointed Director of Bacteriological Services for the City of Edinburgh. Between this year and the outbreak of the Second World War in 1939, he recruited to the academic staff an impressive number who went on to obtain professorial chairs or directorships of laboratories in the United Kingdom and abroad[43,44]. Dr Cecil A. Green (1933) specialised in streptococci and carried out early work on the Griffith types. He was subsequently appointed to the Directorship of the Naval Research Foundation of the Empire Rheumatism Council; later he became Clinical Bacteriologist at the Royal Victoria Infirmary, Newcastle-upon-Tyne; and then finally succeeded to the Chair of Bacteriology at Durham University. Dr Scott Thomson (1934) worked on scarlatina in close liaison with the City Fever Hospital, and on immune responses in mice. He left the department to become County Bacteriologist for Dumfriesshire and subsequently became Professor of Bacteriology at Cardiff University.

In 1935, another appointment indicated Mackie's awareness of the need for new research. He recruited Dr C.G. Anderson, a highly qualified biochemist who had been working at the London School of Hygiene and Tropical Medicine. Dr Anderson worked on lipoids with special reference to antigens for serological tests for syphilis and these were amongst the earliest studies of this kind carried out in Britain. His *Introduction to Bacteriological Chemistry*, published in 1938, was one of the earliest books in this new area of research (Anderson, 1938). Anderson went on to join the staff of the South African Institute for Medical Research, Johannesburg. He was succeeded in 1938 by Dr Sydney Challinor, a chemist, who also came from the London School of Hygiene and Tropical Medicine.

Another new member of staff in 1935 was Dr Andrew J. Rhodes who was in charge of the Public Health Laboratory for some time and became a close research collaborator with Dr C.E. Van Rooyen. Jointly they published in 1940 their textbook *Virus Diseases of Man* (Van Rooyen and Rhodes, 1940). The book was described as "the first encyclopaedic volume on the virus diseases of man". Dr Rhodes left the department during the Second World War to become pathologist to the Shrewsbury Emergency Medical Service. Later he joined the staff of the London School of Hygiene and Tropical Medicine. He left for Canada in 1947, and became director of a succession of laboratories in Toronto and subsequently Professor of Microbiology at the University of Toronto in 1972.

After the end of the 1939-45 war, Dr Van Rooyen also left for Canada. In 1937 he had revised Richard Muir's *Atlas of Bacteriology*. In 1947 he was appointed Professor of Virus Diseases in the University of Toronto's School of Hygiene and from 1956-73 was Professor of Microbiology at Dalhousie University and Director of the Nova Scotia Government Public Health Laboratories and the Department of Microbiology in its Medical School.

In 1936 Dr Helen Wright, a part-time member of the staff since 1931, became a full-time member. Her work on diphtheria typing and her many years in charge of the Public Health Laboratory are referred to later. During the 1937-38 academic year, Dr C.P. Beattie was appointed to the Chair of Bacteriology in the University of Baghdad and, after nine years there, became Professor of Bacteriology at the University of Sheffield. Amongst other new staff who joined the department about this time was Kenneth A. Bisset who had taken a First Class Honours BSc degree in bacteriology in the department's course. His work as bacteriologist to the Scottish Salmon Fishery Board and as a demonstrator in the department's teaching staff

43. *(Left to right) Dr Scott Thomson, Dr C.A. Green, Professor T.J. Mackie,*
Dr C.P. Beattie and Dr C.E. Van Rooyen.

44. *Dr C.E. Van Rooyen and Dr A.J. Rhodes*

provided him with material from which he gained his Doctorate of Philosophy degree. The subject of his thesis was bacterial variation. This was to become Dr Bisset's life's work and he published three books and very many papers on bacterial cytology (see, for example, Bisset, 1970). After the 1939-45 war he joined the staff of the Bacteriology Department of Birmingham and became Director there in 1966.

At the beginning of the 1938-39 session, Professor Mackie recorded that since his appointment, two hundred papers had been published by members of staff. New subjects of research at this time included *Bacillus salmonicida* in fish; conjunctivitis in coal-face workers; the gastric mucosa and pathogens; the pathogenicity of the meningococcus and other related organisms; and rheumatic carditis. During this session Professor Mackie was elected Vice-President of the Third International Congress of Microbiology in New York. This event and the honour conferred on Mackie signifies how far bacteriology had developed generally since his appointment fifteen years before and not least in his own department[45]. The number of academic staff for this year totalled fourteen. There were probably as many technical staff. New members of staff at this time included Dr John C. Ives and Dr Gilbert Ludlam, both of whom were eventually to take up important posts elsewhere. Dr Ives, after two years in the department, took up service during the Second World War in the Royal Army Medical Corps which involved periods in Orkney and Rangoon and membership of a penicillin research team in the 14th Army's Central Laboratory. After returning to the department and being in charge of the Public Health Laboratory, Dr Ives in 1950 became a lecturer in bacteriology at Glasgow University and Bacteriologist to Glasgow Royal Infirmary. Dr Gilbert Ludlam remained on the departmental staff for nine years, principally involved in the supervision of the Public Health Laboratory and doing research on many problems arising from the diagnostic work and including neonatal infections. In 1948, Ludlam joined the Public Health Laboratory Service as Consultant Bacteriologist in charge of the Nottingham diagnostic laboratory. He was appointed director of the newly established Leeds Public Health Laboratory in 1954, eventually relinquishing this post to concentrate on his work on toxoplasmosis begun at Edinburgh.

The Second World War: Wartime Research and Development

For the academic year 1939-40 Mackie begins his record with the simple statement: "War started 3rd September 1939. Department became Central Laboratory for South East Scotland Emergency Bacteriological Services 10th September 1939". These few words heralded the department's entry into an era that made challenging demands on those members of staff, academic and technical, who were not called to the Services. The department's resources were to be fully stretched. Within weeks of the outbreak of the war, staff were either being called up for war service, volunteering for various branches of the Services, or finding themselves in a "reserved occupation" and therefore required to remain in the department to provide the services demanded by its new designation.

There was a general sense of awareness or anticipation of new laboratory procedures that would be required in a war-time situation. A consequence of the possibility of enemy air raids was the setting up of a reserve laboratory equipment store at the Department of Genetics at King's Buildings. Emergency or base hospitals with their laboratories were established at Bangour Hospital in West Lothian, Peel Hospital in the Borders, Stracathro Hospital in Angus, Ballochmyle

AN INTRODUCTION TO
PRACTICAL
BACTERIOLOGY
AS APPLIED TO MEDICINE AND PUBLIC HEALTH

*A Guide to Bacteriological Laboratory Work
for Students and Practitioners of Medicine*

BY

T. J. MACKIE
M.D.(Glas.), D.P.H.(Oxford)
*Robert Irvine Professor of Bacteriology, University
of Edinburgh ; late Wernher-Beit Professor of
Bacteriology, University of Cape Town*

AND

J. E. McCARTNEY
M.D., D.Sc.(Edin.)
*Lecturer in Bacteriology, University of Edinburgh ;
late Fellow of the Rockefeller Institute for
Medical Research, New York*

EDINBURGH
E. & S. LIVINGSTONE
16 & 17 TEVIOT PLACE
1925

BACTERIOLOGICAL
ATLAS

A SERIES OF COLOURED PLATES
ILLUSTRATING
THE MORPHOLOGICAL CHARACTERS OF
PATHOGENIC MICRO-ORGANISMS

By RICHARD MUIR
DEMONSTRATOR OF PATHOLOGICAL AND BACTERIOLOGICAL
METHODS IN THE UNIVERSITY OF EDINBURGH.

EDINBURGH :
E. & S. LIVINGSTONE, 16-17 TEVIOT PL.
1927

An Introduction to Bacteriological Chemistry

BY

C. G. ANDERSON
PH.D.(BIRM.), D.BACT.(LOND.)
LEWIS CAMERON TEACHING FELLOW,
BACTERIOLOGY DEPARTMENT, UNIVERSITY OF EDINBURGH

EDINBURGH
E. & S. LIVINGSTONE
16 & 17 TEVIOT PLACE
1938

OXFORD MEDICAL PUBLICATIONS

VIRUS DISEASES
OF MAN

BY

C. E. van ROOYEN, M.D. (EDIN.)
*Sir Halley Stewart Research Fellow
Lecturer in Bacteriology, University of Edinburgh
Extra Bacteriologist to the Royal Infirmary of Edinburgh*

AND

A. J. RHODES, M.B., CH.B. (EDIN.), M.R.C.P.E.
*Lecturer in Bacteriology, University of Edinburgh
Formerly Assistant Bacteriologist, and Assistant Pathologist
to the Royal Infirmary of Edinburgh*

WITH AN INTRODUCTION BY
T. J. MACKIE.
*Professor of Bacteriology
University of Edinburgh*

OXFORD UNIVERSITY PRESS
LONDON : HUMPHREY MILFORD
1940

---

45. *Early publications*

Hospital in Ayrshire, and Bridge of Earn Hospital in Perthshire. The considerable task of initially equipping these laboratories and maintaining their support was undertaken by Professor Mackie and Mr A.B. Cheyne who made regular visits to the laboratories. Mackie seconded members of staff including Dr R.K. Oag, Dr J.P. Duguid, and others to relieve Emergency Medical Service hospital pathologists absent through illness or on vacation. The department at Teviot Place provided a central source of culture medium and reagents. Amidst such emergency preparations, the department's teaching commitments had to be maintained and training was given to those who had taken up the posts in the emergency hospital laboratories.

The Scottish Command Laboratory

In March 1940 the Scottish Command Laboratory was established in the department in what are now rooms 781 (for long, Professor Mackie's own research laboratory and now an annexe of Classroom C) and 775, Laboratory 13, with sterilisation and culture media preparation facilities available in the department's own rooms. The Army laboratory was under the direction of Major George Montgomery who was later to become Professor of Pathology at Edinburgh University. His assistant was Lieutenant Riddell. The laboratory was a training unit for army medical laboratory assistants and also provided a diagnostic service for army personnel in South East Scotland. In June 1940, Dr C.E. Van Rooyen was commissioned as a Major in the Royal Army Medical Corps and appointed in charge of a laboratory at Peebles. Dr J. Ives was similarly commissioned and served initially at Kirkwall. Dr K. Bisset took up a commission in the Royal Marines and was on service in Europe and Africa. From the technical staff, Robert Weir, Douglas Annat and William Bertram were amongst the first to join the services.

Despite the war, the relative depletion of staff and the emergency conditions, new members joined the staff. Dr George Dempster, having taken his BSc Honours in the department, was appointed lecturer in 1941 and subsequently worked for a period in the Public Health Laboratory. After war service in North Africa and his return to the department, Dr Dempster taught the BSc Bacteriology Course and in 1956 was appointed Professor of Bacteriology at the Medical College, Saskatoon, Canada. In 1942 Dr Cranston Low, a noted dermatologist and former Superintendent of the Royal College of Physicians' Laboratory, joined the staff. A gifted artist, Dr Low collaborated with Mr T.C. Dodds, the Chief Technician in the Pathology Department and later director of the University's Medical Photography Unit, in producing an important colour atlas of bacteriology, with photographs of a very high standard (Low and Dodds, 1947). In 1946, Dr S.W. Challinor resigned to join the staff of the Research Station, Long Ashton, Bristol. He played an important part with Dr Jean McNaughton and later Dr J.P. Duguid in early studies in penicillin therapy and the production of the antibiotic in the department. Dr Challinor was succeeded by Dr Hugh King who came from Boots, Nottingham, after studying at the Lister Institute, London. In the same academic year, Dr J.C. Gould joined the staff. He was to carry out very important studies of antibiotics, especially of sensitivity test methods. Dr Gould worked closely in this field with Dr J.H. Bowie, the bacteriologist in the department's Royal Infirmary laboratory. In 1961, Dr Gould was appointed Director of the Central Microbiology Laboratory at Edinburgh's Western General Hospital.

Production and Testing of Penicillin

Despite the great disruption and the severe restrictions caused by the outbreak of the Second World War, the department's work continued in teaching and in the services of the diagnostic laboratory. The training of many people who came for short periods before taking up war-related posts was an important additional service. Basic research continued, and several important developments were stimulated by the emergency situation. The most important work done during the war merited a reference and commendation by Sir James Howie in the chapter on "Public Health Microbiology Services" which he contributed to *Aspects of Scottish Health Services 1900-1984* by Sir John Brotherston, published in 1987 (see Howie, 1987). Sir James wrote: "Reference could reasonably be made, however, to the fundamental early work of Duguid in Edinburgh on the mode of action of penicillin". Dr J.P. Duguid took a BSc honours degree in the department in 1943. He was then awarded a Crichton Research Scholarship in bacteriology and reserved from war service by the Central War Committee for training in bacteriology. He joined the staff as a lecturer in 1944. In the same year, he was joint author with Dr I.W.J. McAdam and Dr S.W. Challinor of a paper: "Systematic Administration of Penicillin". A series of papers followed between 1944 and 1946 on various aspects of penicillin administration, one of these jointly with Professor James R. Learmonth, of the Department of Surgery who had given considerable support to this work. The University Court made a substantial grant for the encouragement of a team of academic[46,47,48,49] and technical staff. In 1943 Dr S.W. Challinor and Dr Jean McNaughton had actually produced quite substantial batches of penicillin in Czapek-Dox culture medium and this had been used therapeutically in the Royal Infirmary. A detailed survey of this important work on penicillin was given by Professor Mackie in his Honeyman Gillespie Lecture delivered in the Royal Infimary on 19 July, 1945 and is the subject of a later Note. Another member of staff, Dr H. de Waal, carried out a survey of the value of penicillin compared with other agents in the treatment of wounds and burns. About this time, early work was also being done on streptomycin and Dr C.E. Van Rooyen was testing the effect of antibiotics on certain viruses.

Special mention should be made of the role of the British Army "Penicillin Control Unit" whose function was to distribute the new drug in the Central Mediterranean Force, to instruct surgeons in its properties, demonstrate its use, set up investigations and collect results on its efficacy. The surgeon in charge was Lt-Col. J. S. Jeffrey and the pathologist in the team was Scott Thomson who had been a Crichton Research Fellow and Lecturer in Bacteriology in the Edinburgh department from 1934 to 1940. Scott Thomson was co-author of several important papers on topics such as penicillin in battle casualties, treatment of compound fractures with penicillin, and the control of infection in recent wounds by surgery and local chemotherapy. As the bacteriologist of the Penicillin Research Team set up by the War Office in 1943, Scott Thomson investigated the problem of wound infections in battle casualties for nearly three years in North Africa, Sicily, Italy and Austria. As the war progressed and centred upon Italy in September 1943, the bulk of British penicillin was sent there for the studies. Thus, for a short and significant period in the development of the clinical use of penicillin, Scott Thomson effectively controlled the world supply of the new drug.

Bacteriological Studies of the Air of Occupied Premises

Soon after the outbreak of war, quite large communal air raid shelters were built by the local authorities, frequently in the backgreens of tenements in the city. In London at that time, regular air raids were so frequent that many of the public retired every night to sleep in shelters, but in Edinburgh shelters were not so used. Nevertheless, the public health authorities sought to determine the effect on the atmosphere of twenty or thirty people sleeping inside concrete shelters with special reference to humidity, droplet infection and the possible spread of infection. Over a considerable period therefore, men from some of the home defence services slept in the 24-bunk type of shelters overnight, the bunks being close to each other. During the night, humidity readings were taken and culture plates were exposed at regular intervals; after incubation the total count and types of colonies were studied. This work was published in 1942-43 by Professor Mackie who made visits to night shelters during the trials. The findings in this work led to much further and varied studies on droplet infection by Duguid, in collaboration with Challinor (see Appendix B3). A brief entry in Professor Mackie's log book for June 1942 reads simply "Awarded C.B.E. for services to Civil Defence".

Smallpox Epidemic 1942

In the midst of the war emergency situation, an added and serious challenge to the city's medical service resources was presented by a serious outbreak of smallpox that started on 1 November, 1942 and continued until 18 December of that year. There were thirty-six cases, of which eight died. No case of smallpox had occurred in Edinburgh since 1920. The outbreak had been preceded by one in Glasgow some months earlier and another in Fife a month before the first Edinburgh case arose. All three outbreaks were considered to have emanated from one case: a seaman who arrived in Glasgow from Bombay on 29 May of that year. In view of these two outbreaks, public health services in Edinburgh were on the alert. Vaccination was offered to the Edinburgh population and 274,000 people responded (64.3% of the city's population).

A special corrugated iron "smallpox hospital" was used for the isolation of the cases and this was situated a little westwards of the City Hospital main buildings at Colinton Mains. While all the nursing staff of the City Hospital volunteered to look after the smallpox cases, thirteen were selected along with a number of auxiliary staff. All lived in complete isolation during the duration of the outbreak, cooking their own food as well as that of the patients and having no physical contact with any other people. The nursing was of a very high standard. After the outbreak, parts of the temporary hospital were set on fire and destroyed. The homes of the smallpox cases were disinfected by spraying with 40% formaldehyde; and clothing, personal papers and money were disinfected or destroyed. Dr R.P. Jack of the city's Public Health Department worked out his disinfection methods in consultation with members of the Bacteriology Department staff.

Overcoming Shortages: Recycling of Culture Medium

Quite soon after the outbreak of war, some constituents required in the preparation of culture medium were in short supply or quite unobtainable. To cope with this situation, recycling of used culture medium was introduced, when feasible.

EDINBURGH WORKERS ENGAGED IN EARLY COLLABORATIVE RESEARCH ON PENICILLIN

46. *Professor J.P. Duguid*

47. *Dr Jean McNaughton (née Wiseman)*

48. *Dr S.W. Challinor*

49. *Professor Sir James Learmonth*

Unfortunately, blood agar plates could not be so treated. The method was to scrape off all colonies on the plate with a bent Pasteur capillary pipette. The scraped colonies were autoclaved in a disinfectant. The remaining culture medium was scooped out with a spatula or scalpel into a very large beaker. When a considerable quantity of the used medium had been collected, the beaker was covered with Kraft paper or foil and sterilised in a steamer for 1½ hours. The molten medium was then treated with charcoal and filtered through Cellosene wadding in a large Buchner funnel. The clear filtrate was tested for its ability to solidify and, if necessary, a small percentage of agar fibre or powder was added. The pH was readjusted.

The recycled culture medium was not used for diagnostic work but for teaching purposes. Its deficiencies were appreciated. In the context of the present day's Health and Safety Act and the Codes of Practice governing bacteriology laboratories (Howie Code, 1978), it is certain that the potentially dangerous technique described (performed without the wearing of a face mask but with rubber gloves) would have been condemned. The wartime shortages simply seemed to necessitate desperate measures.

Alternative Agars

When Japan entered the war and hostilities spread to the Far East, it was feared that the natural type of agar-agar used in so many solidified culture media, and mainly obtained in shredded seaweed form from the sea in the new area of conflict, might soon become unobtainable. Most commercial firms, while forced to ration or curtail supplies, did continue to supply agar in powdered form, made from other types of seaweed. Considerable work was done in Scotland to determine the suitability of light-coloured seaweeds from native shores. Dr Joyce Coghlan did many of the bacteriological laboratory trials required. Certain types were suitable to some degree but others presented problems as regards a satisfactory solidification temperature, clarity when dissolved in nutrient broth or other fluid media, and other features. The Scottish products were not used in diagnostic work.

War-Time Research and Staffing

Despite the very considerable orientation of the department's work towards the demands of the war situation and the depletion of staff who entered the forces or undertook service in emergency laboratories, much basic research continued. This included studies on: haemolytic streptococci in acute rheumatism, use of convalescent serum in acute rheumatism, diphtheria types, war wound infections, trials with the Kahn Verification Test in the laboratory diagnosis of syphilis, and penicillin therapy. Very many papers continued to be published. In 1942, the sixth edition of Mackie and McCartney's textbook appeared.

In his 1945-46 academic year's records, Professor Mackie noted the following totals of higher degrees gained by staff and students since his appointment just over twenty years before:

M.D. Theses:	17, 7 of these with Gold Medals and 7 Highly Commended.
D.Sc. degrees:	4
Ph.D. degrees:	10
B.Sc. (Honours):	31, with 17 first class awards.

Post-War Development

At the end of the war, Drs Van Rooyen and Ives returned to the department and after a few years took up appointments elsewhere. In 1950 Dr John Ives was appointed William Teacher lecturer in the University of Glasgow and later Honorary Consultant Bacteriologist to Glasgow Royal Infirmary from which posts he retired in 1978. Dr Ives served on very many important committees including the Scottish Standing Advisory Committee on Laboratory Services, of which he was Chairman from 1971 to 74, and the Central Pathology Committee of the Department of Health and Social Security. Dr Kenneth Bisset who served in the Royal Marines, did not return to the department but took up a post in the Department of Bacteriology at Birmingham University and in 1966 became head of that department.

In 1946 Miss Joyce Cranfield, who had taken an Honours BSc degree in bacteriology, joined the staff. She became responsible for the examination of milk and other dairy products and of Edinburgh's drinking water supply. In 1952, Miss Cranfield was awarded the degree of Doctor of Philosophy. After her marriage, Dr Joyce Coghlan became interested in certain of the zoonoses, investigating outbreaks of pasteurellosis, leptospirosis and brucellosis. She co-operated with the Brucellosis Working Party of the Public Health Laboratory Service when the brucellosis eradication scheme was under way, helping to investigate serological techniques and doing studies on the Coombs anti-human globulin test in the diagnosis of chronic brucellosis.

In 1946 Dr Archie Wallace joined the staff, his appointment involving attachment to the City Hospital laboratory. Dr Wallace carried out much specialised research on tuberculosis with Professor Sir John Crofton and, from 1948 to 1974, was bacteriologist at the City Hospital (see separate Note).

Dr John Tinne who had been in charge of the City Hospital laboratory in 1941 while a resident physician there, joined the department after war service and then returned to work in the City Hospital laboratory for a short period under Dr Wallace before eventually joining Dr Ives at the Glasgow Royal Infirmary Bacteriology Laboratory. In 1947, Mackie recruited Dr R.H.A. Swain with a view to a more systematic development in the department of its virology laboratory. Dr Richard (Dick) Swain had been trained in virology by the late Professor Bedson at the London Hospital.

Dr T.F. Elias-Jones joined the staff in 1948 and after experience in the Public Health Laboratory became Consultant Clinical Pathologist for the Ilford and Barking Hospital group before his appointment as Consultant Bacteriologist to the Greater Glasgow Health Board and Director of Glasgow City Laboratory from 1962 to 1981.

Dr Pat Edmunds was appointed a lecturer in 1950 and, after carrying out considerable pioneering work on the development of a serological test for leptospiral jaundice, became bacteriologist to the Astley Ainslie Hospital in Edinburgh in 1954. In 1960 he was appointed Consultant Bacteriologist to the Fife Hospitals based at Kirkcaldy. Dr Edmunds died in 1984.

During the 1948-49 academic year Dr Hugh King, bacteriological chemist, resigned to join the staff of the Biochemistry Department at Liverpool University, and after some years there was appointed to the combined Chair of Biochemistry and Agricultural Biochemistry at the University College of Wales at Aberystwyth. Dr King was succeeded in the department by Dr John Wilkinson. Dr Wilkinson, with Dr Ian Sutherland, formed a teaching and research group in microbial physiology in the large Laboratory 3 on the north-east area of the top floor (subsequently to become part of the Microbial Pathogenicity Research Laboratory). In 1964, Dr Wilkinson and his team moved out to the Department of Microbiology in the College of Agriculture at the King's Buildings, where Dr Wilkinson was appointed to the Chair of Microbiology. Dr Sutherland became Reader and subsequently Head of Department there. He was promoted to Professor in 1991.

In 1949 Dr John Bowie joined the department as a lecturer and was appointed Senior Bacteriologist at Edinburgh Royal Infirmary under Professor Mackie's direction. Bowie had already had a notable career in the Indian Medical Service, having served as Medical Officer to the 20th Lancers and the 1/3 Gurkhas. After his return from India, he had spent a year with Professor Colin Beattie at the University of Sheffield. Dr Bowie with Dr J.C. Gould made important pioneering contributions to antibiotic sensitivity testing by the disk diffusion method. His work on hospital sterilisers and innovations in relation to the sterilisation of hospital materials and surgical instruments, carried out with his chief medical laboratory technologist, Mr James Dick, earned him an international reputation. This is recorded in more detail in Appendix B5.

Dr J.C. Gould was associated with the department as an undergraduate in 1942, working on various research projects. During 1943-44 he worked with Dr Challinor and others on the production of penicillin. Dr Gould did further research in 1946 and after service in the Royal Army Medical Corps returned to the staff of the department in 1948. A year later, following the death of Dr William Logan and prior to the appointment of Dr J. Bowie, Dr Gould was appointed Senior Assistant Bacteriologist in the Royal Infirmary Bacteriology Department. Two years later, he was appointed lecturer in the department where he carried out studies on antibiotics, staphylococcal epidemiology and respiratory infections. He made important observations establishing that contact on inhalation of antibiotics spilt into the hospital environment was related to the high proportion of hospital staff carrying antibiotic-resistant bacteria. Cam Gould, as he was affectionately known, was a man of great energy and dynamism. In his heyday, he would run up the stairs from the quadrangle to Lab. 4 at the top of the North West corner of the building "in one go" – and often demonstrated this to a junior colleague on night duty. He was a fearless and highly skilled rally driver. And he was a splendid teacher. He became Director of the Central Microbiological Laboratory at the Western General Hospital in 1961.

In 1950 Dr Helen Wright was appointed in charge of the department's Public Health laboratory and also as Honorary Consultant Bacteriologist to the South-East Regional Hospital Board in the then recently constituted National Health Service. Further reference is made to Dr Wright later. During the same year the department also acquired a new member of staff who was to gain a high reputation in various areas of bacteriology. This was Dr R.R. Gillies who joined the department a few years after graduating in medicine. Dr Gillies has been described as a superb teacher[50,51]. His textbooks *Bacteriology Illustrated*, produced in collaboration with Mr T.C. Dodds (Gillies and Dodds, 1965), and *Lecture Notes in Medical Microbiology* (Gillies, 1968) were used throughout the world. Dr Gillies collaborated with J.P. Duguid in developing important investigations on bacterial fimbriae. He did other important work on bacillary dysentery, colicine typing and pseudomonas typing in addition to research on pneumococci, streptococci, biochemical test media and hospital infection. Dr Gillies was for nine years Associate Dean in the Faculty of Medicine and for a period was in charge of the bacteriology laboratory in the Royal Infirmary. Appointed to the Chair of Clinical Bacteriology in Queen's University, Belfast, in 1976 he soon made an impact in that department. Sadly he died suddenly in July 1983.

One of the Honours graduates of 1950, Miss Margaret Kelly, remained in the department as a Demonstrator. Subsequently appointed Lecturer, Miss Kelly worked in the diagnostic laboratory and did a number of related research projects. After her marriage to an Edinburgh medical graduate, Dr William Allan, who also worked for a short time in the department as a Research Assistant, they moved to Wolverhampton where Dr Allan became a consultant haematologist. Margaret died there in 1988.

Electron Microscopy

With the acquisition of an electron microscope in 1951 the virology laboratory, under Dr Swain's direction, was able to make a widening contribution to the department's research, training and diagnostic work. A large laboratory on the ground floor which had been part of the Department of Gynaecology was acquired and equipped as the virology laboratory. The electron microscope was housed in a room opposite the virology laboratory, now an office, and was maintained by Mr George Wilson, an electrical engineer[52,53].

Professor Mackie's log book began to record an increasing number of papers on electron microscopic studies of viruses and spirochaetes. In 1953, the virology team was strengthened by the appointment of Dr F. Leonard Constable, who had been registrar in microbiology at the Royal Victoria Infirmary, Newcastle-upon-Tyne. Dr Constable contributed to the department's researches on bacterial fimbriae, and did work on a wide range of viruses. In 1961, he returned to Newcastle as Consultant Microbiologist to the Area Health Authority. In 1975 he was appointed Honorary Physician to HM The Queen and in 1985 became a Commander of the Order of St. John. The first technician to be attached to the Virology Laboratory was Robert Lindsay from 1953 to 1956, and the first Senior Medical Laboratory Technologist in this laboratory was Miss Nan Anderson who, from 1956, contributed greatly to the steady development of the laboratory and the training of junior technical staff in the discipline. Nan Anderson eventually became a Senior Tutor in the Department of Microbiology, University of Toronto, and an authority and author on electron microscopy.

In 1955 Dr J.G. Collee was appointed lecturer after hospital experience at Haddington, service with the Royal Army Medical Corps and a period in general practice in Shropshire. Dr Collee in 1963-64 was World Health Organization Visiting Professor of Bacteriology at Baroda Medical College in India, being one of the Edinburgh team there and collaborating with Professor Robert Cruickshank. He returned to the department as a Senior Lecturer and Honorary Consultant. In 1970, Dr Collee was appointed Reader under Professor Marmion and was awarded a Personal Professorship in 1974 in recognition of his research work in clinical anaerobic bacteriology in which he earned an international reputation. As is described in more detail later, Professor Collee eventually succeeded Professor Marmion to the headship of the department.

50. *Dr R.R. Gillies tutoring overseas postgraduate students*

51. *Dr R.R. Gillies and Miss Margaret Kelly Schick-testing medical students*

52. *George Wilson*

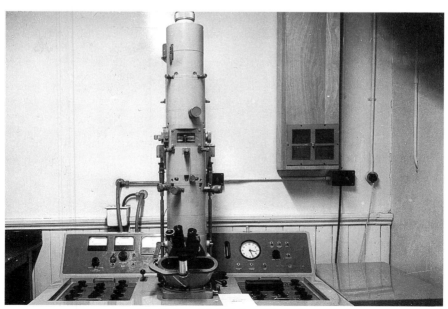

53. *Early model of Electron Microscope*

While Professor Mackie was responsible for so much of the department's progress in teaching, research and the development of the diagnostic service, he was also responsible for considerable expansion of the department's facilities and accommodation. Reference has already been made to the acquisition of various laboratories, the recruitment of biochemical expertise, the development of the virology laboratory, and the installation of the electron microscope. During the 1949-50 academic year further accommodation was also obtained in rooms vacated by the Pharmacology Department on the top floor on the north side of the Medical School. In the following year, the spacious two-tier lecture theatre which the department had shared with Pathology was laminated to produce a third top-floor classroom, Classroom C, entered opposite the lift. This teaching area was eventually to become part of the extensive new Preparation Suite created by Professor B.P. Marmion in 1969-70.

Death of Professor Mackie

Professor Mackie's faithfully kept log book records ceased at the end of September 1955. An entry in Dr Swain's handwriting reads "On 6 October 1955 Professor Mackie died suddenly in his home of a coronary thrombosis". Dr Swain's note continues: "He had done a normal day's work in the department and had, as Dean, introduced Professor Kennedy to the University on the occasion of his inaugural lecture. He died in harness and the suddenness of this parting saddened all his staff for he was greatly respected and loved. He had kept these records for 33 years".

One of Professor Mackie's great and distinguished collaborators, mentor and friend, Professor Carl H. Browning, in a joint tribute with Dr Swain, wrote that Britain had lost one of its ablest bacteriologists. It is hoped that the foregoing record provides considerable evidence to substantiate this statement. T.J. Mackie's directorship of the department over thirty-three years is recounted in the obituary referred to above and published in the *Journal of Pathology and Bacteriology.*[*]

Over his long years in charge, Mackie trained a picked staff. Before being caught up in a welter of senior committees, University Court, Faculty of Medicine, professional and governmental, which sought to draw upon his expertise, he worked long hours in his own research laboratory and undertook a heavy schedule of meticulously prepared lectures. He had an intimate grasp of the wide variety of work going on in the department. During his virtually daily tours of the laboratories, many readers of this account will still recall the door opening and the Chief's entry with the inquiry "Anything interesting?". He would frequently sit down at the bench and study results. He had an unusual flare for anticipating the line of new developments. He was one of the first British bacteriologists to promote the study of viruses and greatly stimulated C.E. Van Rooyen and A.J. Rhodes in the publication of their *Virus Diseases of Man* (Van Rooyen and Rhodes, 1940). He was a pioneer in recruiting a chemist to his staff, foreseeing the importance of bacteriological chemistry. He was a great teacher and eagerly looked for promising young potential bacteriologists, hence his special interest in developing the department's BSc Honours Course for science and medical students. Professor Mackie's primary research interests were the classification of gram negative coliform intestinal pathogens; the mechanisms of immunity; syphilis serology, especially complement

---

[*] Obituaries referred to in the text are listed at the end of this book in Appendix D6.

54. Soon after the accession of Her Majesty Queen Elizabeth II to the throne, the newly appointed Chancellor of the University, His Royal Highness the Duke of Edinburgh, led representatives of the University to present a Loyal Address to Her Majesty The Queen – thus exercising the University's traditional privilege of direct access to the Sovereign. This occurred on 21st May, 1952, at Buckingham Palace.

The photograph shows Principal Sir Edward Appleton our Vice-Chancellor (centre) with (clockwise from left) Sir Alexander Fleming (Rector), Mr George Robertson (Convener of the Business Committee of the General Council), Mr Charles Stewart (Secretary to the University) and Professor T.J. Mackie (Dean of the Faculty of Medicine).

fixation and various flocculation tests; the inactivation of tetanus spores in catgut; bactericidal agents and the early sulphonamides; the biochemical reactions of *Vibrio cholerae;* diseases of fish; animal diseases: he made important contributions to the work of Government Committees, especially the Scottish Agricultural Research Council and the Hill Farming Committee. Membership of these bodies brought him the additional pleasure of tramping his much-loved Scottish hills.

Apart from his collaboration with Dr J.E. McCartney in the publication of the textbook which became essential reading for all bacteriology teachers, students and laboratory workers, Mackie also took part in the revision of his predecessor's textbook the *Muir and Ritchie* from the eighth to the eleventh editions. He published a very large number of papers. Very much "a committee man" and a greatly valued one, he served on the University Court as a Curator of Patronage. He was Assistant Dean of the Faculty of Medicine for twenty years and latterly Dean for a short period[54]. He was awarded the CBE; he was appointed a Corresponding Member of the Royal Academy of Medicine, Rome; he was a Fellow of the Royal Society of Edinburgh; and he was awarded an honorary LL.D. by his *alma mater,* Glasgow University. Indeed it saddened him that what has been described as "the phenomenal collection of medals" that he won at Glasgow was stolen.

Yet this man described as quick, eager, restless, energetic, highly methodical and exacting, still found time occasionally to switch off by golfing, fishing, cycling, sailing, listening to Gilbert and Sullivan and playing the piano. He enjoyed the dinner parties often held in his home at Mortonhall Road for his colleagues in various branches of medicine. His daughter, Dr Joan Mackie, who became a consultant obstetrician and gynaecologist, cherished a folio containing many relics of her father's off-duty ploys, including, in his distinctive (and, to many, quite illegible!) bold handwriting, dinner table place mats with amusing literary quotations and written caricatures of his often distinguished dinner guests. Unfortunately, one of the interesting memorabilia has been lost. This was the musical score for piano composed by Professor Mackie's close friend, Professor Donald Tovey of the Department of Music who, when quite seriously ill with an *Entamoeba histolytica* infection, called upon Professor Mackie's diagnostic skill and clinical attention. On his recovery, he expressed in music his bodily conflict with the amoeba, the rise and fall of his pyrexia, and the pastoral calm as he recovered.

Something of Professor Mackie's rich sense of humour and fascination with unusual characters and situations was evident when a student asked him if he might be granted leave of absence to take his seat in the House of Lords. "Certainly" was the reply, "we always grant leave on occasions of that sort". A tribute to Professor Mackie was published in the University Gazette of December 1955.

First Inter-Regnum 1955-58: Dr R.H.A. Swain

Following Professor Mackie's death, Dr Richard Swain, Senior Lecturer and virologist, was invited by Professor George Montgomery, Dean of the Faculty of Medicine, to take charge of the department. By 1955, seven years after his appointment, Dr Swain had steadily developed the virology section in relation to the teaching of the subject, research and the pioneering of a virology diagnostic service, while he maintained the general running of the department. As is frequently the case during an inter-regnum, major decisions regarding the progress of the department and the engagement of staff had to be postponed until a new Head of

55. *Dr R.H.A. Swain*

56. *Leptospira icterohaemorrhagiae*

Department was appointed. Dr Swain continued to keep Professor Mackie's "log book" for a short time, but this ceased and it is difficult now to trace all the features of the department's development during the period.

There was virtually no significant change in staffing except for the resignation of Dr P.N. Edmunds who was appointed bacteriologist at the Astley Ainslie Hospital in Edinburgh. After five years' service there, Dr Edmunds became Consultant Bacteriologist to the Fife Hospitals. Considerable research continued and the first paper was published by Duguid, Smith, Dempster and Edmunds on fimbriae in *Escherichia coli*. This classic paper (Duguid *et al*, 1955) was the forerunner of much subsequent work on the subject by Dr Duguid and Dr Gillies which became of international importance. Dr Joyce Coghlan published several papers in collaboration with Mr John Norval and officials of Edinburgh Corporation Public Health Department and Sanitary Department on leptospiral jaundice. In conjunction with this work, Dr Swain published an electron microscopical study of the anatomy of *Treponema pallidum* and *Leptospira canicola*[55,56]. A further electron microscope study of the psittacosis virus was also published. Several papers on the Newcastle virus followed. A number of staff members contributed to the publication of the ninth edition of the Mackie and McCartney textbook at this time.

In February 1957 a serious fire during the night destroyed the ground floor virology laboratory, laboratory No. 8. Permanent virological laboratory facilities did not become available again until the establishment of a new virology laboratory on the second floor in premises vacated by the Pathology Department (principally in that department's large classroom) which had moved to the new south-west block of the Medical School opened in 1960. During the 1957-58 academic year Dr Swain was appointed Reader. During the inter-regnum, Miss Campbell Renton was appointed a demonstrator. She had taken a science degree in Oxford where she had worked with Florey and Chain in the development of penicillin production.

CHAPTER SEVEN

PROFESSOR
ROBERT CRUICKSHANK

57. *Professor Robert Cruickshank*

When Professor Mackie became the department's second professor in 1923 much of the first decade of his reign had to be devoted to the basic development of the department and this in two principal respects: the acquisition of increased accommodation and the appointment of additional staff. Furthermore, the department was for long to function in a period when infectious diseases such as scarlet fever, diphtheria, tuberculosis, whooping cough, various enteric fevers and, particularly at one point, smallpox were prevalent in the city. When his successor, Professor Cruickshank[55], was appointed to the Chair in October 1958 he acquired a department in many respects already well established. Additionally, many of the infections referred to above had been virtually eradicated or greatly reduced through improvements in hygiene, better nutrition, vaccination, mass X-ray campaigns, antitoxins, chemotherapy and antibiotics. To a large extent, the department in common with others throughout the world had entered a new era. Professor Cruickshank was very much a man of this era. As a result of the relatively substantial progress which had been made in preventing or combating infectious disease in this country, the health authorities in Britain were able to make a contribution towards world health. The campaign against disease on an international front was led by the World Health Organization. Professor Cruickshank was to play an important part in the far-flung work of this agency.

Robert Cruickshank came of Aberdeenshire farming stock and was the second son of a large family. He was keen on the possibility of further education from an early age and in due course graduated MBChB with Honours at Aberdeen University in 1922. As the most distinguished graduate of his year he was awarded the Anderson Travelling Scholarship, which he used to work for two years with Professors Robert Muir and Carl Browning at the Pathology Department of Glasgow University. Robert Muir, it will be recalled from an earlier chapter, was the first formally appointed lecturer in bacteriology at Edinburgh's Medical School, under the aegis of the Pathology Department in 1894. Professor Carl Browning had been a close friend of Professor Mackie. Robert Cruickshank spent the third year of his scholarship working with Professor John Cruickshank (no relation) of the Department of Bacteriology at Aberdeen University, and this influenced him greatly.

Pneumococcal Studies

After graduating MD with Honours at Aberdeen, Robert Cruickshank returned to Glasgow for two years as a resident medical officer in paediatrics and infectious diseases at the Royal Hospital for Sick Children and the Belvedere Hospital. He was greatly affected by the experience of treating children from deprived social backgrounds, especially those who contracted infantile pneumonia. Indeed, it was said that this period of working with such children contributed much to the compassion that he always retained and expressed for the sick and his belief that a bacteriologist should maintain very close relations with the clinicians. Sir James Howie in his "Portraits from Memory" describes his personal friendship with Robert Cruickshank during his period in Glasgow and provides interesting reminiscences (Howie, 1988). The large number of pneumonia cases which Robert Cruickshank saw in Glasgow, especially children who were treated with antiserum long before the availability of the sulphonamides and the antibiotics, fired his interest in pneumococcal infections. Indeed, during his period as bacteriologist at Glasgow Royal Infirmary in 1928, the trials in which he participated of Felton's serum in lobar pneumonia were the most extensive made in Britain. He later lectured on this subject to the Royal College of Physicians in London in 1933.

In 1936 Robert Cruickshank was appointed Director of the London County Council Group Laboratory at the North West Fever Hospital in London and there his interests became more and more concerned with the mode of the spread and control of infections. When the Central Public Health Laboratory was established at Colindale in 1946, on account of his experience and reputation, he was considered the obvious choice for Director, a post which he held for three years. Numerous colleagues at Colindale were to remark how "Robert Cruickshank created a kind of camaraderie that has never quite left the place".

Of the next stage in his career, Sir James Howie has written: "Inevitably he became a professor. His Scottish ancestors virtually compelled him to aspire to such a title". Thus in 1949 he was invited to succeed Sir Alexander Fleming in the Chair of Bacteriology at St. Mary's Hospital Medical School in London. In 1955 he took over from Fleming as Principal of the Wright-Fleming Institute of Microbiology. Much has been written of Professor Cruickshank's influence on the staff and the work at "Mary's": his contributions to seminars, more important often than they seemed to be at the time; his knack of getting his junior staff known in microbiological circles; his gentle yet skilful guiding of so many into their most effective field of work and the development of their potential (see Howie, 1988). He had considered himself fortunate to survive a chest infection in 1939-40 and following this always had the utmost consideration for any of his staff who became ill, keeping them in touch and gradually bringing them back into the department's work.

In 1945, following the Second World War, Professor Cruickshank had become more and more deeply concerned with the development of the microbiological services and the epidemiology and control of infectious disease, both in post-war Britain and the developing countries of the Third World. It was from this period that his increasing commitment began to the problems of world health and the work of the World Health Organization in which as an expert and consultant he played such an important part.

Appointment to Edinburgh Chair

In 1958, three years after Professor Mackie's death, Professor Cruickshank was appointed to succeed him in the Edinburgh chair. His eight year period as Head of Department has been described and assessed by many commentators. He continued his long-held policy of seeking to link clinician and bacteriologist – or virologist – more and more closely. He always saw his subject in relation to patients. He was once described as "a much more *in vivo* than *in vitro* man". He could convey the importance and relevance of his branch of laboratory medicine so well that someone once commented: "He makes even the surgeons think they understand bacteriology!" The impressions from his work with sick children in Glasgow never faded. He was particularly concerned with the production of a safe and effective whooping cough vaccine and also one for measles.

Professor Cruickshank's involvement in the problems of world medicine[58,59] and his many travels under the auspices of the World Health Organization made him an enthusiastic promoter of and participant in the joint Edinburgh University/World Health Organization sponsored links with the medical school at Baroda in India[60], where he and his wife, along with the then Dr J.G. Collee, Dr Sydney Selwyn, William

58. *D.T.M. & H. Class* 1965 *with Dr (later Professor) Gillies, Professor Cruickshank,*
Dr Joyce Coghlan and Dr (later Professor) Collee

59. *Professor R. Cruickshank tutoring D.T.M. & H. students*

THE W.H.O. EDINBURGH-BARODA PROJECT IN MEDICAL EDUCATION 1963-69

60. Members of the first Baroda team: (left to right) Dr George Boyd (short-term consultant), Dr Geoffrey Walsh, Dr Jim Farquhar, Mr Bill Marr (short-term consultant), Dr Philip Myerscough, Dr Irving Delamore and Professor Robert Cruickshank (short-term consultant and adviser to W.H.O.)
Absentees: Dr Gerald Collee took the photograph and Dr Raymond Mills was reporting to Delhi

Marr, and the late John Brennan of the department's technical staff spent various periods of time in the mid-1960s. Professor Cruickshank wrote that the objectives of Edinburgh Medical School's participation in the Baroda project included the raising of the standards of undergraduate and postgraduate medical education there. It was hoped that, as a result, it would not be necessary for Indian doctors to seek their basic qualifications overseas and that overseas studies could be confined to acquiring specialised knowledge in certain fields. Senior teachers from clinical, paraclinical and preclinical departments in Edinburgh Medical School participated in the Baroda project, and the Bacteriology Department took its part.

Extension of Premises

Despite his intensive involvement with WHO and his considerable travels, Robert Cruickshank brought about significant developments in the work of the department and influenced it radically. He rearranged and extended the departmental accommodation. The virology laboratory previously located on the ground floor had been completely destroyed by fire in 1957. Professor Cruickshank was able to obtain a large classroom on the second floor when the Pathology Department moved to accommodation in the Medical School's new south-west block above the Middle Meadow Walk in 1960. The electron microscope was transferred from the ground floor to rooms adjacent to the new virology laboratories. The former Midwifery Department's museum room on the ground floor became a virus research laboratory. Dr R.R. Gillies took over the original virology laboratory which was re-built for bacteriological work. The department's animal house, for long in unsatisfactory premises in Charles Street Lane adjacent to the Wilkie Surgical Research Laboratory, was transferred to the top floor of the new southwest block. The new animal house facilities were a great improvement.

The Preparation Rooms were extended in area and new autoclaves and other steam sterilisers installed. In 1965 as a consequence of the thalidomide disaster, the financial assistance of the Distillers Company allowed a new laboratory known as the Virus Research Laboratory, to be opened on the roof of the Royal Infirmary, above the courtyard in front of the east entrance to the medical corridor.

In 1956, Miss Margaret Moffat, one of that year's Honours Graduates, was appointed a Research Assistant in the department. After studying at the State Serum Institute in Copenhagen, Miss Moffat returned to Edinburgh and was awarded a PhD in 1960. Dr Moffat joined the staff of the then newly established Wellcome Virus Research Laboratory, subsequently the Regional Virus Laboratory, at the City Hospital. In 1967, she was appointed Lecturer in the Department of Bacteriology, University of Aberdeen, and subsequently Senior Lecturer in the Virology Laboratory.

A number of new members of staff during Professor Cruickshank's period eventually took up important appointments elsewhere. In 1958 Dr Douglas Sleigh was recruited from the Bacteriology Department at the Western Infirmary, Glasgow, to a lectureship at Edinburgh. He did research on urinary tract infections and became an Honorary Senior Registrar to the South-East Scotland Regional Hospital Board. He was a dedicated teacher and a very loyal member of the department. In 1965, after a succession of posts in the west of Scotland, Dr Sleigh became Reader and Consultant Bacteriologist to the Royal Infirmary, Glasgow. He was co-author with Dr M.C. Timbury of *Notes on Medical Bacteriology* first published in 1982, and he became Professor and Head of Department at Glasgow in 1989.

In 1959, Dr Guy Boissard came to the department from the Virus Reference Laboratory at the Central Public Health Laboratory, Colindale. Dr Boissard, initially a London University College Honours Graduate in physiology, also graduated there in medicine in 1951 after service in the Second World War. At Colindale he specialised in poliomyelitis. Following two years working with Dr Swain in the department, in 1961 Dr Boissard was appointed in charge of the Wellcome Virus Research Laboratory. Soon afterwards he left to take up an appointment with Burroughs Wellcome.

Dr Ben Davies joined the department as a lecturer in 1960 and, having published a number of papers on urinary infections, was appointed Consultant Microbiologist to Edgware General Hospital, London in 1971. Four years later he became a Specialist in Microbiology and Head of the Regional Public Health Laboratory in Heerlen, The Netherlands.

Dr Peter Brown who joined the department in 1961, after a succession of posts in Africa and London, left to become Consultant Clinical Pathologist to the Regional Thoracic Centre, Papworth Hospital, Cambridge in 1963. Dr Brown did a considerable amount of research and published many papers on pulmonary tuberculosis in Africa and this country. He was subsequently appointed Consultant Microbiologist to the Queen Elizabeth Medical Centre, Birmingham.

Immunology

In 1961, an indication of Professor Cruickshank's appreciation of the increasing importance of immunology in relation to bacteriology was the appointment to the staff of Dr Donald Weir. Following his graduation in medicine in Edinburgh in 1955, Dr Weir subsequently held a succession of posts in England, notably as a Research Fellow of the Arthritis and Rheumatism Council at the Medical Research Council's Rheumatic Research Unit at Taplow, Bucks. Such was the development of immunology in the department, in teaching and research, under Dr Weir's direction, that a purpose-built laboratory was erected for its work. In 1983, Dr Weir was appointed to a Personal Chair in Microbial Immunology.

In 1960 Dr Helen Wright retired from her post as Senior Lecturer and Honorary Consultant Bacteriologist to the South-East Scotland Regional Hospital Board. Dr Wright's service to the department, initially as an expert on diphtheria typing, and then from 1946 until her retirement, as bacteriologist in charge of the department's public health laboratory, is the subject of a more detailed note.

In 1961 Dr J.C. Gould was appointed Director of the new Central Microbiological Laboratory at the Western General Hospital. In 1963 one of the department's senior lecturers and research workers, Dr J.P. Duguid[61], who had played an important part in the development of the department first under Professor Mackie and then under Professor Cruickshank, became Professor of Bacteriology at the University of St. Andrews and in 1967, at the University of Dundee. He worked on a very wide range of demanding research in the department. Of special note is his work on the early production and administration of penicillin, and on the mode of action of penicillin, and later his important research and observations on bacterial fimbriae and adhesiveness. Professor Duguid made many contributions to the work of a host of important committees and working parties.

Dr Alastair Wilson[62], who came to the department in 1965 as Senior Lecturer in Tropical Microbiology and Immunology and later became Honorary Consultant to

61. *Professor J.P. Duguid*

62. *Dr Alastair Wilson*

63. *Dr Sydney Selwyn*

64. *Dr Leela Ganguli*

65. *Dr M.A. Latif*

66. *Dr S.K. Biswas*

67. *Dr R.B. Singh*

68. *Dr Isabel Smith*

69. *Dr J. F. Peutherer*

the South-East Scotland Regional Hospital Board, had held posts at the Radcliffe Infirmary, Oxford; Stoke Mandeville Hospital; as Reader and Head of Department of Medical Microbiology, Makerere University College Medical School; and Professor of Bacteriology, University of Ibadan, Nigeria. Dr Wilson was seconded as Consultant Bacteriologist to Edinburgh City Hospital during 1974-75. For some time, he was in charge of the department's public health laboratory.

Dr Sydney Selwyn[63] was initially appointed a Research Fellow in Bacteriology in 1960 and later Research Fellow in Virology. He became a lecturer in the department in 1962. He published a number of papers on bacteriology and virology and in 1966 was seconded as Senior Lecturer from the department to become, under the auspices of the World Health Organization, Visiting Professor in Bacteriology in the Medical School at Baroda, India. Dr Selwyn became Honorary Consultant Bacteriologist at Westminster Hospital in 1967. In 1979 he was appointed Professor of Medical Microbiology in London University at Westminster Medical School. Apart from his prolific authorship of papers on a wide range of research subjects, Professor Selwyn has contributed to many television programmes on microbiology and has been Vice-President of the British Society for the History of Medicine.

"The Great Eastern Laboratory"

As a result of Professor Cruickshank's work abroad with the World Health Organization he had visited very many bacteriology laboratories. An obituarist wrote of these journeys: "He was always and everywhere looking for promising young men who could accept leadership in new undertakings. Many of those he met or had heard of, he invited to come to his Edinburgh department for further experience". Of these, a considerable number were Indians. Indeed, at one period during Professor Cruickshank's reign one room in which a succession of Indians were always to be found working was known familiarly to other staff and with a kindly joviality as "The Great Eastern Laboratory".

Amongst the several Indian doctors[64,65,66,67] who came to carry out postgraduate studies in the department was Dr S.K. Biswas from Calcutta who gained a PhD degree for his thesis on a subject of special interest to Professor Cruickshank. This was the Treponema Immobilisation Test, at the time regarded as the ultimate specific laboratory diagnostic test for syphilis. While medical men who had graduated overseas came to the department, so too did a number of medical women. One of these was Dr Leela Ganguli, a graduate of Madras University. Dr Ganguli's research included a study in collaboration with Dr Douglas Sleigh of bacteriuria in pregnancy. Her thesis in this subject gained her a PhD degree. After a succession of posts on leaving the department, Dr Ganguli became Consultant Microbiologist and Head of the Department of Microbiology at the Hope and Associated Salford Hospitals, Manchester.

Development of Virology

Professor Cruickshank's appointment in 1958 freed Dr Swain, who had been Acting Head of Department during the inter-regnum, to develop further the department's virology laboratory. In 1962, Miss Isabel Smith[68] who had graduated with Honours in the department's course of 1951 and after a short period on the staff had taken up a post at the Marine Laboratory in Aberdeen, returned to the department and soon afterwards gained a PhD degree. She joined Dr Swain's virology group and later became a Senior Lecturer. In 1963 Dr John Peutherer[69] took up the Research

Assistantship made available by Dr Smith's staff appointment. He in turn also joined the virology group and was eventually to succeed Dr Swain as Senior Lecturer and Honorary Consultant in Virology. In 1967 Dr Swain, in collaboration with Mr T.C. Dodds, Director of the Medical Photography Unit, published *Clinical Virology*.

Under Professor Cruickshank's direction the department had developed steadily in general microbiology, in virology and in immunology. Its accommodation and facilities had very greatly improved. Developments had proceeded in many new spheres in keeping with a new era, all within Professor Cruickshank's relatively short term of eight years. An example of this was the development of the Wellcome Virus Research Laboratory at the City Hospital in the early 1960s. In 1966 he was awarded a CBE and he retired in the same year. Two years later, his old *alma mater,* Aberdeen University, recognised his distinguished career by the award of an Honorary LL.D.

Rather than resting on his laurels, which many might have considered he deserved to do, Professor Cruickshank's deep interest in the development of medicine in other parts of the world led him to accept an invitation to set up a new department of Social and Preventive Medicine in Kingston, Jamaica. This challenge he took up with characteristic energy and enthusiasm. While in Kingston he also travelled to other parts of the West Indies and South America to advise on the setting up of public health laboratories. His successor at Kingston paid high tribute to him, stressing how his integrity, intellectual honesty, personal charm, keen sense of humour and good fellowship had made him an ambassador of international repute.

Death of Professor Cruickshank

Professor Cruickshank died in Edinburgh in 1974. Tribute was paid to him from a wide range of colleagues in many branches of medicine. So many aspects of his work and approach were highlighted: how he was primarily concerned, behind whatever research was going on, with patient care; how he saw his department as a family. If some considered him paternalistic, then his close friend, Sir James Howie, in his contribution to the *British Medical Journal* series: "Portraits from Memory" said he would rather settle for the simple term "fatherly". "He walked easily but with grace in the corridors of power" wrote another two colleagues. And he used his influence, contacts and considerable prestige in microbiology and wider circles to advance the careers of his staff.

In an era that enjoyed much more departmental socialising than was common in Professor Mackie's day, Robert Cruickshank took special pleasure in departmental parties and in the kindly "At Homes" which he and Mrs Cruickshank often had at their charming house in Greenhill Gardens. He was held in high esteem by so many medical colleagues and by his technical staff and auxiliary workers. Professor Cruickshank's early teacher and mentor, Professor John Cruickshank of Aberdeen apparently "did not distribute praise readily". However, he is on record as having once said of his former pupil and protégé later in his career: "Of course he is quite the nicest man in bacteriology today". There must have been very many others who would have echoed these words.

Second Inter-Regnum: 1966-68

Following the retiral of Professor Robert Cruickshank in 1966, Dr Swain again took charge of the department during this second inter-regnum, this time for two years until the appointment to the Chair of Professor Barrie P. Marmion in October 1968. As is so often the case, and as has been stated before, during such an inter-regnum, no major appointments were made to the staff nor significant alterations to the department's premises. Decisions which might have been required on important matters had to be left in abeyance.

Miss Heather Muir, an Honours Graduate of 1968, during which year she married, after a brief period as a physicist in the Royal Hospital for Sick Children, returned to the department as a postgraduate student in 1969. Her special studies were of the human papilloma virus, the subject of her MSc thesis. Mrs Cubie became a part-time, later full-time, member of staff of the Regional Virus Laboratory, which evolved from the Wellcome Virus Research Laboratory at the City Hospital. She gained her PhD in 1989.

Death of Dr R.H.A. Swain

Dr Swain retired from his post as Reader in Virology and Honorary Consultant Virologist to the Royal Infirmary and the City Hospital in 1975. He died six years later aged 71. Dr Swain had certainly made a substantial contribution to the firm establishment of virology as a major section of the department's work and had been responsible for training a considerable number of staff, academic and technical, in this special discipline.

Dr Richard Henry Austin Swain was born in Wimbledon. Following his education at Cheltonian College and at Streatham and Dulwich College he had studied for three years at Downing College, Cambridge, gaining an arts degree. He graduated in medicine at St Bartholomew's Medical School, London in 1937, and was trained in the still relatively new discipline of virology by Professor L.P. Garrod at St. Bartholomew's and especially by Professor S.D. Bedson at the London Hospital.

During the Second World War, Dr Swain served as special pathologist with the British Forces in Tunisia, Sicily and Florence. After the war, he returned to Hillend Hospital, St. Albans, which was associated with St. Bartholomew's, and was in charge of the pathology, bacteriology and public health laboratories. He joined the staff of the Edinburgh University Bacteriology Department in 1947. In his development of the department's resources in virological teaching and research and in providing a diagnostic service, perhaps the most important feature was the establishment of the Electron Microscopy Unit in 1951. This was the first such unit in Scotland.

Many obituary tributes to Dr Swain noted that he was a kindly and patient colleague, with a lively sense of humour. He was painstaking in training and encouraging his research students. He was a ready and sympathetic listener, especially when administering the department during two difficult inter-regnum periods. His interests were wide in art and literature, reflecting his early studies at Cambridge. He was proud of his wife Margaret's award of an honorary degree by Edinburgh University in recognition of her international reputation in needlework and its history. His two sons followed him into medicine and his daughter entered law.

CHAPTER EIGHT

PROFESSOR BARRIE PATRICK MARMION

70. *Professor Barrie Patrick Marmion*

Professor Barrie Patrick Marmion[70] was appointed to the Chair in 1968. During a decade he was to have a very great influence on the development of the department and he gave it new direction and purpose. He resigned to return to Australia in 1978.

Barrie Marmion was born in Alverstone, Hants, on 19 May, 1920. He graduated in Medicine at University College and University College Hospital in London and gained a Doctorate of Medicine in 1947. From 1943 to 1962 he was Bacteriologist in the Public Health Laboratory Service at Leeds. During this period, he was awarded a Rockefeller Travelling Scholarship at Walter and Eliza Hall Institute, Melbourne, Australia, and this experience considerably influenced him. In 1962 he became a Fellow of the College of Pathologists and in the following year gained a Doctorate of Science from London University. In the same year, he was appointed Foundation Professor of Microbiology at Monash University, Melbourne, holding this post until his appointment to the Edinburgh Chair in 1968. Having become a Fellow of the Royal College of Physicians of Australia in 1964, he became a Fellow of Edinburgh's Royal College of Physicians in 1970, and a Fellow of the Royal Society of Edinburgh in 1976. In 1984 he was honoured by special election to the Fellowship of the Royal Australasian College of Physicians.

When Professor Marmion delivered his Inaugural Address in February, 1969, bacteriology was firmly established as an important branch of medical science. Choosing as the subject of his address: "What kind of Microbiology?", he expressed his gratitude to the University, and especially to the Faculty of Medicine, for financial assistance towards remodelling and refurbishing the department's accommodation. The intensive application of the germ theory of disease in the nineteenth and early twentieth centuries, Professor Marmion said, along with the work of the hygienists such as Hardwick, had led to the conquering of the epidemic and mortal diseases. In due course this early work had been crowned by the more recent discovery of powerful chemotherapeutic and antibiotic agents. However, the revolution of one age, Professor Marmion continued, becomes the tiresome orthodoxy of the next. Some people had reached the conclusion that all the infectious disease problems had been solved. This was quite erroneous.

Discussing the relative meanings and scope of "bacteriology" *vis-à-vis* "microbiology", Professor Marmion commented that the latter term had been used by Pasteur as early as 1882. He also drew attention to one of the features of Pasteur's researches – the inspired guess to explain phenomena well in advance of experimental evidence. Amongst Pasteur's very many comments was that which insisted that there is no division into pure and applied science . . .

Professor Marmion drew attention to the important work of Duguid and Gillies at Edinburgh on fimbriae. He then referred to the need to teach microbiology in the context of the new biochemistry and biology of the subject, including molecular genetics. There was still uncertainty about how best to teach medical students on what he called "the laboratory aspects of medicine".

A New Era

The wide spectrum of development and advance heralded in Professor Marmion's Inaugural Address was no mere conjecture. Indeed, between the date of his appointment to the Chair and his Address, he had already begun to reshape the department.

His introductory theme "The intensive application of the germ theory of disease in the nineteenth and early twentieth centuries" had been the primary force that impelled Professor James Ritchie in the department's establishment and early years. The progress was accelerated during Professor T.J. Mackie's thirty-two years in the Chair, as more and more knowledge became available for teaching, research and laboratory diagnostic methods. With Professor Robert Cruickshank there was a period of consolidation of considerable achievement and exciting progress in the fields of chemotherapy and antibiotics. Even so it might have seemed that the graph of advancement, that had risen so steeply, would level out into an indefinite period of "tiresome orthodoxy". To imagine that this situation would obtain in the department was to reckon without the driving force of Professor Marmion who led his staff into a new era.

Remodelling and Refurbishing

While he had also indicated in his Inaugural Address that the department was already engaged in "remodelling and refurbishing", only those who had first-hand involvement in these processes were aware of just how sweeping and dynamic the programme was. The department's resources and facilities were updated and increased in order to further its work and to initiate and promote new areas of development.

New Preparation Suite

Each floor and every room in the department was assessed for its current function and maximum potential. The "remodelling" followed a logical sequence. A bacteriology department's hub and nerve centre is its culture medium preparation area and sterilisation suite. While certain improvements to these areas had been made during Professor Cruickshank's time – the first changes for many years – these had been made largely within the confines of the department's traditional accommodation. Greatly increased teaching facilities had resulted from the flooring over of the former large galleried combined lecture theatre of the Pathology and Bacteriology Departments to create a relatively large additional practical classroom – Classroom C. Professor Marmion rearranged and reconstructed the rooms and laboratories at the southern-most end of the classroom area corridor to create sufficient teaching and class preparation accommodation to allow the construction of a new washing-up, sterilisation and preparation suite in the former Classroom C area.

Imaginative planning and special funding from the University provided a wide range of modern equipment for the sterilisation suite, including an automatic glassware washing machine. The fact that the large machine and its accessories could not be transported into the room by means of the stairways and lift did not deter Professor Marmion, who, with characteristic determination, had the machine lowered through an opening in the roof, from a crane operating from Middle Meadow Walk.

Floor by floor the department was remodelled, with major changes. Further along the ground floor corridor, what had been for some years a virus research laboratory became the G.P. Diagnostic Laboratory. Eventually this large laboratory was laminated, providing a small seminar room and a study room above.

Immunology and Virology Laboratories

Soon after Professor Cruickshank's appointment in 1958, what had been the Pathology Department's main laboratory, semi-circular, and overlooking the Middle Meadow Walk, situated halfway between floors 1 and 2 (and originally Richard Muir's laboratory) was vacated and became the Bacteriology Department's Immunology Laboratory, with certain partitioned rooms created. High on Professor Marmion's list of "remodelling" was the erection of a new building in the back quadrangle to house the Immunology Laboratory and a new Seminar Room.

The vacated Immunology Laboratory between floors 1 and 2 became the Virus Research Laboratory. A laboratory of this designation had originally been established in 1965 in a prefabricated building erected on the roof of the Royal Infirmary above the courtyard beside the entrance to the Medical Corridor. This building and a group of small laboratories of several departments within it, and much of the equipment, had been funded by the Distillers Company, following the serious physical damage to several children whose mothers had been given the drug thalidomide during pregnancy.

At the end of the little passageway outside the Academic Staff Common Room on the second floor a semi-circular small research laboratory was sub-divided into a new office for the department's Senior Chief MLSO in Administrative Charge and an Accounts Office with, for the first time, a member of the secretarial staff in charge of this section. The adjacent store room was upgraded and refurbished and a photocopying office was set up in another adjacent small room. This complex, with the professorial suite, was to become the administrative heart of the department.

At the south-west corner of the department, on the second floor, the Virus Diagnostic Laboratory was upgraded and new equipment and safety cabinets provided.

The reconstruction of the classroom area and the construction of the new preparation and sterilisation areas have already been described. What in Professor Mackie's latter days had been his own research laboratory and then for some time the Honours Students' laboratory (Room 781), became a quality control laboratory for the preparation suite. The top of what had been one of the Biochemistry Department's stairways was floored over to create a small study room for the Honours Students.

The sequence of small laboratories to the east of the large laboratory, originally "Lab. 3" and used for a variety of purposes over the years, was altered to form one long laboratory, designated the Microbiological Pathogenicity Research Laboratory (MPRL) under the direction of Dr J.G. Collee. The adjacent large laboratory was also used for the work of the MPRL, while within it, the two instrument and centrifuge rooms were refurbished and new high-speed centrifuges and other equipment installed.

The departmental workshop, located under the Tower Landing staircase, for long a small single room, was extended by the acquisition of an adjacent room previously occupied by the Biochemistry Department. The adjoining wall was removed to create an invaluable departmental workshop.

Departmental Safety Committee: Category "A" Laboratory

In 1978, towards the end of Professor Marmion's tenure of office, and following the publication of the important and far-reaching Howie Report "A Code of Practice for the Prevention of Infection in Clinical Laboratories and Post Mortem Rooms", relevant codes of practice were laid down. Microbiological laboratory procedures were codified and laboratories were classified and designated according to the Report's provisions and according to the type of work done in them. In 1977, to implement the Health and Safety at Work Act of 1975, a departmental Safety Committee had been formed and this duly published a detailed Code of Practice for all of the department's laboratories and procedures. The University also set up a central Safety Committee under the convenership of Professor J.G. Collee. Close liaison was thus assured with the University Safety Officer from the outset.

While the new emphasis on safety had its practical implications for most laboratories in the department, very special attention was given to the possibility of its having to deal with Category "A" pathogens such as the agents of Lassa fever, Ebola and Marburg disease, spring-summer encephalitis and smallpox. By the time of his resignation in 1978, Professor Marmion had designed a Category "A" laboratory to be established in a laboratory in the Tower landing. There were special safety procedures for entering and leaving the laboratory. A purpose-built double-entry autoclave was installed. A shower was fitted for the disinfection of the operator when returning from the infected area to the clean area; the water used in the shower passed first into a collecting tank where it was heated to inactivate any infecting agents before discharge into the drainage system. Arrangements were agreed with the city Fire Brigade for procedures to be adopted in the event of a fire occurring in the special containment area.

A Widening Spectrum of Research and Service

During Professor Marmion's term of office, the department's resources of accommodation and research facilities were thus completely reorganised. Much new and expensive equipment was installed and several new members of staff were recruited. The decade saw the development of a wide spectrum of work in the service and research laboratories, with much significant progress. Research initiatives were aligned with team leaders. Some of the projects and achievements are summarised here; many were presented at scientific meetings[71].

In the beginning of this period of radical development, an infection was to demonstrate yet again how rapidly a department of medical microbiology has to be prepared to change and to meet a new challenge.

Hepatitis Reference Laboratory

In 1970, two years after Professor Marmion's appointment to the Chair, a serious outbreak of serum hepatitis (hepatitis B) occurred amongst members of the Royal Infirmary staff and in other parts of Edinburgh. Professor Marmion's experience in this field was crucial and he was appointed Chairman of the Advisory Committee set up by the S.E. Regional Hospital Board. In this assignment, as in many others, he combined his special expertise with determination to deal with the many problems that had to be faced. For three months, he took personal charge of the precautionary measures adopted not only in the Royal Infirmary but in the other Edinburgh hospitals and laboratories. In a historical account of the Royal Infirmary, published in 1984, the author comments upon the hepatitis outbreak: "the handling of that alarming situation by all concerned, under Professor Marmion's leadership, was

71. *Meeting of the Scottish Society for the Study of Infectious Diseases in company with visitors from the Infectious Diseases Society of America, 1970*

internationally applauded" (Catford, 1984). The author further remarks that during the episode "Professor Marmion was then, undoubtedly, the right man in the right place at the right time". As a consequence of the recommendations of the Advisory Committee which Professor Marmion chaired, very many new practical safety measures were made mandatory in hospitals, clinics and laboratories.

Another consequence of the hepatitis B outbreak was the setting up of the Hepatitis Reference Laboratory. This was established in what had been the Virus Research Laboratory in the Royal Infirmary roof-top premises. Dr Chris Burrell from the University of Sydney, Australia, was appointed in charge. Dr Burrell joined Dr John Peutherer and other virological colleagues in the teaching of basic virology and clinical virology to undergraduates, the supervision of postgraduate students in virology and a variety of research studies in hepatitis B including the prevention and possible means of immunisation against this infection. Some time later he was joined by Miss Pat Mackay who gained a PhD degree for her thesis "A study of structural and antigenic components of hepatitis B surface antigen". The hepatitis team flourished[72,73,74,75,76].

Structural Changes and the Development of New Classrooms and Laboratories

The "Inner Quadrangle" Building

The Immunology Laboratory's new premises facilitated an increased research programme under Dr Donald Weir's direction. Dr Bill McBride joined Dr Weir in 1971, and in addition to sharing the heavy teaching commitment in immunology, began his studies on *Corynebacterium parvum* and its immunological potential. These were to assume considerable importance in relation to cancer research. Dr Weir's own research interests were concerned particularly with immunological recognition mechanisms which had begun several years before joining the departmental staff. This work was specially related to auto-immune disease and to research on rheumatism which he had previously undertaken at the MRC Rheumatism Research Unit at Taplow.

The General Practitioners' Diagnostic Laboratory (the old "Lab. 4" of earlier days) occupied a laboratory on the ground floor. The laboratory was under the direction of Dr Alastair M.M. Wilson from 1965 to 1975 and carried out a wide range of diagnostic tests. John Brennan was the Chief MLSO. During the lamination of this laboratory, work was transferred to the Royal Infirmary Bacteriology Laboratory and after the completion of the alterations it was decided that the diagnostic service should be absorbed permanently into that of the Infirmary laboratory.

The lamination of the former diagnostic laboratory had created a ground floor laboratory and a study room and seminar room on the new upper floor reached by a staircase from the corridor. The laboratory became the Research and Development Laboratory. For some time, Dr Hugh Young, a member of the Royal Infirmary Bacteriology Laboratory staff and Dr Caroline Blackwell, an American science graduate and Lecturer on the University department staff, collaborated on studies on the laboratory aspects of the epidemiology of gonorrhoea – developing techniques for improving the specificity of the traditional laboratory tests for this form of sexually transmitted disease and for the classification of gonococci.

REVIEWS OF INFECTIOUS DISEASES • VOL. 4, NO. 3 • MAY-JUNE 1982
© 1982 by The University of Chicago. 0162-0886/82/0403-0001$02.00

Dialysis-Associated Hepatitis in Edinburgh; 1969-1978

B. P. Marmion, C. J. Burrell,
R. W. Tonkin, and J. Dickson

From the Department of Bacteriology, Edinburgh University
Medical School, Edinburgh, Scotland; and the Division of
Medical Virology, Institute of Medical
and Veterinary Science, Adelaide, South Australia

In 1969-1970 there was a sharp outbreak of hepatitis associated with hemodialysis in two Edinburgh hospitals; mortality was 24% among renal patients and 31% in staff members. The epidemiology of the outbreak, the measures taken to control it, and the efforts made to exclude hepatitis B virus infections during an eight-year period after the outbreak, were reviewed in the light of a retesting of stored specimens by modern diagnostic techniques for hepatitis A and B viruses. This review reveals that the outbreak involved some dual infections with both hepatitis B and non-A, non-B hepatitis viruses and that the occurrence of two infections at once was probably related to the exceptional virulence of the outbreak. The review also reaffirms that the routine serotesting of renal patients and staff members and the dialysis of infected patients in a geographically separate isolation facility are effective methods of controlling the spread of hepatitis B virus in hemodialysis units.

72. Paper: Dialysis Associated Hepatitis in Edinburgh: 1969-1978
Reprinted by kind permission of the Editor, Reviews of Infectious Diseases, *and the University of Chicago Press*

73. *Professor B.P. Marmion*

74. *Dr Chris Burrell*

75. *Dr Ralph Tonkin*

76. *John D. Dickson*

Virus Research Laboratory

When the Virus Research Laboratory was transferred from its roof-top premises in the Royal Infirmary to the vacated Immunology Laboratory between floors 1 and 2, Dr John Mackay was appointed in charge in 1971. Dr Mackay was a graduate of the Royal (Dick) Veterinary College where he had a distinguished undergraduate career. After work in a veterinary practice, he obtained a PhD for his thesis on liver diseases in animals. After various other posts, he joined the staff of the Animal Diseases Research Association at Moredun in Edinburgh, where he established and developed a tissue culture laboratory. This work, along with other experience in virology in animal diseases, was a valuable background for joining the University department's Virus Research Laboratory. Dr Mary Norval, an Honours graduate, joined the laboratory's team in 1971.

In August 1975 the departmental staff and his very many contemporary and former colleagues in the world of veterinary medicine, were deeply saddened by the death of Dr John Mackay who had joined the department in 1971. Some reference has already been made to Dr Mackay's important contribution to virology.

The Virus Laboratory, under Dr R.H.A. Swain's direction, provided a diagnostic service. In addition, members of the laboratory team pursued their research interests. Dr John Peutherer's initial studies were on herpes simplex and he subsequently specialised in hepatitis B and HIV, while Dr Isabel Smith worked on herpes simplex and chlamydiae.

In 1979, Dr Elizabeth Edmond, Consultant Virologist at the City Hospital was appointed a Senior Lecturer, attached to the Virus Diagnostic Laboratory. Her special duties were in relation to hepatitis B reference work and the diagnosis and control of viral infections in immunosuppressed patients undergoing transplant surgery. Dr Edmond collaborated with Dr Helen Zealley in a programme of rubella immunisation. When Miss Nan Anderson, who had been the Senior MLSO in the Virus Diagnostic Laboratory, eventually took up a post in Toronto, she was succeeded by Mr John Dickson, whose responsibilities became greatly increased.

The Electron Microscope Suite provided a service to various members of the research staff and to workers from other departments. In the Thin Section Laboratory, the ultramicrotome provided facilities for many research workers. A new Hitachi Perkin Elmer instrument was installed in 1974 with the financial assistance of the Lothian Health Board. The classrooms were gutted and painstakingly redesigned[77].

In the classroom teaching area, the phased replacement of the older types of microscopes was undertaken. Many new audio-visual teaching aids were introduced, including tape-slide tutorial material. The sterilisation and media preparation areas were completely redesigned and re-equipped. From its establishment, the greatly enlarged preparation and sterilisation suite proved an invaluable resource for the whole department.

The Microbial Pathogenicity Research Laboratory (MPRL) occupying the new laboratory created by the removal of the dividing walls of several laboratories in the east corridor, and under the direction of Dr J.G. Collee, was concerned with wide-ranging studies on anaerobes of clinical importance, work which gained for Dr Collee an international reputation. The research team consisted of Dr Andrew

77. *A refurbished practical classroom*

Fraser, Dr Brian Watt, Dr Michael Rutter and Dr Ian Poxton. For a period, bacteriological studies in relation to dentistry were also done. Mr Robert Brown was the Chief Medical Laboratory Scientific Officer appointed to this laboratory. The MPRL also had facilities in the adjacent large laboratory. Here Dr Philip Ross continued his research on pathogenic streptococci and throat infections. In 1973 Dr Brian Duerden joined the MPRL team.

Another important section of the department's work, the Animal House, was upgraded and its management reorganised. Modern cages were installed and other necessary new equipment acquired.

Staff Changes

The decade of Professor Marmion's stewardship of the department thus saw a transformation in its structure and its function. During this time, there were many staff changes. In September 1975 Dr Dick Swain retired after twenty-eight years service during which, as has been detailed above, he had consolidated the foundations of the virological diagnostic and research work and had for two periods been acting Head of Department.

Dr Leela Ganguli, who had joined the staff during Professor Cruickshank's period became a Senior Registrar in Manchester Teaching Hospital in 1971. In the same year, as has already been noted, Dr Ben Davies was appointed Consultant Microbiologist at Edgware General Hospital, London. In 1973, Dr Brian Watt, who had joined the department just before Professor Marmion's appointment and worked in Dr J.G. Collee's team, gained an MD for his thesis "Studies in bacterial anaerobiosis: the recovery of clinically important anaerobes on solid media". In the same year he was appointed Consultant Microbiologist at the Central Microbiological Laboratories, Western General Hospital, subsequently becoming Consultant Microbiologist at the City Hospital Bacteriology Laboratory. Dr Brian Duerden, who had joined the staff in 1973, had specialised in studies in collaboration with Mr W.P. Holbrook, a dental surgeon postgraduate student, on bacteroides, and had also made a comparative study of laboratory diagnostic methods for urinary tract infections. Dr Duerden, who worked under Dr Collee's direction in 1976, was appointed Lecturer in the Department of Medical Microbiology, University of Sheffield Medical School and in 1983 was appointed Professor and Head of Department there. He subsequently went to the Chair of Medical Microbiology at Cardiff in 1991.

Dr Michael Rutter, a veterinary graduate who worked in the MPRL research team with Dr Collee, left to take up a post at the Institute for Research on Animal Diseases at Compton, Berks., and subsequently joined the Directorate of MAFF Veterinary Medicines at New Haw, Weybridge.

Dr Joyce Coghlan (née Cranfield)

In another of the ground floor laboratories, Dr Joyce Coghlan had carried out routine milk and water examinations along with other research and diagnostic work already described. Some of the diagnostic work Dr Coghlan had established was eventually taken over by the Royal Infirmary Bacteriology Laboratory.

Dr Coghlan's important research studies on leptospiral disease merit special mention. She worked closely with Mr John Norval who was Chief Veterinary Officer for the City of Edinburgh. John Norval was a dedicated investigator and he collaborated with workers in various sections of the department. He and his colleagues (Sanitary Inspectors in those days) were tireless enthusiasts. Mr Willie Valentine and Mr Alistair Orr and their colleagues earned the respect of the microbiologists who worked with them. Dr Coghlan and Mr Norval were able to show that leptospirae harboured by pigs were responsible for previously undiagnosed flu-like illnesses in piggery workers. Joyce Coghlan left the department in 1974 to take up an appointment at the Central Public Health Laboratory, Colindale, where she subsequently became Director of the Leptospirosis Reference Laboratory.

Dr J.G. Collee Awarded a Personal Chair

In the spring of 1974 the University announced that Dr Collee had been awarded a Personal Chair. This honour was significant in several respects. It was an indication of the development and expansion of the department's work under Professor Marmion and the consequent need for the latter to be able to share his increased and heavy responsibilities with Professor Collee. But not least, it signified recognition of Collee's important research contributions, primarily in the field of clinical anaerobic bacteriology. In the official citation of the award of a Personal Chair special reference was made to the work of Professor Collee and his research colleagues which had constituted significant contributions to current knowledge on the isolation, culture and characterisation of pathogenic anaerobes.

Dr Robert Reid Gillies

Dr Gillies[78], in the Epidemiology Unit, whose research had embraced classical studies on bacillary dysentery and colicin typing, streptococci and pneumococci, pioneer work with Dr J.P. Duguid on fimbriae, and notably important studies on pseudomonas typing, was joined by Dr John Govan, and subsequently, Dr Sebastian Amyes, both science graduates. This laboratory's work assumed great importance. In due course, Dr Govan developed the pseudomonas research, with major contributions to the respiratory disease in cystic fibrosis, and Dr Amyes built up a separate research group to investigate bacterial drug resistance.

In the autumn of 1976 Dr Gillies, Senior Lecturer and member of staff for twenty-four years, resigned to become the first Professor of Clinical Bacteriology in the Queen's University, Belfast, where he is remembered with much affection. Some reference has already been made to Dr Gillies' valuable contributions over such a long period to the department's teaching and research commitments. He served under three professors. Five years after joining the department in 1952 under Professor T.J. Mackie, Dr Gillies was awarded a Doctorate in Medicine with commendation for his thesis on "The fimbriae and fimbrial antigens of *Shigella flexneri*". He had collaborated with Dr J.P. Duguid on this new and important field of study which had gained international attention. In 1962 Dr Gillies had been Visiting Professor and Head of Department at Ibadan, Nigeria, for a short period. He was a most popular lecturer and he carried an immense workload. In addition to his teaching duties and his considerable research programme, he was Associate Dean in the Faculty of Medicine for nine years. He attracted many recruits to work on departmental research projects and he fired them with enthusiasm. For a short period before his resignation he had acted as Senior Bacteriologist in charge at the Royal Infirmary Bacteriology Laboratory, following Dr Bowie's retiral. Dr Gillies was the author of several textbooks, including *Bacteriology Illustrated* which bears witness

78. *Professor Robert R. Gillies*

to his lucid style and to the photographic talents of Mr T.C. Dodds, his co-author, and his colleague, Mr Jim Paul. Professor Gillies died in 1983.

In June 1976 Dr Andrew Telfer Brunton joined the staff as a Lecturer. After graduating at Edinburgh University and holding brief clinical appointments at the Royal Infirmary and the Northern General Hospital, he was a Lecturer in the Department of Clinical Chemistry at the Royal Infirmary. While in the Bacteriology Department he was co-author of a number of publications on campylobacters and antibiotics. In 1980 Dr Telfer Brunton was appointed Director and Consultant Microbiologist at the Public Health Laboratory, Royal Cornwall Hospital, Truro.

Dr A.M.M. Wilson

In November 1975 Dr Alastair Wilson, who had joined the department in 1965 as a Senior Lecturer in Tropical Microbiology and Immunology, retired to become Consultant Bacteriologist to the Edinburgh City Hospital. Dr Wilson's wide range of experience had included appointments at the Radcliffe Infirmary, Oxford; the Post-Graduate Medical School, Hammersmith; Stoke Mandeville Hospital; and many years in various laboratories in Africa, including the Professorship of Bacteriology and Head of Department in the University of Ibadan, Nigeria. For a short period Dr Wilson was Professor and Head of Department of Medical Microbiology at the University of Malaya. In addition to specialising in the teaching of tropical bacteriology, Dr Wilson's wide research interests included considerable study of *Bordetella pertussis* and the efficacy of whooping cough vaccination in Britain.

Retiral of Dr John Bowie

Dr John Bowie, for twenty-seven years Senior Bacteriologist at the Royal Infirmary Bacteriology Laboratory and Senior Lecturer in the Department, retired in 1976. Dr Bowie's most important contribution to the efficiency and development of hospital sterilisation at the Royal Infirmary and in many other hospitals, is described later. Shortly after his retiral, Dr Bowie went to the Medical School at Salisbury, Rhodesia (now Zimbabwe) to assist in the bacteriological services there. Dr Bowie died there in 1984.

Resignation of Professor Marmion

In 1978 Professor Marmion resigned in order to return to Australia where he was appointed Director, Division of Virology, Institute of Medical and Veterinary Sciences in Adelaide and subsequently honoured there[79] by the University of Adelaide. His contribution to the reorganisation, development and advancement of the department has been presented in outline. The responsibility to maintain and foster these advances represented a daunting challenge for his successor, Professor J.G. Collee, who was appointed on 1 May, 1979. In addition to the vast programme of overhauling and restoration of the department undertaken by Professor Marmion and virtually completed during his term of office, not the least of the many legacies which he left was a new system of management that was overdue and essential for the functioning of the department in an age of high technology. He had introduced a new code of practice for the purchasing of equipment and materials and an accounts system to control budgets for the department's routine work, its many research grants, and its service laboratories.

Only brief reference is made at this point to Professor Marmion's early and continuing efforts to upgrade the inadequate premises of the Royal Infirmary Bacteriology Laboratory at Westgate which made coping with the laboratory's steadily increasing workload very difficult. He improved facilities and working conditions for the day-to-day work of the laboratory and he managed to provide better staff-room facilities which were much appreciated. By the seconding of the Medical School staff to the hospital laboratory for a widening of training and experience, Professor Marmion greatly facilitated the integration of the sections of the department that were separately located in the hospital and Medical School. This was a valuable preparation for the eventual transfer of the hospital work and staff to the Teviot Place building by Professor Collee shortly after he succeeded to the Chair.

Professor Barrie Marmion was honoured in 1990 by the University of Adelaide in recognition of his distinguished service.

Professor Barrie Patrick Marmion

Doctor of the University

Through the degree of Doctor of the University, the University of Adelaide confers a signal honour on individuals who have rendered it distinguished service over many years.

This year, the degree was awarded to Professor Barrie Patrick Marmion, Visiting Professor in the Department of Pathology. It was conferred at the Fourth Ceremony, on Tuesday 1 May, in the presence of the Governor-General, the Honourable Bill Hayden, AC. The Chancellor, Dame Roma Mitchell, presided.

In the Citation, delivered by the Vice-Chancellor, Professor Kevin Marjoribanks, reference was made to the great expansion in the diagnostic work of the Division of Medical Virology and its research in the areas of hepatitis, Q Fever and mycoplasma infections. This was attributed to the catalytic effect of Professor Marmion and his colleagues Dr Christopher Burrell and Dr Eric Gowans who went with him from Edinburgh.

---

79. *Professor Marmion's Australian Honour*
With acknowledgement to the Editor of the University of Adelaide News Magazine 'Lumen', 15 June, 1990

CHAPTER NINE

PROFESSOR
JOHN GERALD COLLEE

80. *Professor J. Gerald Collee*

On 1 May, 1979 Professor J.G. Collee[80] was appointed to the Chair of Bacteriology and to be Head of Department in succession to Professor B.P. Marmion. Having joined the department in 1955 under Professor T.J. Mackie, Collee contributed to its development during the reign of three professors, each of whom had left his own stamp in three distinctive eras. With the constantly evolving roles of bacteriology, virology and immunology in relationship to clinical medicine, Professor Collee was well aware that yet another era was beginning under his professorship. This was clearly evident in his Inaugural Address delivered in April 1975 following his appointment to a Personal Chair in the department.

Gerald Collee was born in Bo'ness, West Lothian, in 1929 and educated at Bo'ness Academy and the Edinburgh Academy. He graduated in Medicine at Edinburgh University in 1951. A hospital post at Haddington was followed by National Service as a Captain in the Royal Army Medical Corps and as RMO to the 5th Royal Northumberland Fusiliers and 81 HAA Royal Artillery at Newcastle. He then entered general medical practice at Shifnal in Shropshire.

While in the army, Collee had published papers on *Clostridium perfringens* food-poisoning and on glandular fever. In 1955, he was invited by Professor Mackie to join the staff of the Bacteriology Department as a Lecturer. From the outset, Collee's research interests lay primarily in clinical anaerobic bacteriology. He gained a travelling scholarship to study statistics at the London School of Tropical Medicine and Hygiene, and to work on bacterial toxins at the Wellcome Research Laboratories, Beckenham. In 1963-64 he was appointed a World Health Organization Visiting Professor of Bacteriology at Baroda Medical College, India.

Following his return to the department, Collee was appointed a Senior Lecturer and Honorary Consultant. Continuing his studies on the culture, isolation and characteristics of pathogenic anaerobes, he and his research team made significant contributions to current knowledge in this clinically important field and their continuing research was of great relevance to the investigation and management of patients with post-operative wound infections. Mechanisms of microbial pathogenicity with special reference to anaerobes continued to form the basis of the work of the department's Microbial Pathogenicity Research Laboratory, under Collee's personal direction and with Robert Brown as the Chief Medical Laboratory Scientific Officer in technical charge.

Inaugural Lecture: April 1975

In 1970 Professor Collee's important research contributions were recognised by his appointment to a Personal Chair. In his Inaugural Lecture, Professor Collee's theme was "Medical Microbiology: Opportunities, Challenges and Degrees of Freedom". Although thus presented four years before his subsequent appointment to the Chair of Bacteriology and Headship of Department, the lecture nevertheless provides a valuable insight into his approach to the wide-ranging opportunities and challenges which were to confront him.

Professor Collee stated that one of the greatest problems was to keep pace with an ever-increasing rate of change. The speed was bewildering and the unpredictability was worrying. At the outset, the Professor paid tribute to his research colleagues: Dr Michael Rutter, Dr Brian Watt, Dr Brian Duerden, Peter Holbrook, Dr Gadalla from Egypt, Dr Andrew Fraser and Robert Brown. He also indicated that the important work on fimbriae, originally by Duguid, Isabel Smith, Dempster and Edmunds, and published principally by Duguid and Gillies of the departmental staff, had been a stimulus. Duguid, Gillies, Swain, Helen Wright, Gould, Constable, Wilkinson and Sandy Cheyne had contributed much to his training and his transition from general practice to the specialisation of bacteriology.

Professor Collee illustrated the clinical importance of the work he and his colleagues had carried out on anaerobes and also the relevance of the phenomenon of bacterial attachment to cell surfaces. In studies on pathogenicity and modes of infection, molecular biology and biochemistry held keys to our increased understanding. Wider insight had been afforded to him by his association with Professor George Boyd of the Chair of Biochemistry, who became his close friend.

As regards the progress of bacteriology and the contribution to be made by students of special intellectual potential, Professor Collee stressed the value of the department's Honours school. In the field of clinical microbiology, there were rapid and continuing developments and the increasing importance of opportunist infections in compromised patients called for constant vigilance.

In other aspects of the work of the clinical bacteriologists and other medical scientists, Professor Collee suggested restraint in the proliferation of committees and working parties. He called attention to the disproportionate amounts of time that these demand, creating diversions from the real priorities. He was willing to concede that no matter the demands of professional commitments – it is important to be more than a microbiologist. There are other values. At the outset of his lecture Professor Collee had remarked how, when he might well have left the department, Professor Barrie Marmion had given him new inspiration and conviction to remain in bacteriology at Edinburgh. He also paid tribute to the outstanding contribution to medical microbiology that Professor Marmion had made after seven years in office. Professor Collee left his audience with "the demanding spirits of Inquiry, Truth and Action . . ."

Transfer of Royal Infirmary Laboratory to Medical School

As most of the department's physical requirements of accommodation and facilities had been met through Professor Marmion's substantial programme of alterations, Professor Collee was able to turn his attention to the essential functions of the department's teaching, research and diagnostic services. However, a major and historic rearrangement of premises was effected by the transfer of the Royal Infirmary's Bacteriology Laboratory from its Westgate building to a suite of specially constructed and designed laboratories in the former Pharmacology and Biochemistry Departments on the north side of the Teviot Place building. This new accommodation on several floors provided substantially increased space and greatly improved facilities for the clinically associated work of the department.

The Royal Infirmary's Bacteriology Laboratory is the subject of a separate chapter in this work. It is of some historical interest to note two points. Firstly, when Professor Mackie was able to obtain increased accommodation for his department in 1931, this was made possible by the acquisition of several laboratories on the top floor of what was then the Medical Chemistry Department, some of whose work was transferred to the King's Buildings campus. Some years later, further accommodation was acquired from what was then the Materia Medica Department (subsequently named Pharmacology Department) on the top floor of the north side of the building. It was the ultimate transfer of the Pharmacology Department to its purpose-built premises in George Square and later of the Biochemistry Department to the Hugh Robson Building in George Square that was to pave the way for the transfer of the Royal Infirmary Laboratory to these vacated areas. Soon after Professor Mackie's appointment to the Chair in 1923 and his designation as Bacteriologist to the Royal Infirmary he proposed to the Managers of the Royal Infirmary that, to enable him more effectively and conveniently to carry out his responsibility for the Royal Infirmary's bacteriological requirements, the hospital's laboratory and its work should be incorporated within his department in the Medical School. Shortage of accommodation however, prevented – or delayed – this arrangement. Thus, Professor Collee negotiated a move that was heralded in 1924 and effected in 1982. This section of the department was named the Clinical Bacteriology Laboratories.

Clinical Virology Laboratories

In 1981, shortly before the transfer of the Royal Infirmary Laboratory to the Medical School, laboratories in what had been the Biochemistry Department were altered and equipped to house the Hepatitis Reference Laboratory which had previously been situated in the prefabricated laboratories on the roof of the Royal Infirmary. In 1982, the Virus Diagnostic Laboratory was also transferred to the area adjoining the Hepatitis Reference Laboratory. The vacated premises on the second floor in the Middle Meadow Walk side of the building were allocated to Dr John Govan and his colleagues for pseudomonas research, previously accommodated on the ground floor. In turn, the ground floor laboratory was altered to provide a new departmental staff-room shared by academic, technical, secretarial and auxiliary staff. This development was facilitated by the new legislation that followed in the wake of the Howie Report on safety in laboratories, and the recognition of the need for "clean" staff-room areas.

The department's Safety Committee continued its important role of systematically monitoring the hazards of work carried out in each laboratory and area. In its work and its discussions, it was particularly well informed and effective because its Convener, Professor Collee, was the first Chairman of the University's Central Safety Committee when this was established in 1975, a position he held for some years.

Staff Changes

A month after Professor Collee's appointment, the staff were deeply saddened to learn of the death of Mr Sandy Cheyne, the department's first Chief Technician. A memorial service was held in Greyfriars Kirk, the University's "parish church" in November 1979, attended by his family and a wide representation of past and present staff, and medical and technical staff from many other departments of medicine. Professor Collee paid public tribute to one who had made a prodigious contribution for over 40 years to the development of the department and of bacteriology in Edinburgh.

In 1980, Dr Andrew Telfer Brunton was appointed Director and Consultant Microbiologist to the Public Health Laboratory at the Royal Cornwall City Hospital, Truro. Dr Pat Mackay joined Dr Telfer Brunton there. Dr Chris Burrell became a Medical Specialist at the Division of Medical Virology, Institute of Medical and

Veterinary Sciences, Adelaide, Australia (later to become its Director of Virology). In the following year the staff were greatly saddened when Dr Dick Swain died. In July 1982, Charles Smith, Senior Chief Medical Laboratory Scientific Officer in Administrative Charge retired, and was succeeded by Mr W. Marr. In July 1983, with a deep sense of shock and regret, the staff learned that Professor Robert Gillies had died suddenly while on holiday in Perthshire.

Personal Professorship for Dr Weir

In 1983, Dr Donald Weir[81] was awarded a Personal Chair. Dr Weir had joined the staff in 1961 and was appointed Reader in 1978. An Edinburgh graduate, after a number of clinical appointments he had been a Research Fellow of the Arthritis and Rheumatism Council, working at the Medical Research Council's Rheumatism Research Unit at Taplow. There he had played a major part in producing a definitive test for systemic lupus erythematosus, resulting from work begun on self recognition in auto-immune disease. In his Inaugural Lecture delivered on 8 May 1984, Professor Weir discussed the range and variety of host defence mechanisms. After dealing with the better-known processes of defence against infection, he referred to the work that he had done in collaboration with the City Hospital staff on the relationship between blood groups and urinary tract infections and infection with *N. gonorrhoeae*. This relationship was also being studied in reactive arthritis. Professor Weir indicated that the main theme of his lecture was the mononuclear phagocyte system and how the phagocytes distinguish "friend from foe". He presented many illustrations of the varied action of phagocytes and the factors involved in this, with special reference to receptor theory. One of Professor Weir's colleagues had shown that the mucoid material produced by *Pseudomonas aeruginosa* affects the function of alveolar macrophages in a way that had important consequences in relation to the pathogenesis of cystic fibrosis. Interesting studies had also been done on the effect of the diabetic state on the immune response which might possibly have important practical implications in relation to infections in diabetic individuals. Throughout his lecture, Professor Weir paid tribute to the collaboration he had received from Dr Caroline Blackwell[82], Dr Dennis Kinane, Dr Ray Brettle, Mr Peter Winstanley and others. Professor Weir's *Handbook of Experimental Immunology* is an invaluable addition to the literature on the subject and his textbook *Immunology: An Outline for Students of Medicine and Biology,* is in use all over the world. In 1984, Professor Weir's close colleague, Dr Bill McBride, resigned after over ten years on the staff of the department to become Adjunct Professor in the Department of Radiation Oncology, University of California, Los Angeles. He was succeeded by Dr John Stewart.

In April 1984 Dr John Bowie died at Ruwa, Zimbabwe. Soon after, on 8 December, 1986, Dr Elizabeth Edmond, Senior Lecturer and Honorary Consultant Virologist, died. She had joined the staff of the department in 1979 and had done research on urinary tract infections and atypical mycobacteria. From 1963 to 1967 she was a registrar in microbiology with Dr J.C. Gould at the Central Microbiological Laboratories at the Western General Hospital. She was amongst the first to gain the membership of the Royal College of Pathologists by examination. Deciding to specialise in clinical virology, Dr Edmond was appointed registrar in virology at the City Hospital in Edinburgh in 1968 and some years later, a Consultant Virologist there.

81. *Professor Donald M. Weir*

82. *Professor Donald Weir and Dr Caroline Blackwell examine a culture plate for meningococci*

The Department's New Name

Under Professor Collee's direction, the work of the department, wide-ranging in its research programme and with heavy demands made upon its diagnostic services in clinical microbiology and clinical virology, was to evolve rapidly to cope with many new challenges. In October 1990 the University authorities granted permission to change the name of the Department of Bacteriology to the Department of Medical Microbiology. For some time, it had been recognised that the current name did not indicate the wider interests and responsibilities of the department and the range of expertise.

In addition to his departmental responsibilities, the range of Professor Collee's other appointments and membership of statutory bodies and committees was wide and demanding. They included Chief Bacteriologist to Edinburgh Royal Infirmary; Consultant Adviser in Microbiology to the Scottish Home and Health Department; member of the Committee on the Safety of Medicines and Chairman of its Biological Sub-Committee; member of the Scottish Health Service Planning Council's Advisory Committee on Infection; member of the Joint Committee on Vaccination and Immunisation (UK) and Chairman of its Sub-Committee on Adverse Reactions to Vaccines and Immunising Agents; member of the Panel of Assessors of the Animals (Scientific Procedures) Act 1986; member of the Scottish Home and Health Department Working Party on Services for Patients Infected with AIDS; Convenership of the University Steering Committee on Safety and subsequently first Convener of the University Safety Committee, with Chairmanship of its Sub-Committee on Infection and Genetic Manipulation; member of the Royal Infirmary Working Party on Tetanus Prophylaxis and Treatment; and member of the Chief Scientist's Biomedical Research Committee.

Professor Collee went on to chair a special Working Group to advise the Committee on Safety of Medicines on possible human hazards of bovine spongiform encephalopathy. As chairman of the Faculty Learning Resources Committee at Edinburgh, he was concerned to maintain the standard of teaching aids and help available to lecturers through the Medical Illustration Service, with which he had close links. Professor Collee's research interests included: Studies on the action of bacteria at cell surfaces with special reference to possible mechanisms of microbial pathogenicity; bacterial neuraminidases; the clostridia; fundamental problems of anaerobiosis; the characterisation of clinically important anaerobes; *Clostridium perfringens (Cl. welchii)* food poisoning; quantitative aspects of sampling of pathogens on swabs; and blood culture methodology. A member of many learned societies, Professor Collee was also involved in much editorial work: as Senior Editor and formerly Chairman of the Editorial Board of the *Journal of Medical Microbiology;* abstracter and reviewer of selected papers and books in English or French for various journals; a member of the Editorial Board of and contributor to *A Companion to Medical Studies* (Blackwell); Co-editor of Mackie and McCartney's *Medical Microbiology;* and of *Practical Medical Microbiology;* and contributor to many other textbooks. His main interests were in anaerobic bacteriology, microbial pathogenicity, practical immunisation and antimicrobial drugs. In 1991 he was awarded a CBE in recognition of his contributions to Medicine.

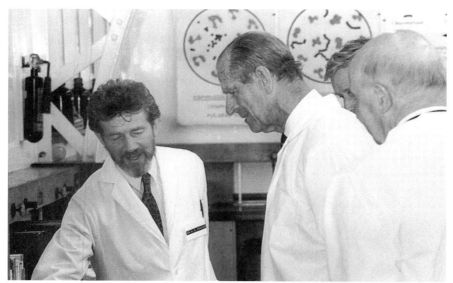

83. *H.R.H. Prince Philip with Dr Andrew Fraser at one of the classroom exhibits*

84. *The Duke of Edinburgh with Professor Collee and (centre) Professor Cairns Aitken,*
Dean of the Faculty of Medicine (29th May, 1991)

Royal Visit

On Wednesday 29 May 1991, the department was honoured by a visit from His Royal Highness, Prince Philip, Duke of Edinburgh, Chancellor of the University of Edinburgh[83,84]. The Duke saw exhibits depicting the many aspects of the work of the Department and then visited the recently refurbished Microbial Pathogenicity Research Laboratories to see a working laboratory.

Retiral of Professor Collee

Professor Collee retired on 30 September 1991[85]. A presentation and supper to mark the occasion was held in the Playfair Library Hall, Old College, on 6 September, 1991[86,87,88], and was attended by many members of staff, colleagues and friends, past and present. Professor J.P. Duguid, formerly of the Chair of Bacteriology at the University of Dundee, spoke warmly of his former colleague of several years in the Edinburgh University Bacteriology Department. Professor John Richmond, President of the Royal College of Physicians of Edinburgh and formerly Professor of Medicine and Dean of the Faculty of Medicine at the University of Sheffield, then paid tribute to Professor Collee, first in an academic context and then as his close friend. Professor Richmond recalled their collaboration when the Edinburgh clinical curriculum was being reformed and how by his courteous persuasion Professor Collee had ensured that bacteriology did not lose teaching time.

Collee was a man of varied learning and interests, and he possessed some artistic versatility. His paintings could provide an impressive exhibition; he could entertain on the fiddle, and some other instruments with lesser ability! He displayed ingenuity as an amateur engineer. More time available in his workshop and in his art studio would be welcome pleasures of his retirement. Professor Richmond said that what had once been said of the first incumbent of the Chair, Professor James Ritchie, could likewise be said of Professor Collee "that he could not recall his ever saying an unkind word about anyone".

To the present writer and to other former members of staff present in the gathering who could also recall Professor Collee's early days in the University Department with Professor T.J. Mackie, there seemed to be about this evening's memorable occasion in the Playfair Library Hall, amidst so many guests from far and wide, something of the sense of the end of an era, from the closing days of Professor T.J. Mackie's reign to Professor Collee's retiral.

85. *Staff, Research Workers, Students, Technical and Clerical Staff with Professor J.G. Collee, 1991*

86. *Professor Collee receiving a presentation from Mrs Joan Collins and Dr Andrew Fraser*

87. *The author and editor of* **Edinburgh's Contribution to Medical Microbiology:** *Charles J. Smith and J. Gerald Collee*

88. *Mrs Norma Marr who prepared the original typescript and disks for this publication, and Mr Bill Marr who acted as Production Manager over eight years.*

CHAPTER TEN

THE BACTERIOLOGY LABORATORY AT THE ROYAL INFIRMARY

An account has already been given in the opening pages of this history, of Edinburgh's first bacteriological laboratory, established by Joseph Lister in a small room in the old Royal Infirmary in Infirmary Street in 1876 with his assistant Dr William Watson Cheyne. Various simple bacteriological procedures were done with very basic culture media and somewhat primitive laboratory equipment. This was after Lister had relinquished the Chair of Surgery at Glasgow University, where he had carried out his important work using a carbolic spray, and returned to occupy the Chair of Clinical Surgery in Edinburgh. He was to resign from this post a year later and return to London. This small bacteriology laboratory therefore had a brief existence, but it was the Edinburgh Royal Infirmary's first.

After Lister's departure for London in 1877, we have no evidence that the little laboratory continued to function under his successor, Professor Thomas Annandale. Certainly the deep and practical interest shown by Lister and Watson Cheyne in the relatively recent discoveries of Pasteur and Koch and the science of bacteriology in relation to surgical technique was retained and developed by one "who had been one of Lister's ardent and faithful supporters". This was Professor John Chiene who was appointed to the University's Chair of Surgery in 1882. Such was Chiene's conviction about the importance of bacteriology that immediately on his appointment he established a small bacteriology laboratory in his Department of Surgery in the partially completed Medical School in Teviot Place. In 1884, he read a paper to the annual meeting of the British Medical Association entitled "On the Desirability of Establishing Bacteriology Laboratories in Connection with Hospital Wards" (Cheine, 1884). John Ritchie in his *History of the Laboratory of the Royal College of Physicians of Edinburgh* (1953) comments that Chiene's laboratory "was said to have been the first teaching bacteriological laboratory in the United Kingdom". It was for "the training of the Royal Infirmary residents and medical students as an adjunct to their surgical ward work but a certain amount of research was also carried on from time to time".

While Professor Chiene's laboratory was situated in the Medical School in Teviot Place and thus not in the Royal Infirmary – by 1882 the then fine new hospital in Lauriston Place, designed by David Bryce and opened in 1879[89] – the bacteriological work which it undertook was directly related to the surgical work of the hospital. This laboratory remained until Professor Chiene's retiral in 1909. It may be referred to as the Royal Infirmary's second bacteriology laboratory.

Other Early Bacteriological Work

The records are sparse and it is not clear who might have provided some kind of wider diagnostic and monitoring service for the many cases of infectious disease admitted to the Royal Infirmary, firstly when it was situated at Infirmary Street, and then after its establishment at Lauriston Place. After the hospital had moved to Lauriston in 1879, the City Hospital for Infectious Diseases was opened in the former Infirmary Surgical Hospital building at Drummond Street and it remained there until the opening of the new purpose-built City Infectious Diseases Hospital at Colinton Mains in 1903. However, patients who developed infections were still admitted in large numbers to the Royal Infirmary itself. We can trace no clear record of a bacteriological laboratory carrying out diagnostic and monitoring work for these patients.

In 1887, eight years after the Royal Infirmary had been opened at Lauriston, the first Edinburgh Royal College of Physicians' Laboratory was opened at No. 7

Lauriston Lane, just westwards of the hospital. This property belonged to the Infirmary Board of Managers who leased it to the College. While John Ritchie, in his history of this laboratory, gives no indication that it carried out work for the hospital, nevertheless he refers to the laboratory as "conveniently near the Royal Infirmary". It is believed that it would have carried out bacteriological examinations for those members of the College of Physicians who were in charge of Royal Infirmary wards.

As already noted, Dr Robert Muir, a member of the University Pathology Department staff, was appointed as Lecturer in Pathological Bacteriology in 1894. He was the first of the staff of the Medical School to lecture formally on the subject. Since Dr Muir had been appointed pathologist to the Royal Infirmary from 1892, it is possible that he also carried out some bacteriological laboratory work in or for the hospital, but this cannot be substantiated. Muir resigned as pathologist and as lecturer in Pathological Bacteriology at Edinburgh when he was appointed to the Chair of Pathology in St Andrews University in 1898.

In many universities and hospitals throughout Britain, it would appear that bacteriology was first practised as an offshoot of pathology until such time as bacteriological knowledge and techniques steadily developed to generate separate bacteriology departments, laboratories and staff. It is a reasonable assumption that this was the case in Edinburgh, in the Medical School and in the Royal Infirmary.

Dr A. Logan Turner in his *Story of a Great Hospital: The Royal Infirmary of Edinburgh 1729-1929*, refers to the Royal Infirmary's first pathologist as Dr Robert Reid, appointed in 1839, and Turner lists Reid's successors until 1929. It may be noted that for long the hospital's pathologists were not necessarily members of staff of the University Department of Pathology. One exception has already been mentioned, namely Dr Robert Muir who for some time was a senior member of staff of the University department and pathologist to the Royal Infirmary. Assuming that, as in other places, bacteriology in the Royal Infirmary would have been an offshoot of its Pathology Department, a search was made of the hospital's Annual Reports and Medical Managers' Committee Minutes for references to the establishment of bacteriology in the hospital as a separate subject.

Bacteriology in 1896

At its meeting in December 1895, attended by Professor John Chiene and Professor William Greenfield of Pathology, members of the Committee were critical of the spirit of rigid economy in the Infirmary which "was causing strain amongst the staff". The earliest reference of relevance to the development of the Pathology Department was at a meeting in February 1896 when the hospital pathologists raised several urgent matters: the need for an extension to their premises; the need for additional scientific and pathological instruments; the need for improved mortuary facilities; and the need for additional assistance. One of the reasons given for the need for more laboratory accommodation was to enable the pathologists to conduct "the chemical examination of pathological fluids". At the same meeting, an urgent plea was made for the provision of a room with requisites for bacteriological examinations. This was the situation in 1896. Later in the same year, the pathologists were provided with "one fair microscope; one good microtome; another small one, plus other two, antiquated and of little use". It would appear that the pathologists were compelled to spend large sums from their own private means on laboratory equipment. In the year referred to, £100 was given for additional equipment. The Minutes note that this new equipment did not include any for bacteriology. In this same year, a request was made for a porter and a boy to be employed in the pathology laboratory and to give special assistance in bacteriology. No further references occur in the Minutes of the Medical Managers' Committee to pathology and bacteriology until 1907 when at a special meeting, an increase of 2/6d per week for "the lab. boy" was requested; 2/- was agreed upon, bringing the boy's wage to 12/- per week. At the same meeting, it was noted that the Edinburgh Public Health Authorities would be taking responsibility "for all cases of infectious or contagious disease unsuited for the Royal Infirmary, especially plague, cholera, anthrax and glanders". By 1907, the new City Infectious Diseases Hospital at Colinton Mains had been open for four years.

Premises

While the Royal Infirmary records from the early 1890s onwards indicate the steady growth of the Pathological Department and its consequent need for increased accommodation and other facilities, no references could be found describing where the department was originally situated, nor when bacteriology began to be done in the department. In early sketches of the new Royal Infirmary, a very small building stands at the north-west corner of the grounds. This is where the pathology and bacteriology laboratories subsequently developed in what came to be known as the Westgate building. Dr A. Logan Turner's classical history provides plans of the hospital's layout. The earliest of these, dated 1891, indicates a small building at the Westgate site, with the Mortuary Chapel at the west end, but the building's function is not indicated. In the latest plan in the book, not dated but presumed to be 1937 (the date of publication), the Westgate building is then designated "Pathological Department" and the premises are shown as much larger than the small building in the original Bryce drawing, and with their gable end very close to the west entrance driveway to the hospital. From the Logan Turner plan of 1937, it is clear that extensions had been added to the original little building. It has been suggested by a number of the hospital's Bacteriology Department staff of long service that the extensions had been added about 1910. There had always been an awareness while working in the building of its original and its new parts. A close inspection of the premises (closed since 1982), made while this historical account was being written, confirmed the above observations. It was decided, however, to seek further confirmation in the Royal Infirmary archives. Amongst very early architect's plans in the keeping of the hospital's Works Department was one of unique interest and value. This was dated 1878, one year before the then new hospital had been officially opened.

Original Plan

The plan provides great detail of what it designates the "Pathological Department" clearly situated at the Westgate site. The premises consisted primarily of a large semi-circular post-mortem room with a gallery from which 200 students could watch autopsies being done by the pathologists in the area below. A number of adjoining laboratories and other rooms are shown. Dr Mike Barfoot, the Lothian Health Board archivist, drew our attention to a note in *The Builder,* an architectural publication, for 20 October, 1877, which recorded that the:

89. *New Royal Infirmary, Lauriston Place, 1879*
The small building on the right, at the West entrance, became the Pathology and Bacteriology Laboratories
(Sketch by David Bryce, Architect)

90. *Dr Theodore Shennan*

Edinburgh Health Society.

HEALTH LECTURES·
For the PEOPLE.

SIXTEENTH SERIES.

No. 6.

KOCH AND HIS WORK.

BY

THEODORE SHENNAN, M.D., F.R.C.S.Ed.,
LECTURER ON PATHOLOGY, SURGEON'S HALL, AND NEW VETERINARY
COLLEGE, EDINBURGH, ETC.

EDINBURGH:
MACNIVEN & WALLACE.
1899.

PRICE ONE PENNY.

91. *Early Lectures by Dr Shennan*

> Pathological Department is in progress: it is to have a frontage of 87 feet to the north and consists of a pavilion two storeys in height, with a high pitched roof and a one-storey block running westward. The theatre, which is to occupy the centre of the block, is 43 feet long by 30 feet wide and 23 feet high and is calculated to accommodate 200 students. To the east of the theatre is a demonstrating room 29 feet square, above which is a room of similar dimensions, appropriated to microscopic observations. To the west of the theatre is a post-mortem room . . .

Again, long-serving members of the laboratory staff could recall the large post-mortem lecture theatre which was eventually laminated to provide additional pathology laboratories and storage space above, while retaining the post-mortem area and a reduced balcony. When, as the Medical Managers' Committee minutes frequently indicate, the duties of the hospital pathologists from 1879 to 1895 were primarily or almost exclusively to perform post-mortem examinations and provide reports, the building as originally designed would serve this purpose quite adequately. When, however, the pathologists were required to participate in diagnostic work, new and additional laboratory facilities were essential. Such demands on the pathologists are not referred to in the records until the early 1890s. According to the Medical Managers' Committee minutes for February 1896, they were then being expected to assist in diagnosis "including the chemical examination of pathological fluids which largely guides the physician to the most helpful treatment of the patient".

To enable the pathologists to carry out their wider duties, increased accommodation was requested. The Committee agreed that two additional rooms be added to the Pathological Department. Space for this extension "is readily to be found on the ground immediately to the east of the present building situated between it and the east [this should have been west] entrance to the hospital". This extension was presumably built soon after February 1896 and brought the east gable end of the Pathological Department building (the future Westgate building) very close to the west entrance driveway to the hospital.

In the minutes for 24 December, 1900, meeting it is noted that there "was still no provision for the bacteriological examination of cases". There is a comment that if it were necessary to decide if a case was one of plague, this could not be done in the hospital's Pathological Department. At the same meeting there was a further comment that "the pathologists' duties long ago far outgrew the dissection of the dead body. There is need for examination of the living body".

In the Royal Infirmary's Annual Report for 1905-06, reference is made to the reorganisation of the Pathological Department. It may have been at this time that a separate laboratory or laboratories were allocated for bacteriological work. In 1906 Dr Theodore Shennan[90] was the pathologist. From the Medical Directory of the time, it is evident that Dr Shennan was also well qualified and experienced in bacteriology, especially in relation to tuberculosis[91]. In 1909, the hospital managers recorded their warm thanks "to those members of staff who provided courses of lectures and instruction to the probationers [nurses]". Dr Shennan was the lecturer in bacteriology. [It is possible that Dr Shennan, while the hospital pathologist, also carried out bacteriology in his department from about 1906. Further data on Dr Shennan's bacteriological experience is provided in Appendix D2.]

Dr William R. Logan

While it would appear that from about 1906 some bacteriological work was being done in the Pathological Department, certainly in 1911 the records indicate that additional support was required for this work still being carried out within the Pathological Department. In the same year the post-mortem room attendant who was being paid 34/- per week was appointed "Chief Laboratory Assistant" and a second laboratory assistant was appointed. In 1914 a memorandum by the assistant pathologists refers to greatly increased laboratory work, "especially in bacteriology and serology, which have more than trebled since 1903". For a few years prior to 1914, Dr W.T. Ritchie had acted unofficially as a clinical pathologist and had done bacteriological work. In 1914, however, the hospital authorities decided to advertise for a clinical pathologist whose duties would be primarily in bacteriological diagnosis. The man appointed was Dr William Robertson Logan[92], who became the Royal Infirmary's first bacteriologist, a post he retained for thirty-four years.

From the sparse information in the records, and more readily from Dr Logan's obituary notice, it has been possible to compile short biographical notes. Dr Logan was a native of Kelso where his education began and was later completed at George Watson's College in Edinburgh. After graduation in Medicine at Edinburgh University in 1909, Dr Logan became primarily interested in pathology and bacteriology. For a short period he was an assistant in the University's Pathology Department under Professor J. Lorrain Smith. In 1913 Dr Logan gained a Doctorate in Medicine for his thesis "A Study of the Normal and Pathological Intestinal Flora of Infants and Very Young Children". Many of the clinical studies were carried out in the Edinburgh Royal Hospital for Sick Children, while the laboratory work was done in the Royal College of Physicians' Laboratory in Forrest Road.

It is recorded that, before taking up the Royal Infirmary post as Clinical Pathologist with special responsibility for bacteriology, Dr Logan had studied for a short period in Paris. His initial service in the Infirmary laboratory was short-lived for, on the outbreak of the First World War, he joined the Royal Army Medical Corps as a bacteriologist in East Madras with the Middle East Forces and later was in charge of the laboratory of the 42nd General Hospital at Salonika. During Dr Logan's war service his post in the Royal Infirmary as Clinical Pathologist in the Pathology Department was held temporarily by a Miss Fitzgerald. When Dr W. Logan first took up his post as Clinical Bacteriologist in 1914, one of his more experienced technical staff was Robert Barr[93] who had joined the Royal Infirmary staff from the Royal College of Physicians' Laboratory in Forrest Road in the previous year. In 1924, a year after Professor T.J. Mackie's appointment as Consultant Bacteriologist to the Infirmary, Dr Logan's designation was changed from Clinical Pathologist to Clinical Bacteriologist. This post he held until his death in 1948. Dr Logan did much to establish bacteriology in the Royal Infirmary Pathology Department, and then from 1925 within the separately established Bacteriology Department. He published several papers, notably in relation to pneumococcal infections.

Professor T.J. Mackie's Appointment

In January 1924, a few months after his appointment to the University Chair in Bacteriology, Professor Mackie began a correspondence with the Royal Infirmary and the University authorities concerning his role and responsibilities as regards the hospital's bacteriology department. The correspondence on this theme was to continue for at least six years. Although the hospital managers had appointed Professor Mackie as Honorary Bacteriologist in response to representations from

92. *Dr William Logan*

93. *Robert Barr*

94. *Informal group photograph of Royal Infirmary Bacteriology Laboratory Staff* (1955-60)

the University, it would appear that confusion frequently arose as regards Professor Mackie's precise role.

Professor Mackie submitted to the Royal Infirmary Board of Managers that he would prefer it if the hospital's bacteriological work could be carried out in his University department but regretted that facilities at the time did not permit this. He was particularly anxious that a regular supply of material from patients in the hospital should be made available promptly for the University's teaching of medical students and also for special investigation and research.

In 1924 Professor Mackie was listed in the Royal Infirmary's Annual Report as Honorary Bacteriologist under the heading of the Pathological Department. From 1925 the hospital's Bacteriology Department was given its own separate heading with Professor Mackie designated Bacteriologist and Dr Logan as Clinical Bacteriologist. In the course of time the staff of the Pathology Department were gradually transferred to the University Pathology Department where eventually all the pathological work for the hospital was carried out. A certain amount of pathology, however, primarily related to the post-mortem examinations was performed in the Westgate building. By the mid 1970s this work was duly transferred to the University department and the building was given over entirely to the hospital's Bacteriology Department. The bacteriological staff of that building had a clear identity and contributed most significantly to the work of the hospital[94,95].

From 1930 Professor Mackie's Senior Assistant in his University Department was appointed to the Royal Infirmary as Extra Bacteriologist. With some exceptions, the Royal Infirmary Annual Reports list a succession of such Extra Bacteriologists nominated by Professor Mackie. The last of these, appointed for a short time in 1945, was Dr C.E. Van Rooyen. In 1946, Dr R.H.A. Swain was appointed Associate Bacteriologist to the Royal Infirmary.

While the correspondence regarding Professor Mackie's precise role and powers as the Royal Infirmary bacteriologist continued for many years, and regardless of whatever confusion there might have been, he made a vital personal contribution to the hospital and the bacteriological service. Professor Mackie's own monitoring and testing of the sterility of surgical sutures, for example, was of national importance in surgery and earned him government commendation for his participation in the framing of legislation governing their manufacture and testing.

While it would appear that Professor Mackie's role in relation to the Royal Infirmary Bacteriology Department was never precisely defined, it may be noted that Professor Robert Cruickshank who succeeded Professor Mackie to the University Chair in 1959, was designated as Chief Bacteriologist to the Royal Infirmary. It was not until more recent times and especially with the "1972 Cost-Sharing Agreement" that the relationships of the hospital's Bacteriology Department and the University Department and its Head were finally clarified.

Dr W. Logan's Successors

Dr Logan remained in his post as Clinical Bacteriologist until his death in 1948. He had had a succession of Assistant Clinical Bacteriologists from 1926 who are listed in the Royal Infirmary Annual Reports. One of these assistants in relatively more recent times was Dr John Telfer Smeall, who was appointed in 1930 and retired in 1946. Dr Smeall, a native of Jedburgh, had been an accountant and had then completed a notable military career before studying medicine in which he graduated

95. *Informal group photograph of Royal Infirmary Bacteriology Laboratory Staff (1955-60)*

in 1912. In the First World War he served in the Royal Army Medical Corps and was awarded the Military Cross with High Commendation. After a short period as a house surgeon in Carlisle he had joined the Royal Infirmary staff.

Dr Smeall was succeeded in the Infirmary laboratory in 1946 by Dr Robert J.G. Rattrie, an Edinburgh graduate who had previously held several clinical appointments in the hospital. He resigned at the end of 1948 to enter the family general practice at Maryport, Cumberland. Tragically, he was killed in a road accident in 1966.

In April 1948, shortly before Dr Logan's death, Dr Thomas B.M. Durie[96] was appointed Junior Assistant Bacteriologist in the Royal Infirmary laboratory. Dr Durie, an Edinburgh graduate, held a postgraduate appointment in the Astley Ainslie Hospital, and then served in the Royal Army Medical Corps from 1944 to 1947. He was involved in the Normandy to Germany Campaign. After demobilisation and various training posts, Dr Durie joined the Royal Infirmary bacteriology laboratory staff as an Assistant Bacteriologist from April 1948 until September 1963, then becoming Honorary Consultant Bacteriologist to the Infirmary from October 1963 until his retiral in September 1984. Dr Durie also held the posts of Lecturer in the University Bacteriology Department from 1952 until 1963 and Senior Lecturer from 1963 until 1984. The application of bacteriology to the field of clinical medicine and the development of rapid laboratory diagnostic systems were his special interests. He participated extensively in the teaching of nurses and collaborated in the publication of many papers.

In May 1948 Dr Ralph Tonkin[97] was appointed Assistant Bacteriologist. After graduation at Edinburgh he held appointments at the Dunfermline and West Fife Hospital before joining the Royal Navy Volunteer Reserve in March 1946. He served as Surgeon-Lieutenant in a destroyer flotilla of the British Pacific Fleet until April 1948. In the following month he joined the Infirmary bacteriology staff. In 1952 his appointment was combined with a Lectureship in the University Bacteriology Department. In 1953, the South-East Scotland Regional Hospital Board appointed Dr Tonkin Honorary Senior Hospital Medical Officer in Bacteriology to the Royal Infirmary. In 1968 he became a Senior Lecturer in the University Department and Honorary Consultant in Bacteriology to the South-East Scotland Regional Hospital Board. Apart from his involvement in the Infirmary's bacteriological laboratory diagnostic service, Dr Tonkin had particular responsibility for the bacteriological aspects of several surgical and clinical areas of the hospital, notably the surgical wards of Professor Sir Michael Woodruff, the wards of the Department of Thoracic Surgery including cardiac bypass surgery and the intermittent and acute dialysis units. He also had responsibilities in the Simpson Memorial Maternity Pavilion. His many published papers included studies during the 1969/70 hepatitis B virus outbreak in the Royal Infirmary, work done in the hospital's Intensive Care Unit, and observations on the Kahn Universal Serologic Reaction. Dr Tonkin retired in 1983.

Dr John H. Bowie

Following Dr Logan's death in July 1948, the post remained vacant for some time. Dr R.H.A. Swain of the University Department was nominated by Professor T.J. Mackie to take temporary overall charge of the laboratory. On 1 April 1949 Dr J.C. Gould was appointed Senior Assistant Bacteriologist, again on Professor Mackie's nomination to the Infirmary authorities. Dr Gould joined the University Bacteriology

96. *Dr Thomas B.M. Durie*

97. *Dr Ralph Tonkin*

Department as a Lecturer in October 1950 by which time Dr John H. Bowie had been appointed Senior Bacteriologist to the Royal Infirmary.

Dr J.H. Bowie[98], a native of Edinburgh, graduated in medicine in 1934. He was soon afterwards commissioned in the Indian Medical Service, holding appointments as medical officer with various regiments including the 20th Lancers and Gurkhas. In 1940 he was appointed Senior Pathologist to the Military Hospital at Dehra Dun. He carried out much research in India, especially on typhus fever, and collaborated with Professor C.P. Beattie in this work. Professor Beattie at one time had been on the staff of Edinburgh University Bacteriology Department before taking up a Chair in Baghdad, eventually returning to Sheffield as Professor of Bacteriology at the University there. Indeed, when Dr Bowie himself returned from India, he held an appointment as a lecturer in bacteriology at Sheffield for a year in Professor Beattie's department.

On his return to Britain, Dr Bowie had the advantage of a very wide range of experience. In addition to his work in India where he had formed The Army in India Penicillin Research Team and for which he was honoured by the Indian government, he had been on special missions in the Middle East, North Africa and Naples; in the latter, he did work on epidemic typhus. After his short period with Professor Beattie in Sheffield, Dr Bowie took up a lectureship with Professor Mackie in 1949 at the same time being appointed Senior Bacteriologist to the Royal Infirmary. With Dr J.C. Gould, he made important pioneering contributions to antibiotic sensitivity testing.

In 1957 Dr Bowie collaborated with the Royal Infirmary Works Department team, and with Manlove, Alliot & Edwards, steriliser manufacturers, to develop the first high pre-vacuum steriliser. He demonstrated a prototype of this with gravity displacement sterilisation at a conference of British surgeons (Bowie, 1958). The introduction of the first rapid cooling (water spray) steriliser for bottled fluids was another of Dr Bowie's important developments. With his Senior Chief Medical Laboratory Technologist, James Dick, Dr Bowie produced the Bowie-Dick Test as a monitor of high pre-vacuum steriliser performance (Bowie, Kelsey and Thompson, 1963). This special tape test soon came into universal use. It was fitting that James Dick's name should have been included since very much of Dr Bowie's important pioneering work on sterilisation was made possible through Dick's dedicated and informed initiative and assistance. Along with one of the Royal Infirmary's engineers Alex Wilson[99] and especially the assistance of Mr Ian Robertson, who was in charge of the hospital's sterilisation unit, the Bowie-Dick team[100,101,102,103] earned a high and internationally recognised reputation. Following James Dick's death in 1972, his successor Mr Ian Samuel, formerly of Moredun Animal Diseases Research Association, continued the close collaboration with Dr Bowie.

Yet another important achievement by Bowie in collaboration with the Royal Infirmary engineers led by Mr B.G. Summers, surgeons and nursing staff, in particular Miss S.R.R. Scott and Mrs M.H.F. Alexander, was the development of the Edinburgh Tray System for the supply of reliably sterilised instruments to operating theatres (Bowie, Campbell, Gillingham and Gordon, 1963) and the concept – translated into practice – of a Theatre Service Centre. Again, these developments were adopted by hospitals in Britain and abroad. For his distinguished contribution to hospital clinical and surgical practice, including also the design of theatre and patient isolation accommodation, Dr Bowie was admitted to the Fellowships of the

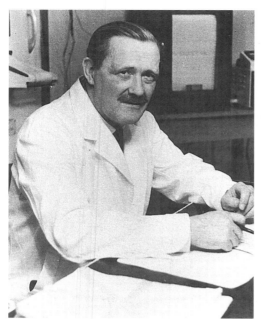

98. *Dr J.H. Bowie, Senior Consultant Bacteriologist, Royal Infirmary,* **1949** *to* **1974**

99. *Alex Wilson*

100,101,102,103. *(Back row) Dr J. Bowie and James Dick, (front row) Ian Robertson and Colin Flynn*

104. *James Robertson*

105. *Ian Samuel*

Royal College of Physicians and the Royal College of Surgeons of Edinburgh. He was also invited to chair several important working parties and committees on hospital sterilisation equipment and procedures. Subsequent tributes paid to Dr Bowie included that of his being a "latter day Lister".

A Snapshot of the Sixties

Professor Collee offers the following snapshot from his viewpoint on the academic terracing.

John Bowie, Tom Durie, Ralph Tonkin, Jimmy Dick, Ian Samuel and their associates were a powerful force in the Royal Infirmary over the years. Many stories testify to the regard in which this team was held. The individual commitment and industry of these men, and their capacity for determined single-mindedness (sometimes bordering, it may be said, on fierce obstinacy) were legendary. John Bowie would not compromise; Tom Durie would worry about patients, attending meticulously to all aspects of bacteriology in the laboratory and with the house staff on the wards – and he would not go home. Ralph Tonkin, most loyally supported by Jimmy Robertson[104], would worry endlessly about his patients on the renal wards or in the Special Care Baby Unit – and he would track down outbreaks of infection with relentless and painstaking investigations. Through all of this, and around the constantly questing movement of this microbiological team, James Dick, and subsequently Ian Samuel[105], would strive to keep the remarkable pack in daily order. These were stirring times.

Other Members of the Staff of the Royal Infirmary Laboratory

Dr R.R. Gillies

After Dr Bowie's retirement on 1976, and during Professor B.P. Marmion's occupancy of the University Chair of Bacteriology, Dr Robert Gillies acted as Senior Bacteriologist in day-to-day administrative charge in the Royal Infirmary laboratory, while continuing to carry out his considerable university department responsibilities in teaching and research, in addition to those of Associate Dean of the Faculty of Medicine. When Dr Gillies resigned to become the first holder of the Chair of Clinical Bacteriology in Queen's University, Belfast in 1976, he was succeeded in the Royal Infirmary post by Dr Rex Miles.

Mr Robert Barr

Reference has already been made to Robert Barr, who according to James Dick's informal historical account of the Royal Infirmary laboratory, was recruited as a young laboratory assistant from the Royal College of Physicians' Laboratory in about 1913, and who eventually became the laboratory's first Chief Technician in 1923. In Robert Barr's earliest days in the laboratory, training in medical laboratory techniques was only beginning. The Pathological and Bacteriological Laboratory Assistants' Association was still to be developed – in no small measure due to the pioneering initiative of Richard Muir, the chief technician (although he did not have this title) in the University Pathology Department, and for a short time in the University Bacteriology Department. Muir's experience and skill earned him the grading of Demonstrator in Pathological and Bacteriological Methods and he was the first in Britain to introduce training and organised classes enabling the early "lab boy" to begin on the long road towards the high professionalism of the Medical Laboratory Scientific Officer of modern times. In his early efforts, Richard Muir had enjoyed the encouragement and active support of Professor William Greenfield of the Pathology Department. Muir's successors at Edinburgh, Bobby Barr and Sandy Cheyne, continued to strengthen the foundation of technical staff training, and tribute must also be paid to Dan Kilgour of the Royal Infirmary Pathology laboratory. A former "lab boy" of the Edinburgh University Departments of Pathology and Bacteriology, Duncan Colquhoun, became one of the pioneers of training in Glasgow.

James Dick

In more modern times, James Dick, who in 1955 succeeded Bobby Barr as the Infirmary Bacteriology Laboratory Chief Technician, certainly admirably upheld and continued the efforts of Edinburgh's pioneers in advancing the standards of laboratory technical staff. He served for long as a dedicated and effective voluntary teacher in evening classes. His efforts were recognised by the Secretary of State for Scotland when he was appointed a member of the Medical Laboratory Technicians' Board at its inception and on which he remained until his death in April 1972 at the end of nearly fifty years service in the Infirmary Bacteriology Laboratory.

James Dick was succeeded by Mr Ian Samuel who had been on the staff of Moredun Research Institute for Animal Diseases, Gilmerton. Mr Samuel was Mr Dick's close collaborator for many years in the teaching of Medical Laboratory Scientific Officers. Following Mr Samuel's retiral in August 1982, he was succeeded by Mr Gerald McInnes who had joined the Royal Infirmary Bacteriology Department as a junior MLSO in 1957.

Relocation and Consolidation

In 1982 the Royal Infirmary Bacteriology Laboratory, which for long had endured quite inadequate space and facilities for the constantly increasing scope of its work in the Westgate building, was transferred to the Medical School, to occupy the commodious, refurbished and redesigned premises once part of the Departments of Biochemistry and Pharmacology. Renamed the Clinical Bacteriology section of the Department of Bacteriology, the laboratories provide a service for the Royal Infirmary and associated hospitals, Simpson Memorial Maternity Pavilion (SMMP) and the Princess Alexandra Eye Pavilion (PAEP), as well as a general practitioners service for the local area. In the same year the Clinical Virology laboratories were consolidated in new premises within the Medical School and adjacent to the Clinical Bacteriology laboratories. For the first time in its history the entire Bacteriology Department became united under one roof. In the year 1991-92 the clinical laboratories processed 175,610 bacteriology specimens and 38,036 virology specimens. At that time the total staff of the clinical laboratories exceeded eighty persons.

A further significant step forward was the formal recognition at this stage of the role of the Control of Infection Nurse by the Health Board and the setting up of infection control teams in their hospitals, including the Royal Infirmary which played a leading part in this initiative. The federation was completed in October 1990 when the Department of Bacteriology changed its name to the Department of Medical Microbiology in recognition of the wide range of interests and the quality of the expertise that it now embraced and commanded.

CHAPTER ELEVEN

OTHER EDINBURGH LABORATORIES

The Royal Hospital For Sick Children

Edinburgh's first Sick Children's Hospital was opened in a house at No. 7 Lauriston Lane in February 1860. Lauriston Lane ran parallel to and a little east of the present Archibald Place. Small as it was, the hospital had a management committee and visiting and resident physicians and surgeons, many of whom later enjoyed distinction in the Edinburgh medical world and beyond. Very many of the first children admitted were suffering from "fevers". Very soon the Lauriston Lane house became too small and in 1862 the hospital moved to Meadowside House at the southern end of Lauriston Lane, on the verge of the Meadows, east of where the Simpson Memorial Maternity Pavilion came to be built. It duly received Royal patronage and became the Royal Hospital for Sick Children. By 1870, ten years after its establishment, 44,962 "poor, sick children", had been treated as in-patients or out-patients. From the outset, a major problem was the management and treatment of children with infectious diseases. Not until 1885 were all such cases transferred to Edinburgh's City Hospital for Infectious Diseases in the former Surgical Hospital of the Royal Infirmary in Drummond Street. Dr Douglas Guthrie, distinguished Edinburgh medical historian, in his valuable account of the Royal Hospital for Sick Children (Guthrie, 1960), recounts early but unsuccessful efforts by a Dr Charles Wilson to have a separate fever hospital for children established in Edinburgh. Very soon after the opening of the Meadowside House hospital, large numbers of children were being admitted suffering from scarlet fever, diphtheria, typhoid fever, typhus fever, measles and "febricula" (fever of undetermined origin).

Early Laboratory Work

It has not been possible to trace where, if at all, bacteriological laboratory diagnostic work may have been carried out on specimens from children before and after their admission to Meadowside House. As we have seen, the discoveries of Pasteur and Koch were not to lead to the introduction of bacteriology to Edinburgh until the opening of Lister's small laboratory in the old Royal Infirmary in 1876 and then only for work related to surgical cases. It is possible that Professor John Chiene's small bacteriology laboratory, opened in the University Department of Surgery in 1882, may have done some work for the Sick Children's Hospital. Certainly this early laboratory was involved in work associated with a scarlet fever epidemic in 1886. Soon after the Royal College of Physicians' Laboratory was opened in 1887, a small amount of diagnostic bacteriology was done for general practitioners in the city, and this would have led to children with infections being admitted to the hospital; possibly this laboratory also did work for such cases after admission. We have no documented support for these suppositions.

Guthrie lists the successive "Pathologists and Bacteriologists" appointed to the Sick Children's Hospital from 1870. Since early bacteriology was first practised as an offshoot of pathology, it is possible that the pathologists who were attached to the hospital may have provided some basic or elementary bacteriological services.

In due course the hospital facilities at Meadowside House proved quite inadequate, a situation further complicated by a typhoid outbreak amongst the staff. While a new hospital was being built in Sciennes, where it is today – patients and staff were transferred temporarily from 1890 until 1895 to Plewlands House, the former Morningside Hydropathic and subsequently Morningside College for Boys at the top of Morningside Drive. Of incidental interest is the fact that the visiting

106. *Royal Hospital for Sick Children, Sciennes*

107. *Dr Agnes McGregor*

Consultant Surgeon at the Plewlands House hospital was the famous Joseph Bell, at one time the teacher of Edinburgh medical student Arthur Conan Doyle, who was so impressed by his tutor's powers of observation and deductive diagnostic skill that he immortalised him as the prototype of his famous detective Sherlock Holmes. In a bacteriological context, an observation made by Bell from his experience with children illustrates the perceptive mind which so impressed Conan Doyle. In Bell's book, *Surgery for Nurses* (Bell, 1888), he makes the observation: "Children suffering from diarrhoea of a wasting type sometimes take a strong fancy for old green-moulded cheese and are able to devour it with the best effect. Is it possible that the germs in the cheese are able to devour in their turn the bacilli of tuberculosis?" Surely a quite remarkably early anticipation of antibiosis!

Describing the fine new purpose-built hospital in Sciennes[106] after its opening in 1895, Guthrie includes a reference to the impressive new facilities, in particular the Pathology Department, being above the Out-Patient Department entered from Sylvan Place. He compares this laboratory with that of the early days – presumably at Meadowside House – when it was "an unattractive dark little room . . . the equipment minimal".

When Dr Robert Muir took up his chair in St. Andrews, he was succeeded by Dr W. Carnegie Dickson. Dr Dickson also appears in the University Calendar as one of Professor James Ritchie's first two members of staff when he was appointed to the newly created Chair of Bacteriology in 1913. He is listed by Guthrie under the Sick Children's Hospital's "Pathologists and Bacteriologists" as having one (or both) of these designations from 1909 to 1914. It is possible, therefore, that Dr Carnegie Dickson was the hospital's first bacteriologist. From 1914 until 1922, Professor James Ritchie appears under the above headings.

Dr Agnes McGregor

The person who was to earn a high reputation as the hospital's pathologist was not to take up the joint appointment until 1922 and her service to the hospital has been more clearly documented than that of her predecessors. She was Dr Agnes McGregor[107]. When in 1918, Dr McGregor had completed the pathology course and third year of the medical course at Edinburgh University, Professor J. Lorrain Smith, who had been pathologist to the Sick Children's Hospital since 1914, asked her to undertake post mortems and the reporting of biopsies and bacteriological specimens at the hospital for a few months since the regular pathologist was on war service. This was Dr McGregor's first experience of the then little known subject of paediatric pathology, on which she was eventually to become an authority.

After graduating in 1922, Dr McGregor was given a formal part-time appointment as pathologist and bacteriologist to the hospital. Her subsequent full-time appointment as paediatric pathologist she held until her retiral in 1960. Dr McGregor carried out important work on infection in pre-natal mortality in the pre-antibiotic era and in 1938 she published an important paper on pneumonia in the newborn. She rapidly became an authority in these subjects. This latter paper was written in association with Dr W.A. Alexander, one-time President of the Royal College of Physicians of Edinburgh. She also collaborated with Sir Robert Philip, the Edinburgh world authority on tuberculosis, and later with Professor Sir John Crofton, also an international authority on this disease. In the 1920s, quite vital and entirely new research on bovine tuberculosis was done at the Royal Hospital for Sick

108. *Sir Harold J. Stiles*
(From oil painting in R.C.S.)

109. *Sir John Fraser*

110. *James Smith*

111. *John Dow*

Children by Professor Sir Harold Stiles[108] and Sir John Fraser[109], two of Edinburgh's most distinguished surgeons. They studied tuberculous bone and joint disease in children admitted to the hospital, and they questioned Koch's view that bovine tuberculosis was of little human consequence. The validity of their challenge was soon acknowledged. The School of Paediatric Pathology which Dr Agnes McGregor established in Edinburgh earned an international reputation and thrived.

Bacteriology Laboratory Transferred

In 1932, another lady joined the staff of the Sick Children's Hospital as bacteriologist and assistant pathologist, while also working part-time in the University Bacteriology Department. This was Dr Helen Wright who held these posts for eleven years, working in close collaboration with Dr Agnes McGregor, with whom a close and lasting friendship was formed. The two lady doctors became a well-known and highly respected team in Edinburgh medical circles. When Dr Wright subsequently joined the staff of the University Bacteriology Department full-time, her close association with the Sick Children's Hospital continued for some time.

The earliest laboratory technician to be traced was James H.T. Smith[110] who joined the Pathology Laboratory of the Sick Children's Hospital in 1922, becoming Dr Agnes McGregor's assistant when she had just been appointed part-time as the hospital's pathologist and bacteriologist. James Smith had begun training in the Royal Infirmary Pathology Laboratory at the West Gate building in 1920. After a very short time, he joined the staff of the University Pathology Department. It is perhaps of interest that a reference given to James Smith when he left the University Pathology Department in 1922 to work with Dr Agnes McGregor at the Sick Children's was on notepaper headed "Department of Pathology and Bacteriology, University New Buildings, Teviot Place". This is surprising since a separate University Department of Bacteriology was set up by Professor James Ritchie in 1913 and of course remained separate. It is difficult to understand how notepaper designated for the joint departments was used when Professor Ritchie's department had been in separate existence for nine years. James Smith resigned from the hospital laboratory in 1929 to take up a post in the Royal College of Surgeons in Nicolson Street. He was succeeded in the hospital laboratory by John Dow[111] who carried out the technical work in both pathology and bacteriology. Some years later, John Dow was joined by Tom McDonald. In 1952, four years after the inauguration of the National Health Service and a consequent rearrangement of laboratory services in Edinburgh, the work of the Sick Children's Hospital bacteriology laboratory was transferred to the Astley Ainslie laboratory. John Dow took up an appointment at Moredun Research Institute and Tom McDonald eventually joined the staff of the Central Microbiology Laboratories at the Western General Hospital. Dr Agnes McGregor, who had retired as the hospital pathologist in 1960, died in 1982.

The City Hospital Laboratories

Bacteriology

As the architect's plan reveals, the City Infectious Diseases Hospital, opened at Colinton Mains on 13 May 1903, (and subsequently referred to as the City Hospital), was most impressive, built to the latest designs of the time and costing the then relatively high sum of £350,000. It was generally regarded as one of the leading hospitals of its kind in Great Britain. It was Edinburgh's third City Hospital. The first

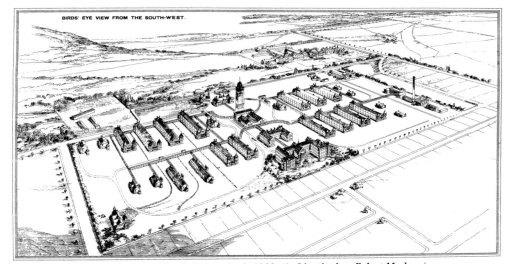

BIRDS' EYE VIEW FROM THE SOUTH-WEST.

112. *City Fever Hospital, Greenbank, 1903 (Architect's plan: Robert Morham)*

113. *Dr Claude Ker*

had been opened in 1870 in what for some time had been the Canongate Poorhouse in the former Queensberry House. The second was established in the former Surgical Hospital of the Royal Infirmary in Drummond Street, vacated when the Infirmary moved to Lauriston Place in 1879.

No records could be traced of bacteriological laboratory examinations having been carried out for the Canongate hospital. With regard to the second City Hospital in Drummond Street, Dr John Ritchie's history of the Royal College of Physicians' Laboratory records that work for this hospital was done in Professor John Chiene's small bacteriological laboratory in his Department of Surgery in the Medical School in Teviot Place, by Dr Allan Jamieson, a consultant physician at the Drummond Street Hospital, and Dr Alexander Edington. During a serious epidemic of scarlet fever in the winter of 1886 and the spring of 1887, Dr Edington isolated a bacillus which they believed might be the causative organism. Interesting as this work may have been, scarlatina was, of course, caused not by a bacillus but by the haemolytic streptococcus. Further laboratory work on this epidemic infectious disease of children was planned to be carried out in the Royal College of Physicians' Laboratory in Forrest Road, opened in 1887, but this was not pursued. It is possible that the RCP Laboratory did other laboratory work for the City Hospital in Drummond Street.

When the new City Hospital opened at Colinton Mains[112] (for long also known as Colinton Hospital, but eventually taking as its address Greenbank Drive), the various wards of the long Florence Nightingale style, of red sandstone to suggest warmth, and running north to south to capture maximum sunlight for hygienic purposes, were designated for the wide range of infectious diseases which would be provided for: ten wards for scarlet fever, four for typhoid and other enteric fevers, and with other calculated allocations for diphtheria, whooping cough, erysipelas, chickenpox, tuberculosis and smallpox. Small buildings, which still remain, were designed for strict isolation of highly infectious cases. The estimates of the various infections expected to occur in Edinburgh, based on the incidence statistics for previous years, for long remained correct although many wards were grossly overcrowded during epidemics, frequently resulting in the allocation of two small children per bed. The advancement towards vaccination, antitoxin treatment, chemotherapy and antibiotics had still to come.

Tables 11.1 and 11.2 indicate the numbers of cases of infectious diseases in Edinburgh for the year 1903 and the "Return of Patients" in the City Hospital for the year ending 1904. The introductory background given and the statistics illustrate the very substantial need for the bacteriological diagnosis of cases before admission to the hospital, confirmation on admission of a provisional diagnosis and the monitoring of patients during treatment and before their discharge. No time was lost therefore after the opening of the new hospital before an attempt was made to carry out the bacteriological work required.

Dr Claude B. Ker[113], Medical Superintendent of the hospital from its opening until his death in 1925 wrote in his first annual report:

> The Bacteriological Laboratory in the hospital was opened in October [1903] and a systematic examination has been made in all cases of diphtheria, scarlet fever and typhoid fever in which the diagnosis has been doubtful. This departure, it is hoped, will tend to prevent the risk of cross-infection in scarlet fever and diphtheria and enable the discharge of patients who have suffered from the latter disease to be regulated on a scientific basis.

TABLE 11.1

Notification of Infectious Diseases in Edinburgh, 1903

Disease.	Jan.	Feb.	Mar.	Apr.	May.	June.	July.	Aug.	Sept.	Oct.	Nov.	Dec.	Total.
Typhus	...	...	...	...	...	1	...	...	...	...	...	...	1
Typhoid, Relapsing, and Continued Fever	17	12	11	5	14	39	35	41	19	17	17	10	237
Puerperal Fever	1	...	1	1	...	...	1	1	1	...	·	1	7
Diphtheria, Membranous Croup	39	50	40	46	52	43	45	51	60	60	49	40	575
Smallpox	...	...	...	...	...	...	1	...	...	...	...	4	5
Scarlet Fever	84	131	175	97	81	72	96	123	143	155	154	104	1415
Erysipelas	48	41	39	26	32	23	34	37	26	44	39	45	434
Total	189	234	266	175	179	178	212	253	249	276	259	204	2674

TABLE 11.2
Return of patients in City Fever Hospital, 1904

Disease	Remained 31st December 1903.			Year 1904.			Remaining 31st December 1904.		
	Adults.	Children.	Total.	Admitted.	Discharged.	Died.	Adults.	Children.	Total.
Typhus - -	...	...	...	6	6	...	...	...	...
Typhoid, Relapsing, and Continued Fever -	9	10	19	174	152	18	15	8	23
Puerperal Fever -	...	...	...	1	1	...	...	...	...
Diphtheria, Membranous Croup -	11	34	45	579	517	41	23	43	66
Smallpox -	4	...	4	170	159	15	...	...	...
Scarlet Fever -	26	189	215	942	985	27	29	116	145
Erysipelas -	13	3	16	136	126	3	23	...	23
Measles -	7	6	13	.587	537	25	7	31	38
Whooping Cough -	...	7	7	135	96	26	...	20	20
Observation -	3	2	5	73	63	8	3	4	7
Chicken Pox -	...	...	...	14	11	...	...	3	3
Quarantine -	...	...	...	...	...	...	...	...	...
Total -	73	251	324	2817	2653	163	100	225	325

The task which Dr Ker had allocated to his laboratory was considerable. Little detail is on record concerning the resources of the laboratory as regards staff and equipment. Dr Haldane P. Tait (1974) records that the City Hospital's bacteriology laboratory did 3000 examinations in 1905; by 1914, the laboratory examinations numbered 10,639. He indicated that the laboratory's work brought to light much valuable epidemiological information.

Early Bacteriologists

In the successive Annual Reports of the Edinburgh Public Health Department, which always included a section on the City Hospital, it is recorded that the bacteriology laboratory continued to function under Dr Ker's interested and active supervision, with a succession of his senior clinical assistants taking day-to-day charge of the laboratory. Some information is provided on these early hospital bacteriologists. There was a Dr Meikle in 1904; Dr T. Lauder Thomson in 1907; and Dr John Ritchie in 1909. By 1910 the laboratory appears to have had a quite significant number of technical staff and to have been carrying out a "wide range of examinations". Dr Ritchie was succeeded by Dr Robertson and during this period Dr Ker refers to his shortage of laboratory staff and how "it was impossible for them to face the volume of laboratory work required, as in the examination of throat and nasal swabs from scarlet fever cases". In 1921 Dr Walter Benson was Dr Ker's senior assistant; he took a particular interest in the laboratory and very many examinations were carried out under his personal direction.

From 1921 onwards, the references in the Edinburgh Public Health Annual Reports to the City Hospital's laboratory become rather sparse and irregular. In 1925 Dr Ker died and the great enthusiasm and drive which had characterised his twenty years as Medical Superintendent were greatly missed. He had earned a high reputation as an authority on infectious disease. In 1929 the first reference is made in the hospital's annual report to a laboratory assistant by name, whose services in that year and for several following years were obviously greatly appreciated. The laboratory assistant referred to was Jimmy Craig, as he was always familiarly known. It proved difficult to obtain precise information on Mr Craig's background and his period of service in the laboratory and the scope of his duties. Accordingly, we sought information from Mr William Webber[114] who first worked with Jimmy Craig and then succeeded him as the bacteriology laboratory's sole assistant for several years. Mr Webber understood that Jimmy Craig had come to work in the City Hospital laboratory shortly after the end of the First World War and that he may have had some war-time laboratory experience, perhaps in the Royal Army Medical Corps. Although Craig may have joined the laboratory staff in about 1920 the first reference to him in the annual reports does not occur until 1929. The records indicate that while Craig carried out the bacteriological work without assistance and simply with the supervision of a senior clinician, from some time prior to 1929 and until 1937 the laboratory was reporting on an average of 10,000 specimens per year.

It should be noted that from the early 1920s while Jimmy Craig was coping with the laboratory work apparently single-handed, there was a close liaison between the City Hospital and the University Bacteriology Department. This was very largely due to the clinical importance of many studies carried out under Professor Mackie's direction. In 1925, two years after Mackie's appointment, Dr Claude Ker, Dr J. McGarrity of the City Hospital, and Dr J.E. McCartney of the University Bacteriology

Department collaborated on work concerning the Dick Test and other aspects of susceptibility to scarlet fever. In 1926 Mackie and McCartney investigated the toxicology of scarlet fever and serological types. In 1930 Dr Helen Wright of the University department began her work on diphtheria typing and virulence testing in collaboration with Dr A.L.K. Rankin of the City Hospital. Indeed, long after the incidence of diphtheria had been greatly reduced, Dr Wright remained an authority on the laboratory diagnosis of the disease, frequently being consulted by City Hospital clinicians. On several occasions during severe epidemics of scarlet fever, Professor Mackie's assistance in offloading work from the City Hospital laboratory is gratefully acknowledged in reports.

It seems, as the annual report's acknowledgements of Jimmy Craig's assistance ceased after 1933, that medical superintendents after this date chose not to refer to laboratory staff by name. Certainly according to Mr Webber's personal recollection Craig was still the sole laboratory assistant in the hospital laboratory until 1937, and remained in charge of technical work until 1945, when he contracted tuberculosis and died a few months after admission to Southfield Sanatorium at Liberton.

Mr Webber himself had become a part-time porter in the City Hospital in 1934. In the course of his duties he became friendly with Jimmy Craig and after some time expressed an interest in helping him in the laboratory. It was agreed by the then Medical Superintendent, Dr Benson, that he could spend time working with Craig providing that this did not interfere with his portering duties. Mr Webber thus began on a part-time basis and was duly to become Chief Medical Laboratory Scientific Officer of the laboratory with a greatly increased staff. In the Second World War, Mr Webber joined the Royal Navy. After demobilisation he returned to work part- and then full-time with Craig in the bacteriology laboratory.

More Modern Times

In 1937 Dr Alexander Joe had become Physician and Medical Superintendent of the City Hospital. He was not unfamiliar with the hospital, having originally joined the staff as Assistant Medical Officer in 1924. After completing a short period as lecturer in bacteriology in the University department under Professor Mackie, Dr Joe's first appointment at the City Hospital was brief. In 1925 he had become Assistant Medical Officer of Health for Edinburgh. During this period he was closely associated with the city's earliest programmes of diphtheria immunisation. He then moved to the North Western Fever Hospital at Hampstead as Medical Superintendent, and he subsequently returned to Edinburgh to take charge of the City Hospital. On account of his experience, albeit short, in Edinburgh University Bacteriology Department, he had retained a particular interest in the subject and became closely involved in the development of the hospital laboratory at first under the technical charge of Jimmy Craig and then Mr Webber. Dr Joe retired in 1960.

From 1941 to 42 Dr John Tinne was the hospital bacteriologist before he went on war service. Dr Tinne recalled that at this time very many specimens were sent to the University's Bacteriological Diagnostic Laboratory in Teviot Place, although the hospital laboratory still undertook a wide range of examinations. He also recalled occasions when the hospital, with a bed accommodation figure of 750, was forced during severe epidemics of diphtheria and scarlet fever to admit around 900 children, with the smaller children lying "spoon and fork" fashion in the beds. The admission of measles cases had at times to be limited.

114. *William Webber*

115. *Bacteriology Laboratory Staff, City Hospital, Edinburgh, 1960*

In 1948 Dr Archie Wallace, a Senior Lecturer in the University Bacteriology Department, through an arrangement between Professor Mackie and the health authorities, was appointed hospital bacteriologist. Dr Wallace's contemporaries in the laboratory and other colleagues were anxious that his very considerable efforts to develop the laboratory and its relationship with the hospital clinical staff should be recorded. Coinciding with Dr Wallace's appointment, Professor Mackie was able to arrange for the hospital laboratory to be upgraded. While the premises in the small red sandstone building immediately eastwards of and now joined to the present-day laboratory were only temporarily improved, much better equipment was made available. For a few years, Dr Wallace was assisted by Miss Margaret Buchanan, an Honours graduate. In 1952, Dr Tinne returned as Dr Wallace's assistant for a brief period. Dr Nancy Conn also worked for some time in the Bacteriology Laboratory.

In 1961 Professor Robert Cruickshank acquired funding from the Wellcome Trust for the establishment of a virology laboratory at the City Hospital "which would have good clinical links". Ward 4A was made available. At the beginning however, it was also decided that the new premises would be shared with the Bacteriology Laboratory (except for its tuberculosis work) until a new prefabricated laboratory had been built, facilitating the then urgently required expansion of the bacteriological work. In 1970 the new Bacteriology Laboratory was opened. When the Bacteriology Laboratory and the then newly established Virology Laboratory occupied the Wellcome Laboratory from 1961 to 1969, Mr W. Webber carried out the technical administration of the Virology Laboratory with Mr James Sutherland as the Senior Technician. In 1970 when the Bacteriology Laboratory took occupation of the newly completed prefabricated premises and vacated the Wellcome Laboratory, Dr Alistair D. Macrae was recruited from Colindale to become the first Consultant Virologist and Mr David Hargreaves the first Chief MLSO in virology at the City Hospital. At the time of writing, the prefabricated building built to cope with the expanding bacteriological work has been superseded by a fine new purpose-built laboratory.

Research Projects

Along with the improvement in the laboratory facilities in 1948, additional technical staff were gradually recruited with appointments being made available for systematic training leading to the professional qualifications of the Institute of Medical Laboratory Technology (now the Institute of Medical Laboratory Sciences) and its members designated Medical Laboratory Scientific Officers (MLSOs). From an early period, Dr Wallace and his staff[115,116] collaborated with Professor John Crofton in many studies of tuberculosis which were of international importance, especially concerning the effectiveness of various new drugs against mycobacteria. Mr Webber was very much involved in the technical assistance of the considerable work done on tuberculosis and he himself obtained the Fellowship of the IMLT for his thesis on the sensitivity of *M. tuberculosis* to para-amino salicylic acid (PAS). Mr Webber's time had to be devoted increasingly to laboratory administration, but his senior technical colleague Jack Clark continued to made a valuable contribution to the various tuberculosis research projects over many years.

When the incidence of tuberculosis steadily declined, Southfield Hospital was closed and the University Department of Respiratory Medicine was established at

116. *Dr Archibald Wallace*

117. *Dr Alastair Wilson*

the City Hospital in 1960 with Professor (later Sir) John Crofton occupying the Chair. He and Dr Wallace turned their attention to the bacteriology of other respiratory diseases. Resulting from the considerable research carried out in this field, a then definitive paper on pneumonia in hospital practice was published. In 1952 Dr Sheila Stewart joined the group as a Research Fellow in Bacteriology, funded by the Royal Victoria Tuberculosis Trust. She worked initially in the laboratory at Southfield Hospital and, from 1960, at the City Hospital when the Professorial Unit was transferred there.

Careful studies by Dr Stewart showed that failure occurred in some patients treated with streptomycin although their bacilli had been found initially sensitive by the current technique. These patients had been previously treated with chemotherapy which in others had resulted in proved resistance. It was therefore suspected that the current Medical Research Council method for testing streptomycin resistance had failed to detect low, but clinically significant, resistance. A new method was devised which showed that these organisms were indeed resistant. This new method correlated well with clinical outcome and came to be generally adopted. These findings led to a systematic study by Dr Sheila Stewart, eventually published in 1963 and covering some ten years' work. Analysis showed that even the lowest measurable degree of resistance to any of the standard drugs often prevented effective action by that drug. This work of international importance involved close collaboration between Drs Julian Bath, G. Boissard, Margaret Calder and Margaret Moffat under the direction of Professor Crofton and Dr A. Wallace. The support of Professor Robert Cruickshank was significant. A similar collaboration existed between the Bacteriology Laboratory and the consultants in charge of the hospital's Infectious Diseases Unit, with many papers published, notably on urinary tract infections.

The City Bacteriology Laboratory Today

After Dr Wallace's retiral in 1974, Dr Alastair Wilson[117] was appointed Consultant Bacteriologist and held this post until his retiral in 1980. Mr Bill Webber retired in 1976 after over thirty years service having greatly assisted the laboratory to enter a new era. Sadly, he died in September 1989. The long tradition of technological competence, so much a feature of the laboratory, is now fittingly maintained under the experienced direction of Mr Webber's successor, Mr Michael Croughan. Dr Wilson was succeeded by Dr Margaret Calder[118] as Consultant in Bacteriology.

In 1980 the Scottish Mycobacteria Reference Laboratory (SMRL) at Mearnskirk Hospital was closed at rather short notice. Dr Margaret Calder forwarded a submission to the Scottish Home and Health Department for the establishment of the SMRL at the City Hospital. The submission was based on the expertise in the bacteriology of tuberculosis available at the hospital and indeed the laboratory's long tradition of important work in this field. The submission was successful. There was considerable upgrading of the facilities to conform with the stringent Health and Safety regulations. In addition the post of Chief MLSO was upgraded to Senior Chief MLSO, extra technical staff were taken on and it was also agreed that a second consultant should be appointed to the laboratory. Dr Brian Watt, who had been Consultant Bacteriologist at the Central Microbiological Laboratories, Western General Hospital, was appointed to the second consultant post in 1982. When Dr Margaret Calder retired in 1986, Dr Watt[119] succeeded her as Administrative Head of Department. Dr Xavier Emmanuel was appointed second Consultant in Bacteriology.

118. *Dr Margaret Calder*

119. *Dr Brian Watt*

From its opening in 1903 and for very many years afterwards, the City Hospital remained primarily an infectious diseases or "fever hospital". Its laboratory was concerned with confirmatory laboratory diagnosis and the monitoring of a wide range of infectious diseases, sometimes of epidemic proportion and occasionally with high risk and requiring special precautions, such as during smallpox epidemics or outbreaks. Eventually, with improvements in housing and nutrition, with the use in the community of various forms of immunisation, the introduction of mass radiography, the availability of chemotherapeutic agents and relatively more recently the antibiotics, the incidence of infectious diseases had decreased greatly and often dramatically. In due course the types of cases admitted to the City Hospital changed and new units were established. All these developments have had their consequences for the laboratory, resulting in the retention of basic bacteriological procedures but also the introduction of many new tests and techniques. With the wide spectrum of cases now admitted to the City Hospital, the range of bacteriological examinations is correspondingly extensive. A laboratory diagnostic service for general medical practitioners in Midlothian is also provided. The laboratory has a national and international reputation for special expertise in areas ranging from antibiotics and anaerobes to tuberculosis and AIDS-related infections. Dr Watt has been deeply involved in these significant developments. Some 50 years after Jimmy Craig was the sole laboratory assistant, the City Hospital laboratory staff consisted of two Consultant Bacteriologists, one Registrar, eighteen Medical Laboratory Scientific Officers, from Senior Chief grade to juniors in training, along with two part-time technicians and auxiliary staff. The number of clinical specimens processed by this laboratory in 1989-90 was 56,432. In addition, the Scottish Mycobacteria Reference Laboratory, based on the City Hospital Bacteriology Laboratory, dealt with 8,141 specimens in the same year.

The Regional Virus Laboratory At The City Hospital

by Dr J.M. (Hamish) Inglis

When Dr Alistair Macrae took up office in 1970 as Consultant Virologist in consultation with Professor Marmion and Mr Alex Welstead, at that time administrator at the City Hospital, it was agreed that the new regional laboratory should serve the hospitals and general practitioners in the Lothians and Borders, except for the Royal Infirmary and any general practitioners who wished to continue sending their specimens to the University diagnostic virology laboratory. They also agreed that since this was a wide remit and because Glasgow already had a similar laboratory situated in Ruchill Hospital named the Regional Virus Laboratory, so it should be named in Edinburgh. The laboratory evolved from the Wellcome Virus Research Laboratory which had historical links with tthe University virologists and the Department[120,121].

At that time (1970) there were three part-time lady registrars in the laboratory engaged on various interests. Only one, the late Dr Betty Edmond[122], was to continue in virology. Dr Winifred Thompson, although showing interest and enthusiasm, responded to the call of general practice but to this day continues to show an interest in the laboratory aspects of viral infections. Dr Helen Zealley[123] made her mark in virology in these early years by having the foresight to see the benefit of long-term studies on schoolgirls who had just been immunised with the newly developed

120. *Dr Guy Boissard*

121. *James A.W. Sutherland*

122. *Dr Elizabeth Edmond*

123. *Dr Helen Zealley*

124. *Dr Alastair Macrae*

125. *Dr Hamish Inglis*

vaccine against rubella. Her initial studies on Edinburgh schoolgirls were expanded and new schedules have evolved to take account of national and international experience. Only those girls with no detectable or low level antibodies receive vaccine. Alas, diagnostic virology's loss was administration's gain when Dr Zealley left to become a Community Medicine Specialist and now, having followed in her late father's (Sir John Brotherston) footsteps, has become Chief Administrative Medical Officer and Consultant in Public Health to the Lothian Health Board. She, too, continues to show an interest in diagnostic virology. Sadly, too, Dr Edmond left the laboratory in 1979, having continued the studies in rubella and initiated studies, especially in students, in relation to glandular fever, to fulfil a desire to be more involved in teaching and research. At that time she took up the appointment of Senior Lecturer in Professor Collee's department where she advanced her interest in immunocompromised patients with cytomegalovirus infections.

On Dr Macrae's arrival in 1970[124] he arranged for structural alterations to be made in the laboratory, transforming four small laboratories into one large well-lit area for serology which was a great improvement. Early in 1971 Dr Hamish Inglis[125], Professor T.J. Mackie's last Honours student, was recruited from the Brompton Hospital where he had set up the diagnostic virology laboratory. With his interest in respiratory virology and the close liaison with the Royal Hospital for Sick Children – especially with Dr Hamish Simpson, now Professor of Paediatrics at Leicester – the isolation of viruses became well established. With the advent of immunofluorescence techniques and the ability to give same-day reports, especially in babies with bronchiolitis, diagnostic virology really "took off" and it was difficult at that time to convince clinicians that it was not possible in all cases to give such a speedy service.

At that time it was our aim to forge good links with as many of our clinical colleagues as possible. Of note in particular were the problem sessions held by the respiratory physicians, namely Professor (now Sir) John Crofton and Dr Andrew Douglas. What a wealth of knowledge and experience both had and how well they taught both undergraduate and postgraduate students alike. Combined clinical and virology research projects were undertaken in patients with chronic bronchitis and pneumonia. It should be remembered that at that time Dr Sheila Stewart had laboratory space within the RVL to pursue her studies in mycoplasmas and she, too, contributed to the above studies. Nor should it be forgotten that the late Dr George Sangster and Dr Jim Gray of the Infectious Diseases Unit again showed great interest and co-operation in the development of the laboratory and in investigating patients with interesting and perhaps unusual viral infections. After such a short time at the helm, Dr Macrae left in 1974 to return south as Consultant Virologist in Nottingham. From that time Dr Edmond took over as director of the laboratory.

With the wide remit that the RVL has, it benefited greatly from the Laboratory Van Service which had been established by Dr Gould at the Western General Hospital for the transport of specimens to the laboratories and the delivery of reports back to the hospitals and general practitioners. The laboratory has grown both in size and complement of staff. Gradually over the years as the workload increased, the number of staff increased and the need for more laboratory and office space also increased.

After Dr Edmond left in 1979, Dr Hamish Inglis was appointed director, but over the years because of the lack of suitable applicants it was found impossible to fill the vacant post of Consultant Virologist and it was not until 1989 that Dr Sheila Burns, who had trained in the RVL and passed her MRCPath examination, was appointed as consultant. Alongside routine diagnostic virology it has always been essential to have on-going research and development, and to this end the laboratory has been fortunate to have Dr Heather Cubie as a member of staff. Dr Cubie, also an Honours graduate from the Bacteriology Department, has had an interest in papilloma viruses for a long time and has become an authority on the subject. Behind all aspects of research and development is the aim to deliver as speedy a service as possible. The newer molecular approaches may help in this direction.

In 1985 Sir John Crofton opened the new extension to the laboratory which included on the first floor a general office and individual offices for senior members of staff together with a large purpose-built room with a reinforced floor to accommodate the many deep freezers required for the storage of specimens. On the ground floor the accommodation comprised a seminar room/library, a staff-room and ample storage rooms. At the time of building the extension it was found possible from within the allocation to fund a computerised system for recording the reception of specimens through to the reporting of results. Mr David Hargreaves, being upgraded to Senior Chief MLSO in 1979, quite apart from showing excellence in all aspects of diagnostic virology, showed particular aptitude in computing and continues to guide and train in this relatively new aspect of laboratory practice. He also shows keen interest in the further education of members of the Institute of Medical Laboratory Sciences. To add to the well-equipped laboratory, it was fortunate that a very cheap and excellent second-hand electron microscope became available which was able to be housed in one of the store rooms created in the extension due to the reduced storage of paper records. Lately, much good work has been done in the diagnosis and epidemiology of Human Immunodeficiency Virus infections and now, through Dr Burns' initiative, a diagnostic service for Pneumocystis carinii infections throughout the region has been established. The number of clinical specimens processed by the Regional Virus Laboratory at the City Hospital in 1989-90 totalled 50,984.

The Astley Ainslie Hospital

This important modern rehabilitation hospital in Morningside[126] was opened in 1923 originally for the reception of convalescent patients from the Royal Infirmary, but after a few years concentrating rather on the positive aspects of rehabilitation. By 1931, there was provision for 120 in-patients. The classification of patients at that time indicated a wide variety of conditions, many of bacterial aetiology and including a considerable number of tuberculosis cases. Children were also admitted. Many of the patients contracted throat, chest and urinary infections while in the hospital. In 1931 Lt.-Colonel John Cunningham[127] was appointed the first Medical Superintendent. He had retired from the Indian Medical Service and had been in charge of several bacteriological laboratories in various parts of India, notably that of the Pasteur Institute in Kasauli. No doubt it was as a result of this experience and his special interest in bacteriology that in March 1931, soon after his appointment to the hospital, a small laboratory was opened there. Its first Annual Report records bacteriological examinations on a wide range of specimens and clinical conditions. From the outset, it seems that "many autogenous vaccines were prepared in the laboratory". In January 1931 in anticipation of the bacteriology laboratory opening, Roderick Ross was appointed laboratory assistant and Robert Hosie "lab. boy".

126. *Aeriel view of Astley Ainslie Hospital*

127. *Lt. Col. John Cunningham*

In the Annual Report for 1931, grateful acknowledgement was made to the Royal College of Physicians' Laboratory and to Professor T.J. Mackie of the University Bacteriology Department "for assistance in the supply of bacteriological culture media which cannot be prepared in the laboratory under existing conditions". It would appear that there was very close consultation between Professor Mackie and Lt.-Colonel Cunningham who were personal friends, and Mackie was always ready to assist the hospital laboratory with materials or provision of temporary staff. From the outset, Lt.-Colonel Cunningham supervised the work of the laboratory, initiating research, including the continuation of work which he had first begun in Indian laboratories.

Within a short time, the laboratory records indicate work on coliform urinary infections, an attempt being made to classify the organisms isolated and "to relate the numerical intensity of the infection with the clinical condition of the patient and improvement under treatment". Studies were also made of "the longevity of certain pathogenic organisms which promises to be of some scientific interest".

Research Studies

In 1932, Drs H.J. Gibson and W.A.R. Thomson undertook work on the possible relationship of haemolytic streptococci to the cause of acute rheumatism and published their findings (Gibson, Thomson and Stewart, 1933). These did not coincide apparently with those of other workers in the same field. In 1933, by which time the hospital had greatly increased in-patient accommodation, the Annual Report drew attention to the frequency of streptococcal throat infections amongst patients. Research was also continuing on the relationship of haemolytic streptococci and rheumatoid arthritis. This hypothesis seemed to be a great preoccupation of certain of the clinicians. (The classical study that considered a possible microbial aetiology for rheumatoid arthritis and demonstrated the weakness of current claims was to be done fifty years later by Professor Marmion, Dr Norval and their research team.)

Lt.-Colonel Cunningham carried out "serological tests in relapsing fever". In the mid-1930s the laboratory took part in studies of ear, nose and throat infections prevalent in the hospital and work was carried out by Dr Helen Wright on coliform infections. Dr Wright was later to join the staff of the University Bacteriology Department. At this time, while working in the Astley Ainslie laboratory, Dr Wright collaborated with Miss May Christison of the University department in a survey on the incidence of diphtheria carriers in a normal hospital population. Some laboratory studies were also made on tuberculosis cases, of which there was always a considerable number in the hospital.

Staff Changes

It is understood that, during the earlier period, Lt.-Colonel Cunningham supervised the laboratory. In 1945, Professor Mackie seconded Miss Davies, an Honours graduate, to work in the Astley Ainslie laboratory which she did for a year. In 1948, with the inauguration of the National Health Service, the Royal College of Physicians' Laboratory in Forrest Road closed. The former RCP staff obtained posts in various Edinburgh laboratories. Those who had worked in the bacteriology section were transferred to the Astley Ainslie Hospital laboratory, where the scope of work was increased, especially later when the laboratory provided a service for hospitals in the th of the city. Dr W.M. Levinthal[128] became bacteriologist in charge and John guson[129] the technician in charge. In 1954 Dr Levinthal retired and Dr P.N. munds[130] who had been on the staff of the University Bacteriology Department ceeded him. In 1960, Dr Edmunds resigned to become Consultant Bacteriologist the Fife hospitals. In the same year, plans were being finalised for the closure of ᵉ Astley Ainslie laboratory. Dr Helen Wright, who had just retired from the iversity department, took charge of the laboratory until its actual closure. In 51, the bacteriological work of the laboratory which had begun thirty years fore, was transferred to the newly opened Central Microbiological Laboratories the Western General Hospital, in which John Ferguson had been appointed a nior Medical Laboratory Technician.*

The Municipal Hospitals' Laboratory Services

This historical account of bacteriology in Edinburgh has devoted special attention and space to the establishment of the first University Chair in the subject, founded in 1913, and the development of the department under its successive professors, and it has done so for several reasons. As a result of the Chair's inauguration, the systematic teaching of bacteriology became more firmly established, not only for medical students but also, in due course, for others whose professional qualifications demanded some knowledge of and practical training in microbiology, as for example, students of veterinary and tropical medicine, public health, dentistry and the Honours BSc course. Such provision and development in the University Department of Bacteriology also contributed greatly towards the establishment of smaller laboratories in hospitals and other institutions in the city and surrounding districts; and indeed, many of the graduates and technicians who took charge of such laboratories had been trained in the University department. Apart from the earliest laboratories already referred to, further developments took place.

Former Poor Law Institutions

In 1929 with the passing of the Local Government (Scotland) Act, the powers and role of local public health authorities were altered. One of the many changes was that while such health authorities had previously been primarily concerned with preventive medicine, especially as regards public hygiene and the spread of infection, and had only been allowed to provide isolation or fever hospitals and Poor Law Institutions, they were now permitted to establish and maintain general hospitals, which came to be known as municipal hospitals.

It was therefore decided that the following Poor Law hospitals at Craigleith, built in 1869 and a Military Hospital during World War I; Pilton built in 1896; Seafield, built in 1907; and Craiglockhart built in 1870, previously administered by the Parish Council, should come under the aegis of the city's Public Health Department. In order to administer these hospitals, which in 1932 had been named respectively the Western General Hospital, the Northern General Hospital, the Eastern General Hospital and the Southern General Hospital, a joint committee was formed of Edinburgh Corporation and the University. One of the provisions of the joint administration of the hospitals was that professors in the Medical School were

---

* For an account of the history of the Astley Ainslie Hospital, "between the streamlet and the town", see Smith (1989b).

128. *Dr Walter Levinthal*

129. *John Ferguson*

130. *Dr Pat Edmunds*

131. *Dr Andrew McCabe*

132. *Douglas Annat*

appointed directors of units appropriate to their specialisations. University staff were appointed to clinical and teaching posts in the new Municipal Hospitals, and medical students of the University and the School of Medicine of the Royal Colleges of Physicians and Surgeons were taught in the hospitals.

After the establishment of these new types of hospitals in 1932, their requirements for bacteriological examinations were met by the Diagnostic Bacteriology Laboratory in the University department in "Lab. 4". As this added considerably to its workload, additional medical and technical staff were appointed. In 1953 a bacteriology laboratory was opened at the Northern General Hospital which took over the service for the Municipal Hospitals. Dr Andrew McCabe[131], formerly of the University Bacteriology Department, was appointed in charge of the new laboratory and Douglas Annat[132] also moved from the University department to become chief medical laboratory technician. The technical staff initially numbered four. In 1961, the work was transferred from the Northern General Laboratory to the new purpose-built Central Microbiological Laboratories at the Western General Hospital, opened in July 1961. Dr McCabe and his staff left the Northern General Hospital to form the nucleus of the new laboratories at the Western General Hospital, and Dr J.C. Gould was appointed Director and Consultant-in-Charge. This was a major development in the evolution of medical microbiology at Edinburgh.

CHAPTER TWELVE

THE CENTRAL MICROBIOLOGICAL LABORATORIES AT THE WESTERN GENERAL HOSPITAL

Development of Clinical Bacteriology towards a Centralised Service

by Dr J.C. Gould

During the late 1950s when the demands on laboratory services, including microbiology, were increasing rapidly it was foreseen that the Health Board would require to provide a greater proportion of these services from its own laboratories. At this time, it will be recalled, there were some small satellite laboratories in the peripheral hospitals having varying associations with the University Department. Thus at East Fortune Hospital there was a clinical laboratory providing basic services and more especially a tuberculosis diagnostic service for Dr Murray and his colleagues who served East Lothian and the Border counties. At Bangour General Hospital the bacteriology laboratory, started during the Second World War, continued under the direction of Dr Isabel Purdie who also kept a watching brief over the East Fortune laboratory. There was a clinical laboratory at the Royal Hospital for Sick Children which was from time to time under the supervision of the University Department but for longer periods co-operating with the bacteriology laboratory at the Astley Ainslie Hospital, first under Dr Levinthal and later Dr Pat Edmunds. This latter laboratory subsequently provided a bacteriological service to the hospitals on the south side of the city. In 1953, a bacteriological laboratory was deemed necessary for the hospitals on the north side of the city under the management of the Northern Hospital Group and this was developed at the Northern General Hospital alongside a clinical chemistry laboratory. Dr Andrew McCabe, a lecturer in the University, was appointed Consultant with Mr Douglas Annat as Chief Technician.

The progressive demand for diagnostic services, from the hospitals, general practitioners and the local authorities, had earlier indicated that there was a need for centralisation of laboratory facilities; as a result it was decided, with Scottish Home and Health Department (SHHD) support, to build a large laboratory within the curtilage of the Western General Hospital which was intended to house a large proportion of the services provided by the South Eastern Regional Hospital Board. For various reasons, including the exponential rise in the demand for clinical chemistry and haematological tests, when the laboratory building was nearing completion, it was obvious that only one major branch of clinical laboratory medicine could be accommodated; this turned out to be bacteriology.

Thus, through amalgamation of the peripheral laboratories already described and the absorption of a proportion of the clinical diagnostic work carried out at the University Department (Lab. 4), the Central Microbiological Laboratories (CML) at the Western General Hospital were formally opened by Sir Kenneth Cowan, then Chief Medical Officer at the SHHD, on 24 July, 1962. The service work had actually started in December 1961 with Dr J.C. Gould[133] as Director and Consultant in Charge, and Mr Douglas Annat, Chief Medical Laboratory Technician. Graduate and technical staff from the laboratories at the Astley Ainslie Hospital, Royal Hospital for Sick Children, Northern General Hospital, and East Fortune Hospital, joined the new laboratories. Within a short time, diagnostic services were being provided for all of the hospitals within the Edinburgh area (except the Royal Infirmary, City and Bangour hospitals) and for the hospitals in East Lothian. In addition, the CML served the majority of general practitioners in the Edinburgh area and was responsible for all of the local authority bacteriology south of the Forth.

The success of such centralisation depended much on a satisfactory specimen collection and report delivery service; this was provided by further extensive development of the Laboratory Van Collection Service of the Health Board which became a model of its kind, providing a collection and delivery service for all the laboratory specialties to the hospitals and individual practitioners, at a total cost of less than one per cent of the laboratory running costs to the Health Board.

The Central Microbiological Laboratories[134] rapidly developed under the local management of the Northern Hospital Group of the South-East Regional Hospital Board and were adequately staffed at all levels to provide a comprehensive and expeditious service to all their users, to recruit and train bacteriologists and technical staff, and to provide much clinical research of value in the fields of clinical bacteriology, mycology and immunology. These laboratories processed a total of 217,542 specimens in 1989-90.

Research Contributions From The Central Microbiological Laboratories

by Dr J.C. Gould

A considerable amount of research work has been done and continues to be done at the Central Microbiological Laboratories. Most has been concerned with the problems of a busy clinical laboratory and directed to improvements in the diagnosis and management of patients with infection and related conditions. For example, cervical glandular enlargement noted in children was shown in some instances to be due to exposure to mycobacteria other than *M. tuberculosis* and diagnosis was facilitated by the differential Mantoux test using both human and avian antigen. The epidemiology of an outbreak of typhoid fever in Edinburgh was fully elucidated by painstaking work in co-operation with community physicians and environmental health officers.

A more general problem investigated was that of the place of quantitative methods in diagnostic bacteriology similar to those used for many years in public health laboratories for the examination of water, milk and food. Such examinations are the basis of standards of safety of items for human consumption. Some laboratories have also been concerned with the enumeration of viable organisms in the dust and air by sampling and this has been referred to elsewhere. The Central Microbiological Laboratories took over responsibility for public health bacteriology in the south-eastern region of Scotland in 1962 and used standard quantitative examination methods for screening some 10,000 water and milk samples for each year. Certain foods have also been examined for the number of organisms they contain in an attempt to relate to wholesomeness. These examinations of milk, water and food were quite distinct from the examinations carried out when necessary, for specific pathogens such as *Salmonella* and *Campylobacter*.

However, most laboratory bacteriological diagnosis has depended on qualitative analysis of specimens such as exudates, body fluids and tissue, and the isolation of organisms recognised as potential pathogens. An exception to this has been the examination of urines which are commonly examined in a quantitative or semi-quantitative manner. As a result, clinical and laboratory experience has attached

133. *Dr J.C. Gould*

134. *Central Microbiological Laboratories, Western General Hospital*

importance to counts of 100,000 per ml, usually regarded as significant of infection. The isolation of any number of bacteria from the blood or cerebro-spinal fluid has been considered significant providing contamination is excluded, since these fluids are organism-free in health. There was, however, little information on the importance of the numbers of different bacteria isolated from specimens such as faeces and sputa which carry commensal flora, and their relationship to the clinical condition of the patient. Accordingly, investigations were done in an attempt to measure the number of bacteria of different types in specimens sent to the laboratory and to relate this information to the clinical condition of the patients, so assisting in diagnosis and specific treatment with antibacterial drugs. The following is a brief account of these investigations carried out at the Central Microbiological Laboratories.

Urinary Tract Infections

Quantitative culture of urine was performed using methods developed in the laboratories. However, the number of organisms is not the only laboratory parameter that should be considered in establishing a diagnosis of infection. Apart from ensuring satisfactory methods of collection of the specimen to avoid contamination, reducing the interval between sampling and examination to a minimum and controlling the holding temperature of the specimen, the quality of the isolate and the amount of antibacterial activity in the specimen are most important. Mixed flora were rarely found in primary infection, but more frequently when infection is secondary to interference such as catheterisation, in post-operative conditions, and following failure of treatment. Counting bacteria in routine urine specimens enabled a better definition of "asymptomatic bacteriuria" and was found to be of particular value in younger patients and in women of child-bearing age. Significant bacteriuria was also found to occur in some patients, particularly young men, with counts less than 100,000 per ml.

The counting of cells as well as bacteria in the urine can also be helpful and was shown to be of great importance in establishing a diagnosis in the new-born and the young child in whom it is often difficult to determine if infection is present, in part due to the clinical difficulty of obtaining uncontaminated specimens. Further investigations showed it was worthwhile to sample directly from the bladder by direct puncture through the abdominal wall, a relatively simple and safe procedure.

The clinical syndrome of prostatitis, occurring in young and middle-aged men, appears to be increasingly common and in most cases it was found difficult to obtain a bacteriological diagnosis. Investigations were made in a large series of patients examining first, middle and last stream specimens of urine, supplemented where possible by specimens of semen and prostatic fluid. The laboratory examinations included prolonged anaerobic culture and attempts to isolate bacterial L-forms and mycoplasmas, in addition to full quantitative studies. In this way, it was possible to establish an association between clinical signs and symptoms and the isolation of a variety of bacteria. This information helped in the choice of specific long-term chemotherapy which was frequently successful.

Respiratory Infections

Several investigations of the effectiveness of antibiotic treatment in respiratory tract infections were supplemented with quantitative bacteriological studies of respiratory exudates. Sputa and swabs, after homogenisation, were examined aerobically and anaerobically for the number of colony-forming units in culture. In some, microscopic examination counted both cells and the main groups of bacteria. These parameters were useful in forming the clinical diagnosis and following the progress of treatment. Bacterial counts showed that the great majority of patients with clinical infection had 10 to 10,000 times the numbers of potential pathogens such as *Haemophilus influenzae,* pneumococcus and haemolytic streptococcus in culture than were obtained from those without infection. An important finding was that increased numbers of *Haemophilus* species, other than *H. influenzae,* were frequently associated with infection.

Quantitative bacteriological studies on swabs from cases of clinical tonsillitis, laryngitis and bronchitis showed significant increases in the counts of potential pathogens in 65% of patients, thus indicating the importance of bacterial infections, whether primary or following initial viral invasion. The significance of this finding was reflected in the clinical success of appropriate antibacterial chemotherapy.

There has long been controversy about the need for tonsillectomy. The opportunity arose to carry out extensive studies on tissue obtained at tonsillectomy in children and these showed that the numbers of *Streptococcus pyogenes* and *Haemophilus* species isolated were very high. Frequently, this was so when pre-operative swabs from the throat and tonsil surfaces yielded no such organisms, or only small numbers. Further, it was shown that systemic treatment with antibiotic prior to removal of the tonsils greatly reduced the numbers of viable organisms, this reflecting the concentrations of antibiotic obtained in the tissues.

The Intestinal Flora

The microflora of the large intestine was known to be numerous and complex; less information was available on the quantity and quality of the flora of the small bowel, in either health or disease. Thus an extensive study was planned in association with the Gastro-intestinal Unit at the Western General Hospital to elucidate the bowel flora in normal individuals and those with malfunction. This work showed that the flora was extremely heterogeneous and often difficult to characterise. Detailed studies compared the numbers of the different groups of bacteria in the normal and diseased bowel, and the ecology of this flora was examined in relation to the range of oxidation-reduction potentials likely to occur in the lumen of the gut. These potentials were shown to be an important factor in influencing the relative numbers of aerobes, micro-aerophiles and obligate anaerobes present at different levels in the gut. Malfunction of the bowel such as intestinal hurry, or the occurrence of "blind loops", was related to changes in oxidation-reduction potentials in the lumen and concomitant alteration of the relative numbers of aerobic and anaerobic bacteria.

Chemoprophylaxis was introduced as an attractive adjunct to surgery of the bowel to help reduce the common complication of post-operative endogenous infection. It was feared that antibiotics used in this way would upset the bacterial flora of the gut leading to untoward secondary effects and infection with resistant bacteria. However, the use of suitable combinations of antibiotics against the intestinal flora, based on careful qualitative and quantitative assessment of the bowel flora in individual patients showed that this need not be so, and the relative effect on the normally predominant anaerobic flora was explained by disturbance of the microbial ecology leading to oxidation-reduction potential changes in the gut. Further, quantitative examination of the faeces in patients receiving chemotherapy showed that the appearance of many abnormal isolates such as pseudomonas, proteus, yeasts and staphylococci was more often spurious as their numbers were small and insignificant, although they might overgrow qualitative cultures and thus appear to be of greater importance.

Aerobiology

Several investigations of the relationship between environmental contamination and sepsis due to *Staphylococcus aureus* were carried out involving quantitative estimations of bacteria in airborne dust and other sources. It was found that there was a general correlation between the incidence of staphylococcal sepsis and the environmental levels of contamination, illustrating the vicious circle upon which cross-infection depends. It was found that the relative proportion of *Staph. aureus* in the environment was more important than the total bacterial count as this reflected ward activities and the adequacy of ventilation.

The levels of bacterial contamination of the environment in maternity units and nurseries were measured over a number of years and showed marked ecological changes that reflected the changing use of antibiotics and antibacterial agents. Similarly, the number of erythromycin-resistant strains of staphylococci in the environment followed the prevalence of infection due to such strains.

The Central Microbiological Laboratories were involved, along with the Royal Infirmary Laboratory, in the design and operation of the first custom-built unit for tissue transplantation. It was considered important to continuously measure the microbial content of the environment of the unit. This served as a check on the efficiency of the ventilation systems and other procedures designed to avoid bacterial contamination and also gave warning of the introduction of any infection source into the unit. This bacteriological monitoring included estimations of the total bacterial content of the airborne and settling dust and analysis for the presence of specific organisms such as *Staph. aureus* and *Pseudomonas*. The aim was to maintain a total bacterial count of no more than 50 colony-forming units per cubic metre and no specific pathogens, so providing as near as possible a pathogen-free environment within the "clean area" of the unit suitable for the treatment of patients highly susceptible to infection. These procedures were shown to be effective in maintaining satisfactory environmental levels of bacteria and preventing exogenous infection in the patients under treatment.

The pattern of infection of orthopaedic units was studied over many years and shown to be relatively constant in quality, *Staph. aureus* being the most frequently isolated pathogen. The evidence, notably that of Charnley, seemed to indicate that infection resulted from contamination of the operation site in theatre. With the increase of major elective operations such as hip-arthroplasty it was important to reduce the chances of infection and its potentially serious consequences. Accordingly, observations were made with unidirectional airflow (laminar) systems in surgical theatres, with detailed bacteriological monitoring of the operation environment and the patient's wounds using quantitative methods. The initial results indicated a reduced rate of deep infection in patients operated on under laminar flow. However, as the rate of infection under conventional theatre ventilation was often as low as 2.5 per cent, a very large number of patients was required to provide results that were statistically significant, taking into account the large number of variables in the procedures of different surgeons. Thus the laboratories and the clinical unit at the Princess Margaret Rose Hospital participated in a major multicentre trial whose results have been fully reported (see Lidwell *et al*, 1982). These show conclusively the benefits of laminar flow over conventional ventilation in reducing infection and the virtual elimination of serious infection when combined with appropriate chemoprophylaxis.

From the results of the above investigations, it is clear that quantitative methods are valuable in many bacteriological examinations. There is need, however, for further studies to encourage the adoption of quantitative methods in routine diagnostic bacteriology and to extend our knowledge of the importance of the numbers of pathogens in other types of specimens, as for example *Salmonella* and *Shigella* in faeces from convalescent and healthy carriers and their relation to infectivity of the individual.

Immunological Investigations at the Central Microbiological Laboratories

by Dr Kenneth C. Watson

In early 1969 Dr K.C. Watson arrived in the Central Microbiology Laboratories to take up a consultant post, having occupied the Chair of Microbiology in the University of Natal. Dr Watson had a particular interest in immunology and had considerable experience of the early days of immunofluorescence. The CML had recently acquired an immunofluorescence microscope but was offering only a limited service to users. During the next few years the immunology service grew rapidly to cover a wide range of immunological investigations, both in relation to microbial diseases and autoimmune disorders. The laboratory developed a special interest in systemic lupus erythematosus and rheumatic diseases, and formed a close relationship with the University Department of Rheumatology. The laboratory also took over the immunological requirements of the University Department of Dermatology at the Royal Infirmary and for many years investigated all biopsy and serum specimens from patients with a wide variety of skin disorders. This work was of great interest to the laboratory because it led to a high degree of expertise in tissue immunofluorescence by members of staff.

A number of research projects were undertaken by Dr Watson in collaboration with Mr E.J.C. Kerr, Senior Chief MLSO in the laboratory. The most interesting of these extended over a period of several years on factors influencing the standard haemolysis inhibition test for anti-streptolysin antibody (ASO), with special reference to the role of cholesterol and other sterols. It was subsequently demonstrated that the ASO-like activity was located in peptide fragments where the cholesterol moiety was exposed in such a way that the spatial orientation allowed the cholesterol to bind freely with streptolysin O (SLO). It soon became apparent that sera with ASO activity could contain both true antibody (ASO) and activity that was related to the presence of suitably exposed cholesterol molecules. Dr Watson and Mr Kerr therefore designated this second activity as ASF (antistreptolysin factor activity). Further investigations showed that ASF activity is derived from the catabolic turnover of beta-lipoproteins. Such activity was found to be present in all sera, a matter of great interest since SLO is only one of a number of related toxin molecules that bind the cholesterol. Others include pneumolysin, cereolysin, tetanolysin and listeriolysin. Dr Watson and Mr Kerr therefore postulated that ASF activity may represent an early non-specific defence mechanism capable of coming into operation before the development of specific antibody production and/or cell mediated immunity. A series of other studies of sera from patients with a variety of suspected autoimmune disorders also suggested the possibility that cholesterol-toxin complexes may render the peptide portion of the complex autoantigenic, with the formation of immune complexes. These may play a role not only in recognised autoimmune disorders, but also in the formation of plaques in atherosclerosis.

For a number of years Dr Watson, Mr Kerr and Miss Maureen Baillie were involved in biotyping strains of *Haemophilus influenzae* from patients with cystic fibrosis. It was possible to show that the same biotype might persist for several months in some patients. In others there were quite rapid changes in existing biotypes. One unexpected finding was that in cystic fibrosis patients there might be four or even five different biotypes present simultaneously, something not found in sputum samples from non-cystic fibrosis patients.

The Clinical Mycology Unit at the Central Microbiological Laboratories

by Dr Leslie Milne

Until the 1960s, routine diagnostic mycology was provided on a rather haphazard basis by clinical bacteriologists in the Edinburgh area. At that time there was an increasing awareness of fungal infections, particularly in relation to deep-seated infections in compromised hospital patients. The introduction of renal transplantation in Edinburgh enhanced this awareness. Around the same period, some clinicians were showing more interest in fungi. For example, Dr Ian W.B. Grant and his team at the Chest Unit, Northern General Hospital, undertook research on aspergillosis and Farmer's Lung and in the process discovered Maltworker's Lung.

Clinical bacteriologists were becoming uncomfortably aware of limitations of their expertise when faced with the widening range of recognised pathogenic fungi and their increasing importance in medicine. Fortunately, Dr Walter Blyth, mycologist at the Botany Department of the University, was both motivated and able to provide specialist help. Dr Blyth contributed much to the research in human fungal disease being undertaken in Edinburgh and also provided a diagnostic service on an ad hoc basis to Dermatology and other clinical departments in Edinburgh. The workload rapidly grew to unmanageable proportions. A local specialist mycology service was required and the prime movers were Professor (later Sir) John Crofton, Professor Patrick ("Paddy") Hare, Drs I.W.B. Grant and J. Cameron Gould.

Accordingly, on 1 September 1970, the Mycology Unit opened under the charge of Dr Leslie J.R. Milne at the Western General Hospital's Central Microbiological Laboratories. The remit of the Unit was to provide a comprehensive mycological diagnostic service to all hospitals and general practitioners in Lothian and beyond, and to undertake a reference function for other microbiology laboratories, principally in the East of Scotland. In addition to these roles, the Unit would undertake research and development, and teaching and training.

Diagnostic and Reference Service

Since its inception the Mycology Unit provided a diagnostic service related as closely as possible to the patient. That is, while many clinicians in hospitals and the community are normally served by their local microbiology laboratories, a direct line of communication was established between the clinicians and the Mycology Unit. This arrangement had the agreement, and often encouragement, of the relevant local laboratory staff. Thus, of the total workload of the Unit, 90% originates outwith the Western General Hospital.

The Unit's work with primary care practitioners provides further evidence of the close relationship between mycology and early patient contact. In the first year of its existence, the Unit obtained less than 1% of its specimens from GPs. Currently, 35% of a vastly increased total number of specimens are submitted directly from the community. The change can be attributed to an active policy to encourage GPs and much credit is due to Dr Duncan McVie, formerly of the University Health Service, who was responsible for formal training of GP trainees in the diagnosis of skin disease and for promoting the benefits of mycological investigation.

During the lifetime of the Unit, deep-seated life-threatening infections have become dramatically more prevalent. The expansion of organ transplantation and other procedures causing immunocompetence has largely been responsible. Thus, close links have been forged with specialties such as haematology, intensive therapy and renal units. Concomitantly, the range of pathogenic yeasts and filamentous fungi has increased beyond all expectations. The emergence of less common species of fungi in pathogenic situations has contributed, in part, to the reference laboratory function of the Mycology Unit. In recognition of the service provided to the East of Scotland and beyond, the Scottish Home and Health Department has designated the laboratory as a National Reference facility.

Research and Development

Research and development has always been an important aspect of the work of the Mycology Unit, with the main thrust on clinical applications such as improvements in therapy and diagnostic techniques. Dr Milne collaborated with Dr Ross Barnetson to develop techniques for the collection of clinical material and the processing of samples in the laboratory. In the latter case, a predominant interest in aspergillosis was encouraged by Drs Ian W.B. Grant and Graham K. Crompton of the Chest Unit at the Northern General and Western General Hospitals. This collaboration led to an understanding of fundamental aspects of the disease and its reliable diagnosis in the laboratory. The advances have been recognised at home and abroad and have formed a major part of contributions to medical texts in which Dr Milne has been closely involved.

The development of antifungal drugs cannot take place without the co-operation of patients, clinicians and clinical mycology laboratories. The Mycology Unit has been associated with work related to almost all of the new antifungals introduced since the early 1970s. The range includes the first antifungal imidazole (clotrimazole); the first oral imidazole to show systemic activity (ketoconazole); the discovery of the combined use of imidazole and a steroid for skin infections; the use of the triazole, itraconazole, in the treatment of aspergillosis; and the emergence of fungal resistance to fluconazole in AIDS patients. Space does not allow acknowledgement here of the clinical and other collaborators that made this possible.

Teaching and Training

Formal teaching commitments exist between the Mycology Unit and the University of Edinburgh, Heriot-Watt University, Queen Margaret College, Glasgow Polytechnic and the University of Wales. In addition a major contribution is made to the annual course in Medical Mycology organised by the British Society for Mycopathology at the University of Leeds. Teaching and practical training in the diagnosis of fungal disease are given to MLSOs from Edinburgh and elsewhere in Scotland. Postgraduate training of medical staff is undertaken for membership of the Royal College of Pathologists and as course requirements for the Joint Committee for Higher Medical Training. The Unit has also supervised students for Doctor of Philosophy degrees.

The number of clinical specimens processed by the Mycology Unit in the year 1989-90 totalled 11,950, with much associated liaison to guide the clinical management of the patients. This is a very significant development.

APPENDIX A

RETROSPECTIVES ON IMPORTANT INITIATIVES

1. The Lister Institute

Had events gone otherwise, the history of the University Department of Bacteriology would have unfolded not in the premises allocated to it in the Medical School, but outwith the University in a proposed Institute which it would have shared with the Pathology Department. This was never to materialise.

In 1894, the Royal College of Physicians of Edinburgh and its sister body, the Royal College of Surgeons, had first jointly considered how they might co-operate more closely. The principal proposal agreed upon was that they might combine resources in building a jointly owned laboratory. This possibility took on added importance after the establishment of the Chair of Bacteriology in 1913 and the appointment of its first incumbent, Professor James Ritchie. Ritchie had been Superintendent of the Royal College of Physicians' Laboratory from 1906 until 1920, for seven years combining his professorial responsibilities with those of the RCP post.

When Professor Ritchie took up his University appointment, as related elsewhere, bacteriology had been carried on within the University Department of Pathology. Pathological Bacteriology had been the subject of a course conducted by Dr Robert Muir of the Pathology Department, who was also the University's first formal lecturer in bacteriology, appointed in 1894. There is some evidence that for several years after his appointment, Professor Ritchie had to develop his new department with facilities provided in the Pathology Department although separate Bacteriology Department laboratories were gradually acquired. Possibly through Professor Ritchie's understandably frequent requests to them, the University authorities became particularly concerned to provide their new department with much more adequate accommodation, while endeavouring to assist the ever-developing Pathology Department in a similar manner.

Memorial to Lord Lister

In 1912, Lord Lister[135] died and the Royal College of Surgeons of Edinburgh, in common with their sister bodies throughout Great Britain, desired to erect a suitable memorial to the world-famous pioneer of antiseptic surgery. Such memorials took various forms. In Edinburgh, where Lister had established the city's first small bacteriology department in the old Royal Infirmary in 1876 and had occupied the University's Chair of Clinical Surgery, it was decided that the most fitting memorial would be the establishment of an Institute of Pathological and Clinical Research. Pathology would include bacteriology. The Principal of the University supported the scheme of the College of Surgeons and at a conference on 19 March, 1913, representatives of the University, the two Colleges, and the Carnegie Trustees prepared a draft scheme for what was provisionally named "The Edinburgh Lister Institute of Pathology". It was agreed that a site be purchased and a building planned. The building would be vested in the University and would provide for teaching and research. All the work of the Pathology and Bacteriology Departments would be carried out in the proposed new Institute. Research would be supervised by a board comprising three representatives of the University, two from the Royal College of Physicians and one each from the Royal College of Surgeons and the Carnegie Trust. The Royal College of Physicians' Laboratory would be closed and its work and staff incorporated in the new Lister Institute. The money obtained from the sale of the RCP Laboratory would be subscribed to the Lister Memorial Fund,

135. *Lord Lister in later years*

136. *Lister Housing Co-operative, Lauriston Place*

to which other donations would be sought widely. It was expected that the new Institute would be completed in a short time.

Plans Laid Aside

Six months after the completion of all the planning, the First World War began. The scheme, like so many others, had to be laid aside. However, perhaps quite unexpectedly, one feature of the Royal College of Physicians' Laboratory's war-time service was to contribute to the Lister Memorial Fund. The Belgian army authorities had appealed for "a supply of vaccines against typhoid and sepsis" as well as antisera for tetanus, dysentery and meningitis. A very large consignment of such vaccines and antisera was prepared at the Forrest Road laboratory and dispatched to the Belgian front. The work was carried out by Dr James Dawson and Dr J.P. McGowan, the latter featuring prominently in the published lists of the laboratory's research in bacteriology. Yet further appeals were received from Belgium and an arrangement was made by which the RCP Laboratory prepared the vaccines for the then well-known Edinburgh pharmaceutical firm of Duncan Flockhart to package and sell commercially. From the financial arrangements that were agreed, the Lister Memorial Fund benefited considerably. After the war and well into the 1930s, the continued collaboration with Duncan Flockhart in vaccine preparation resulted in even greater increase to the Lister Fund. By 1938, £1,440 had been contributed to the Fund, a not inconsiderable sum at that time.

Rather strangely, the plans for the Lister Institute which had not been seriously studied for some time after the end of the First World War, once again had to be laid aside: this time by the outbreak of the Second World War in 1939. Perhaps other factors had intervened between the wars. Professor Ritchie had died in 1923 and when Professor T.J. Mackie succeeded him, he was able to acquire a steady increase in accommodation and facilities for the University Bacteriology Department in Teviot Place. Likewise, the Pathology Department had acquired more satisfactory accommodation and there were long-term prospects for further improvements for both departments.

Original Scheme Abandoned

Thus by 1938, if there was still some discussion of the Lister Institute Scheme, the concept behind it had been modified. By 1945 and the end of the Second World War, there appears to have been little interest by the University authorities and the Royal College of Physicians. From the outset, when the Lister Institute had first been proposed and indeed very soon afterwards strongly supported, the leading advocate of the plan appears to have been Professor James Ritchie, possibly for the reasons given earlier. It is true that Professor Ritchie's colleague and close friend, Professor W. Lorrain Smith of the Chair of Pathology, had shared his enthusiasm. When, in the mid-1920s, consideration of the Lister Institute plans had been resumed, Professor Lorrain Smith had stated that without the inspiration and vision of his friend, he personally did not have the ability to make the scheme a reality.

On account of the two world wars, it may appear that the Lister scheme never "got off the ground"; nevertheless, certain steps had been taken soon after 1914 when the Memorial Trustees began to purchase flats[136] on the north side of Lauriston Place between Graham Street and Heriot Place and the Vennel on the west boundary of George Heriot's School. This was with a view to building the proposed Lister Institute on this site. By 1955, most of the houses had been acquired and although the Memorial Fund had become quite a substantial sum, the plans for the original Institute had long been abandoned. In 1965, the University took over as Trustees for the Lister Fund. After considering whether a new building to house the Postgraduate School for Medicine might be erected on the site, this plan was rejected in favour of the new building being sited at Roxburgh Place where in fact it was built in 1967 and commemoratively named the Lister Institute. The Lister Memorial Fund met most of the cost, supplemented by the Davidson Trust Bequest. What had come to be called the Lister site in Lauriston Place had for long been considered by the University as the possible site of a new Dental Hospital and School but the Edinburgh District Council Planning Committee refused permission for the scheme. In May 1976, Edinvar Housing Association bought the Lister site houses from the University and in September 1976 the Lister Housing Co-operative[136] was formed and took ownership of the site. Thus the memorial to Lord Lister, originally envisaged as an Institute to house the University Department of Pathology and Bacteriology, did not take that form. Today the world-famous surgeon is commemorated by the Roxburgh Place building and the work carried out therein; and his name also lingers on, albeit obliquely, in the finely restored housing complex in Lauriston Place.

2. The Bacteriological Services For The City Of Edinburgh – The First Fifty Years: 1900-1950

Based on a Report by Dr Helen Wright

In 1926, three years after Professor T.J. Mackie had been appointed to the University Chair of Bacteriology, the bacteriological diagnostic services for the City of Edinburgh, provided by a laboratory in the Usher Institute from 1902, were transferred to the University department under Professor Mackie's direction. This work was carried out in one of the three laboratories acquired by Professor Mackie on the first floor of the then Medical Chemistry Department. Consequently, from 1926 until relatively recent times, innumerable members of the Bacteriology Department's academic and technical staff spent varying periods of time working and gaining experience in what became familiarly and widely known as "Lab. 4". This was the room number of the none-too-large laboratory situated on the top floor on the west side of the Medical School. The valuable, and at times unique, experience gained in Lab. 4 – the "Public Health Lab." – was taken by many who had worked there to other departments in various parts of the world and visitors from far and wide were made welcome to work in Lab. 4.

The development of Edinburgh's microbiological services is described in the following account taken from a report by Dr Helen A. Wright to the City of Edinburgh Public Health Department (Report, 1950). Helen Wright had a lengthy and distinguished association with Lab. 4. In 1950, she was appointed Consultant Bacteriologist to the South-East Scotland Regional Hospital Board and was Director of the laboratory from then until her retiral in 1960.

Dr Helen Wright's Report

In her report, Dr Helen Wright vividly described the initial discoveries of Pasteur and Koch which led to an increasing understanding of the aetiology of infectious diseases and the laboratory diagnosis of these during what Professor Topley had described as the riotous growth of the 1880s. Typhoid fever, tuberculosis, erysipelas, cholera, diphtheria and several other fevers were amongst the first to be capable of bacteriological laboratory diagnosis. Dr Wright also placed the growth of the new and important medical science of bacteriology in the context of the work of what she called "the sanitarians"; most notable in Edinburgh being Dr Henry Littlejohn, the city's first Medical Officer of Health, appointed in 1862, who grappled with health and disease-related problems of ensuring pure water supplies; effective drainage; better housing and working conditions; food hygiene; milk examination and inspection of cows. All of these public health factors had important bacteriological dimensions.

Dr Wright referred to Edinburgh's earliest bacteriological diagnostic laboratories at the Royal College of Physicians' Laboratory and later the Usher Institute (described in detail in the early sections of the present writer's account). Reference is also made to the Royal Infirmary's Bacteriological Laboratory and that at the City Hospital. Then in 1926, the city's bacteriological services were centralised under Professor Mackie in the University Bacteriology Department. An interesting and impressive presentation of statistics is given.

Many of the advancements in bacteriological laboratory diagnosis described in the 1950 review were in no small measure due to research carried out in the University Bacteriology Department and the diagnostic laboratory, and in which Dr Wright had herself been involved, e.g., the introduction of tests for leptospirosis, abortus fever, enteric food poisoning and its epidemiology, diphtheria typing and virulence testing. In a Public Health context, Lab. 4 was responsible for the regular testing of the city's water supply; of milk from a wide range of farms and dairies; of food examination not only from outbreaks of food poisoning but in routine sampling in close collaboration with the city's sanitary inspectors, notably in a later period with Mr J. Norval[137], the city's Chief Veterinary Officer, Mr W. Valentine[138] and Mr Alastair Orr. Since the review summarised above was written in 1950, naturally it does not refer to very many other diagnostic procedures introduced into the work of Lab. 4 in subsequent years which became a source of expertise on salmonella infection; the laboratory diagnosis of tuberculosis; VD serology and the monitoring of BCG vaccine before its issue for use, along with routine diagnostic bacteriology.

Hawick Typhoid Epidemic

Perhaps one of the most important and certainly most dramatic episodes in the archives of Lab. 4 occurred in 1938 when it was involved in diagnosing actual cases and tracing carriers in a most serious outbreak of typhoid fever which occurred in Hawick[139]. One hundred cases of the infection were diagnosed bacteriologically, including carriers. There were five deaths. While the initial reporting of the first cases was carried out by Lab. 4, a special field laboratory was set up in Hawick under the personal direction of Professor T.J. Mackie and staff seconded from the University. After very careful investigation the outbreak was eventually traced to a catering trade worker.

Such episodes were fortunately rare. The statistics provided by Dr Wright[140] in her review indicate the steady basic increase in the work of the laboratory. In 1926 when Professor Mackie took over the city's diagnostic bacteriological services, the

137. *John Norval*

138. *William Valentine*

HAWICK TYPHOID EPIDEMIC

First Death: Six New Cases

NEW BACTERIOLOGICAL LABORATORY PLAN

Edinburgh University Experts in Charge

The epidemic of typhoid at Hawick claimed its first victim yesterday, when the death occurred of a young woman who was one of the first cases.

An official bulletin issued last night by Dr James R. Adam, the Medical Officer of Health for Roxburghshire, states that six cases were admitted to hospital yesterday, making the total number 71. The bulletin adds—"No statement can be made as yet regarding the probable source of infection."

All precautionary measures are being taken in connection with the epidemic, and it has been decided to instal a bacteriological laboratory at the Buccleuch Memorial Institute at Hawick. Experts from Edinburgh University Bacteriological Department will have charge of the laboratory. Tests hitherto had been carried out in the laboratory in Edinburgh.

Dr Adam stated yesterday that investigations into the outbreak are being pushed to the limit, and they were getting full assistance from the Department of Health and the Edinburgh University laboratory staff.

"NO PANIC IN THE TOWN"

"There is no state of panic in the town," Dr Adam added. At present no definite statement could be issued, but investigations into the outbreak were continuing, and every practical measure was being taken.

The death occurred yesterday at the Isolation Hospital of Miss Ina Simpson, 12 Ettrick Terrace, Hawick. Miss Simpson, who was 21 years of age, was employed in the office of one of the local hosiery manufacturers.

Mr R. W. Barrie, the former Scottish Rugby Internationalist, and at one time captain of the Hawick Rugby Club, had given three blood transfusions in an effort to save Miss Simpson.

Within the last few days more men have been admitted to hospital than previously. Women patients have been in the majority in the early stages of the epidemic. The cases are not confined to any particular districts of the town. A number of cases are now reaching the critical period of 21 days, and blood transfusions have been necessary.

139. *Extract from the* Glasgow Herald, *26 May, 1938*

TABLE A 2.1

Notification of Infectious Diseases in Edinburgh, 1947

Disease	Jan.	Feb.	Mar.	April	May	June	July	Aug.	Sept.	Oct.	Nov.	Dec.	Total
Diphtheria	7	5	5	5	9	1	1	5	3	4	2	3	50
Erysipelas	16	17	8	17	13	7	9	12	13	9	10	12	143
Scarlet Fever	32	27	41	24	20	11	18	20	21	32	36	28	310
Typhoid Fever	2	..	..	..	..	..	1	..	1	1	..	..	6
Puerperal Fever	3	2	5	4	4	3	4	5	6	12	6	11	65
Puerperal Pyrexia	3	1	1	3	9	..	1	5	2	2	4	3	34
Cerebro-spinal Fever	14	8	13	6	2	3	1	1	3	2	3	1	57
Infective Jaundice	..	..	1	..	1	..	..	..	..	..	..	..	2
Tuberculosis, Pulmonary	49	45	50	54	46	57	37	44	56	57	54	57	606
Tuberculosis, other forms	11	11	7	13	18	10	14	8	17	5	7	10	131
Ophthalmia Neonatorum	..	2	..	2	1	1	1	..	1	..	..	..	10
Malaria	4	2	4	1	1	4	1	3	..	..	2	1	23
Dysentery	13	14	7	5	4	4	3	..	2	13	1	3	69
Acute Primary Pneumonia	48	43	47	29	9	15	3	13	7	14	14	46	288
Acute Influenzal Pneumonia	29	11	11	5	..	..	..	1	..	..	6	2	65
Measles	386	302	119	109	76	95	96	69	50	25	34	42	1,403
Whooping Cough	84	106	114	106	99	83	69	53	21	18	18	19	790
Poliomyelitis	1	..	..	..	..	1	4	38	47	38	18	4	151
Polio-encephalitis	..	..	..	..	..	..	..	..	..	..	..	..	..
Encephalitis Lethargica	..	..	..	..	..	..	..	..	..	..	..	..	..
Totals	702	596	433	383	312	296	263	277	250	232	216	243	4,203

140. *Dr Helen Wright*

141. *Robert K. Farmer*

number of specimens examined in that year was 5,444. Dr Wright cites the figure of 8,000 for 1932; 19,000 for 1937 and 45,000 for 1947, this latter high figure being accounted for by the examinations for the Municipal Hospitals then being at their peak. Table A 2.1 indicates the incidence of various infectious diseases for 1947.

3. Mr Robert K. Farmer – Pioneer Of Technician Training

Many years before Dr Helen Wright was appointed Director of the Public Health Laboratory, indeed as relatively early as 1934, the senior technician in this laboratory was Mr Robert Farmer[141], who had succeeded Mr Alex Drysdale, the original and for long the only technician in the diagnostic laboratory. Farmer was given increased technical staff not only in Lab. 4 whose work was steadily increasing, but also in other sections of the department as more research workers joined the staff. While Mr A.B. Cheyne was the Chief Technician, his classroom duties were so demanding that Farmer undertook the administration and training of junior and senior technical staff.

The experience gained in training the department's junior technical staff when there was no standardised national scheme was drawn upon by Farmer and formed the basis of a training syllabus he drew up, at first adopted by the Pathological and Bacteriological Laboratory Assistants' Association (PBLAA) and later nationally by the Institute of Medical Laboratory Technology (IMLT). At the heart of the department's own training scheme was the valuable range of experience to be gained in Lab. 4.

With a view to raising the basic scientific standards of medical laboratory technicians, juniors who had not reached a sufficient level in mathematics, physics and chemistry at school attended evening courses in these subjects; they could not enter the PBLAA's scheme and later that of the IMLT until they had acquired pass certificates. Junior technicians were rotated through the various areas of the department, e.g. preparation of culture medium; preparation of practical teaching material under Sandy Cheyne's meticulous eye; care of animals; and assistance to various research workers. This system of rotation was also extended outwith the department, juniors spending short periods working in the allied disciplines of pathology, clinical chemistry and haematology, while the juniors from these disciplines came to work in the department (and other bacteriological laboratories). Thus, staff were prepared for the PBLAA's and later IMLT's Intermediate and specialised Final Examinations. In the evening courses as a preparation for the Intermediate Examination, senior technical staff taught on a voluntary basis. In the courses for the Final Bacteriology Examination, held in the University department, the teachers for very many years, again giving one evening per week on a voluntary basis, were Sandy Cheyne, Robert Farmer, and Jimmy Dick and Ian Samuel of the Royal Infirmary Bacteriology Laboratory. These experienced technicians, with others, conducted the local examinations. It is a source of some satisfaction to realise that not only did Lab. 4 have an important part to play in the training and experience of medical and technical staff, but the department's training systems became a model for the country.

4. The Lewis Cameron Fund

For over half a century, lecturers, research workers and certain students in the University Department of Bacteriology have benefited from the Lewis Cameron Fund. This Note traces the origin of the Fund.

At a meeting of Edinburgh University Court on 27 October, 1930 it was announced that the late Mrs A.M. Cameron had bequeathed her estate, subsequently calculated at approximately £80,000, for the establishment of the "Lewis Cameron Fund" to commemorate her late husband. The income from investment would be utilised for awarding an annual prize open to Edinburgh medical students for the best paper submitted on an aspect of bacteriology or the diagnosis of disease. The Court considered the estimated proceeds from the bequest as excessive for a prize and the Business and Law Committee was requested to consider the matter and report back. Legal difficulty was encountered in altering the terms of the bequest. Eventually, permission was granted from Mrs Cameron's trustees to use the proceeds of the Fund for the payment of salaries to lecturers and research workers in medical departments, in addition to the award of the essay prize.

Dr Lewis Cameron, whom the fund commemorated, was a native of Knockando on the eastern border of Elginshire, who gained an MD at Edinburgh University in 1863 and a Licentiateship of the Royal College of Surgeons of Edinburgh in the same year. His MD thesis was: "On Some Forms of Jaundice". Dr Lewis Cameron joined the Indian Medical Service in 1866 as a surgeon and gave notable service in Bengal until his retiral in 1891. He died at St. Hellier in 1927. It was not possible from the data available to discover why the subject of the Lewis Cameron Fund Prize should have been for an essay in bacteriology or the diagnosis of infectious disease.

NOTES ON STUDIES OF HISTORICAL INTEREST

by Professor J.P. Duguid[142]

1. *Streptococcus pyogenes* Infections

Scarlet fever and other serious infections with *Streptococcus pyogenes* were prevalent in Edinburgh, as elsewhere, in the 1930s and early 1940s. Patients filled several large, 24-bed wards at the City Fever Hospital, in addition to even larger numbers nursed at home. Bacteriological research on these infections was stepped up after 1933 by Drs C.A. Green and Scott Thomson, the former introducing to Edinburgh the serotyping method of F. Griffith for the identification of different strains of the streptococcus.

The outstanding study was done by Dr H.L. de Waal, initially with guidance from Dr Green. De Waal prepared a complete set of specific absorbed typing sera and used them to type the very numerous strains isolated in a comprehensive study of throat and nose swabs from patients in hospital (swabbed daily) and the home, and healthy carriers in schools, among home contacts and hospital staff, and in the general community. Among the many interesting results of this monumental work, which was published in 1940 and 1941 (De Waal, 1940, 1941), were: (a) the demonstration that patients in multi-bed wards commonly became cross-infected with a different type of *Streptococcus pyogenes* from other patients and that the serious late complications of scarlet fever were usually due to the cross-infecting strain which was insusceptible to the immune response against the original strain; (b) the demonstration that a healthy person visiting a scarlet fever ward for a few hours usually acquired contamination in his nose or throat with one of the ward strains of *Streptococcus pyogenes,* but usually eliminated the contaminant within 24 hours; (c) the finding that in sequential daily examinations of patients with a persisting infection, a proportion of well-taken swabs failed to detect the organism present.

De Waal was an exceptionally industrious and careful worker with an intense, introverted personality. Unfortunately, when serving as an army pathologist from 1941 to 1945, he became addicted to the consumption of ether and other solvents, and on resuming his appointment as lecturer in Edinburgh in 1946, continued the practice in his locked laboratory in the tower of the department. After he had been found unconscious on the floor by Dr Van Rooyen, his father in South Africa was notified of the problem. The latter came to Edinburgh and supervised his son by sitting all day in the laboratory with him. The arrangement did not prove convenient or effective, and after a month or so he took his son back to South Africa, where he died about a year later, a tragic fate for a researcher of the greatest ability and potential.

In October and November 1942, a severe epidemic of scarlet fever, tonsillitis, rheumatic fever and otitis media broke out in *HMS Caledonia,* the shore-based residential naval training school at Rosyth. Drs C.A. Green and S.W. Challinor and J.P. Duguid demonstrated that there was an extensive aerial infection with the epidemic streptococcus in all areas of the school, mainly related to dust raining from clothing by body movements, and little to droplet-spray-producing activities.

Severe infections with *Streptococcus pyogenes* became much less common after penicillin came into general use in the mid-1940s, but the studies of Dr P.W. Ross in the 1960s showed that this potentially very dangerous streptococcus was still commonly carried in the throats of Edinburgh children.

2. Early Penicillin Studies

After the Florey group had published the Oxford work on penicillin in *The Lancet*

142. ILLUSTRATIVE EXAMPLES OF
PROFESSOR J.P. DUGUID'S RESEARCH STUDIES
IN THE UNIVERSITY DEPARTMENT OF BACTERIOLOGY

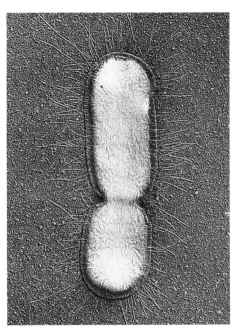

Electron-micrograph of a Flexner dysentery bacillus, showing the filamentous appendages, "fimbriae", which effect attachment to intestinal and other body cells (J.P. Duguid and R.R. Gillies, 1957, *Journal of Pathology and Bacteriology*, 74, 397-411).

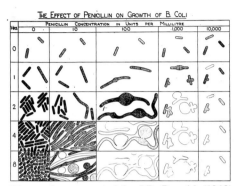

Observations reported by J.P. Duguid (1946) *Edinburgh Medical Journal*, 53, 401-412 suggesting that penicillin kills bacteria by interfering specifically with the formation of their outer supporting cell-wall.

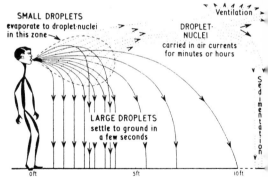

Spread of respiratory infections by droplets and droplet-nuclei. Fig. 8.2, in Mackie and McCartney's Medical Microbiology, edited by J.P. Duguid, B.P. Marmion and R.H.A. Swain, 13th Edition, p.121, Churchill Livingstone, Edinburgh, 1978.

in the latter half of 1941, J.R. Learmonth, Edinburgh's Professor of Systematic Surgery, became very interested in the possible use of penicillin for the treatment of surgical infections. He persuaded Professor Mackie to assign two bacteriologists to produce a supply of penicillin for a clinical trial, and from mid-1942 until the autumn of 1943, Dr S.W. Challinor and Mrs Jean MacNaughton were engaged in this task. Following the method of Florey, they grew penicillium as surface cultures on shallow layers of liquid medium in large numbers of flasks which were incubated for 10 days at 28°C in a hot room in the Wilkie Surgical Research Laboratory. Yields were low, about two units per ml, and much of this penicillin was lost in the procedures of extraction and concentration. By September 1943 their net yield was a small vial of yellow powder comprising one million units, enough to treat a single patient. Professor Learmonth used this supply to treat a patient with staphylococcal septicaemia and brain abscess, initially with great improvement. But after exhaustion of the penicillin supply, the patient died and at necroscopy showed a mixture of bacteria other than the original staphylococcus in her brain abscess.

In October 1943, Learmonth obtained part of one of the first imported batches of American commercial (Pfizer) penicillin to perform a trial of its use in the treatment of acute haematogenous osteomyelitis due to *Staphylococcus aureus*, a condition insusceptible to the available sulphonamide drugs and carrying a fatality rate of about 50% in septicaemic cases. To economise in use of the limited supply of penicillin and allow the treatment of the maximum number of patients, namely 40, Drs McAdam, Challinor and Duguid devised a method of giving the drug by continuous, small-volume intramuscular infusion (McAdam, Duguid and Challinor, 1944). This procedure maintained in the patient's blood a cidal level of penicillin for the extant strains of *Staph. aureus* with the expenditure of only 100,000 units a day, while the alternative method of three-hourly injections of 25,000 units used 200,000 units a day. The findings for 40 patients, 19 of whom were septicaemic on blood culture, were published by McAdam, the Clinical Tutor in Learmonth's unit (McAdam, 1945). Only one patient died, i.e. 5% of the septicaemic cases, and the functional outcome was generally good.

In parallel with that work, Dr Duguid made *in vitro* morphological studies of the influence of penicillin on growing bacteria of a wide range of species. He obtained evidence to suggest that penicillin exerted its effect by interfering with the synthesis of the outer supporting cell wall of the bacteria and that all species possessed the target mechanism, although in the supposedly "resistant" species a high concentration of penicillin was required to affect it. These findings were published in 1946 (Duguid, 1946) and later confirmed when J.T. Park and J.L. Strominger in the USA elucidated the biochemistry of the changes in 1957.

Further important studies on penicillin and other antibiotics were made by Dr J.C. Gould. With Dr J.H. Bowie he published in 1952 (Gould and Bowie, 1952) a comprehensive study of conditions influencing the use and reliability of the disk diffusion method of testing the antibiotic sensitivities of patients' strains of bacteria, a method first suggested by D.C. Morley in 1945. The work of Gould and Bowie popularised and standardised the use of the method in Scotland, a method on which the laboratory control of chemotherapy has mainly depended throughout the last 35 years. Subsequently, after making a series of studies of healthy nasal carriers of *Staphylococcus aureus*, Dr Gould in 1958 published observations (Gould, 1958) showing that the high incidence of penicillin-resistant staphylococci in nasal carriers among hospital staff was due to the staff inhaling and contaminating their fingers and noses with traces of spilt penicillin in the air and dust of the hospital environment. This surprising finding was confirmed by later work in Australia.

3. Airborne Infection

In 1942, Professor Mackie commissioned the construction of a "slit sampler" as designed by Bourdillon, Lidwell and Thomas (1941), an instrument that counted even the smaller bacteria-carrying particles in air with a much higher degree of efficiency (99%) than any other available sampler.

As we have noted earlier, this sampler was used (Green, Challinor and Duguid, 1945) to observe airborne infection in *HMS Caledonia,* the naval school at Rosyth, during an epidemic of scarlet fever in the autumn of 1942. Numerous particles carrying *Streptococcus pyogenes* type 1 were found in the air in a dormitory, schoolroom, recreation room and hall, the numbers reflecting the amount of bodily movements liable to disseminate dried secretion dust from clothing, and not the amount of expiratory activities such as speaking, coughing and sneezing, liable to expel secretion droplets. The significance of the latter finding lay in the different susceptibility of dust-borne and droplet-borne streptococci to the disinfecting action of propylene glycol vapour, an agent shown in the USA to reduce the transmission of the common cold among children in a residential home. Drs Challinor and Duguid showed that tolerable concentrations of the vapour killed the bacteria in freshly sprayed droplets, but not those in dried secretion dust.

Subsequently, Dr Duguid devised a technique employing the slit sampler to recover, count and measure the smaller droplets and droplet-nuclei produced in expiratory secretion spray, a majority undetected by previous methods of observation. He was thus enabled to give for the first time a comprehensive account of the numbers and size distribution of the droplets expelled by different expiratory activities and to show that pathogenic bacteria were likely to be present in only very few of the droplets small enough to remain airborne as droplet-nuclei (Duguid, 1946). In agreement with the findings for *Streptococcus pyogenes,* Drs Duguid and Wallace later showed that infection of the air with *Staphylococcus aureus* from nasal carriers was mainly due to liberation of the staphylococci in dust particles from the skin and clothing during body movements and hardly at all to the expulsion of droplet spray in sneezing (Duguid and Wallace, 1948).

4. Electron Microscopy

On return to work after a six-month convalescence from a first coronary thrombosis in late 1950, Professor Mackie became convinced that the electron microscope would become an invaluable tool in research on viruses and bacteria. He obtained funds to buy one and employ a technician to maintain it. In 1951 he sent Dr J.P. Duguid to visit the Metropolitan Vickers electron microscope development laboratory in Manchester to learn about the operation and use of the instrument. The one then in use and on sale was the EM2, a two-stage magnifier, but the EM3, a more versatile and powerful three-stage microscope, was at an advanced stage of development and Professor Mackie ordered one of the first production models. The EM3 arrived in Edinburgh in 1953 and was installed in a room on the ground floor next to the west entrance to the New Buildings. Mr George Wilson, trained in electrical and vacuum engineering at Heriot-Watt College, was appointed to maintain it.

The staff of the Bacteriology Department were at first slow in exploiting electron microscopy for the purposes of their researches. Virology was the most obvious field of application, but at that time the methods for concentrating and purifying viruses in preparations suitable for EM examinations were not well developed. Indeed, the senior virologist, Dr R.H.A. Swain, made his first EM studies not on the morphology of viruses, but on that of the pathogenic spirochaetes of the genera *Borrelia*, *Treponema* and *Leptospira*, demonstrating the number and position of their axial filaments (Swain, 1955, 1957). His colleague, Dr F.L. Constable, studied growths of the psittacosis chlamydia, then thought to be a virus, and found, contrary to the views of Professor S.P. Bedson, Britain's authority on these organisms, that their elementary bodies often reproduced by binary fission.

Dr J.P. Duguid and Miss Isabel Smith, then a PhD student, studied the flagella of a collection of strains of *Escherichia coli*. In addition to the locomotory flagella they distinguished in some strains a second, small kind of filamentous appendage which they named "fimbriae". The fimbriae were present only in those strains of the collection that three years earlier had been found by Dr G. Dempster to cause haemagglutination by virtue of their adhesiveness for red blood cells. The discovery of these new, adhesive organelles was announced at the Edinburgh meeting of the Pathological Society of Great Britain and Ireland in July 1954, and a fuller account was published in 1955 (Duguid, Smith, Dempster and Edmunds, 1955). In continuation of this work, Drs Duguid and Gillies studied the occurrence, formation and antigenic properties of the fimbriae in dysentery bacilli. They showed that the common type of fimbriae ("type 1") were adhesive for a wide variety of animal, plant and fungal cells and that their adhesiveness was completely annulled by the addition of minute concentrations of D-mannose or alpha-methyl-mannoside, suggesting that the fimbrial adhesion's receptor in animal and vegetable cells consists of mannose residues on the cells' surface polysaccharides (Duguid and Gillies, 1957).

Subsequently, Dr Duguid with D.C. Old, then studying for the PhD degree, extended observations of fimbriae to salmonellae, klebsiellae and other enterobacteria, and identified further types of fimbriae with different adhesive properties. They continued these studies after transfer to posts in the University of Dundee and reviewed the results of twenty-five years' work in an article published in 1980 (Duguid and Old, 1980). By that time research groups throughout the world were studying the adhesive properties of bacteria of all kinds with a view to defining their role in colonisation and infection.

5. Sterilisation Studies

The Edinburgh work on sterilisation merits an entry in these records. The story starts with a series of cases of post-operative tetanus that occurred in the Royal Infirmary in 1926 to 1927. At their meeting on 2 May, 1927, the Board of Managers appointed Professor Mackie to enquire into the circumstances and to submit a report. At that time there had been seven definite cases and one doubtful case of tetanus during the year from April 1926.

Mackie's meticulous work showed beyond doubt that tetanus spores and other clostridial spores were present in catgut used for surgical sutures and that the spores were highly resistant to the disinfecting and sterilising procedures then in use. Mackie noted that most of the cases followed gynaecological operations and he was "struck by the amount of catgut left in tissues in such cases . . . (e.g.) 69 inches and that usually thick gauge" (Correspondence in Departmental file). The common factor in the cases was catgut from a single source, and the series stopped when this was discontinued. Mackie went on to develop methods for the assured disinfection of catgut and to devise a rigorous sterility test for commercially prepared batches of the finished product. Thereafter, on Mackie's advice, the Scottish health authorities required the manufacturers of surgical catgut sutures to have their products disinfected by an approved method and to submit samples at intervals to an approved laboratory for sterility testing. Samples of catgut from the local manufacturers (Merson and later Ethicon) were coming to the University Bacteriology Department for testing as late as the 1960s, and Charles Smith (trained by Mackie) did the testing. This work by Mackie, starting with clinical and epidemiological research, was thus developed to the provision of a sound system of prevention and surveillance (see Mackie, 1928; Mackie, McLachlan and Anderson, 1929).

Up to 1955 in Edinburgh as in most other hospital centres, the sterilisation of surgical instruments and dressings was done independently in each surgical unit in the unit's own autoclave, installed by the hospital engineer and operated under the direction of the theatre sister. That this system was unsatisfactory was shown by a survey of hospital autoclaves made by Dr J.H. Bowie and published in 1955 (Bowie, 1955). He found that over 90% of the autoclaves by reason of faulty design, installation or operation, were incapable of assuring sterilisation of packaged goods without excessively deleterious effects. (J.P. Duguid recalls that he may have stimulated J.H.B. to make this survey by telling him he had seen sterilisation in a professorial surgical unit done in an autoclave without a thermometer and in which the pressure gauge was known to be broken. The procedure was controlled by the theatre sister admitting mains steam to the chamber for a time she *thought* sufficient!)

Bowie's publication induced others to make similar surveys in other regions and these confirmed the generally unsatisfactory state of surgical sterilisation (e.g. Howie and Timbury 1956; Medical Research Council Report, 1964). As a result, efforts were made to define the requirements of design, installation and operation of surgical autoclaves such as to assure sterilisation. To this end Bowie made important contributions, e.g. by his publications on the downward displacement autoclave (Bowie, 1957) and the automatically controlled high pre-vacuum autoclave (Bowie, 1958).

Further contributions to safety in surgery made by Bowie were the development of the Bowie-Dick autoclave tape test to indicate whether a package had been autoclaved (Bowie, Kelsey and Thomson, 1963) and development of the advantageous Edinburgh pre-sterilised "pre-set tray" system for the presentation of surgical instruments at operation (Bowie, Campbell, Gillingham and Gordon, 1963). For long, Bowie's close collaborator was his Chief Medical Laboratory Technologist, James Dick, and subsequently the latter's successor, Ian Samuel.

6. A Laboratory-Acquired Infection

Robert Oag, a Yorkshire man, joined the department as a lecturer about 1938. He was a good teacher of practical classes, organised the BSc Honours course, and gave a voluntary but well attended course on clinical bacteriology to final-year medical students. He arranged that each student should have the opportunity to perform on a cadaver the procedure of lumbar puncture, of which no other practice was given throughout the medical course. In research, he determined the previously unknown thermal death times of bacterial spores exposed to dry heat at various temperatures above 180°C, using an experimental oven borrowed from the Heriot-Watt College, and published the results in 1940.

In August 1944 he was asked to assist pathologists in the Royal Infirmary to establish the cause of death in a man just returned by air from Africa with symptoms suggestive of viral encephalitis. He dissected the remains of the brain to obtain specimens for inoculation into animals, and according to Dr Cranston Low, with whom he shared his laboratory, did so without even rudimentary care against contaminating himself. About 10 days later Dr Oag was admitted to the Royal Infirmary with speech, swallowing, eye and respiratory paralyses indicative of viral encephalitis. Apparently better after 10 days in hospital, he discharged himself so that he could accompany his family on a holiday to Devon, where on arrival he collapsed and died.

It is noteworthy that until about 1970, bacteriologists worked with dangerous pathogenic organisms without any of the elaborate safety procedures and equipment that are now mandatory. Yet there were very few infections recognised as being acquired in the laboratory; in Edinburgh up to 1960, only two non-fatal cases in addition to the fatality in Dr Oag. Dr J.P. Duguid, when an inexperienced research student, was encouraged by Professor Mackie to work with virulent cultures of anthrax and tubercle bacilli, with which he must frequently have contaminated himself. And like other bacteriologists, he frequently visited wards in the City Fever Hospital to collect specimens from patients under conditions exposing him to infection, e.g. collecting the cough spray of tuberculous patients on to slides held in his unprotected hand. Bacteriologists then relied on their natural defence and immunity mechanisms to prevent such contaminations from developing into infections.

7. Dr W. Levinthal and DNA

Dr Walter Levinthal, who spent his later years in Edinburgh, was a distinguished German bacteriologist and had held senior posts in the Robert Koch Institute, Berlin, until his arrest by the Nazis in 1933 (see Appendix D2). His contribution to the discovery of the significance of DNA will not be widely recognised. The matter is of great biomedical interest, as the following outline shows.

In 1909, the German workers Neufeld and Handel published their discovery that pneumococci have different type-specific capsules and can be classified on this basis (Neufeld and Handel, 1909). Thereafter Griffith, in London, found that it is possible to change or transform the type by suitable exposure to "type-transforming substance". Griffith was loath to publish this as he feared that others would think it incredible and suspect that he had contaminated his cultures. Neufeld then visited Griffith's laboratory and was very impressed with Griffith's type transformation experiments. On return to Berlin he and Levinthal repeated and confirmed Griffith's studies. Neufeld wrote to Griffith and urged him to publish. Unfortunately, Griffith discreetly buried his important finding in a long paper on the epidemiology of pneumococcus types; the paper was published in 1928 in the *Journal of Hygiene* (Griffith, 1928). Neufeld and Levinthal published their confirmation (in another journal) in the same year (Neufeld and Levinthal, 1928).

Avery and his co-workers, in the Rockefeller Institute for Medical Research in the USA, struggled for years to identify the chemical nature of the type-transforming substance present in killed extracts of pneumococcus and eventually identified it as DNA. This was published by Avery, MacLeod and McCarty (1944) under the title "Studies on the chemical nature of the substance inducing transformation of pneumococcus types". In their cautious discussion they went only so far as to refer to the comments of Gortner (1938) and Dobzhansky (1941) which *likened the transforming substance to a gene*. Avery's group did not themselves claim that DNA was a gene, but their discovery provided the first evidence that it was so. Later Hershey and Chase showed that the T phages of *E. coli* injected only their DNA content into the bacteria, which acted like a gene and reproduced the phage (Hershey and Chase, 1953).

These were the discoveries that established DNA as the genetic material and stimulated Watson and Crick to elucidate the mechanism of its replication.

THE CONTRIBUTION OF BACTERIOLOGISTS TO TUBERCULOSIS RESEARCH IN EDINBURGH

by Professor Sir John Crofton[143]

Mortality from tuberculosis probably reached its peak in England and Wales in the mid-nineteenth century, when it was one of the major causes of death. The Scottish peak was about ten years later. Thereafter mortality fell slowly, but relatively steadily, as standards of living improved. Elimination of susceptibles by early death, and later the isolation of many infectors in sanatoria, may have contributed.

Mortality and notification rates rose impressively in both World Wars. In the 1939-45 war the increase in Scotland was dramatic. Moreover, almost uniquely in Europe, Scottish rates continued to rise after the war until 1950. Before the introduction of streptomycin in 1947, followed by PAS in 1948 and isoniazid in 1952, about half of all new cases of pulmonary tuberculosis died from the disease. Tuberculous meningitis was always fatal and miliary tuberculosis almost always.

Research in Edinburgh

The University Department of Tuberculosis, first under Professor Charles Cameron and, from 1952, with Professor John Crofton and his colleagues, Drs Norman Horne, Ian Ross, Ian Grant and James Williamson, participated in the now classical co-operative controlled trials initiated by the Medical Research Council in 1947. The first trial was of streptomycin in the treatment of advanced pulmonary tuberculosis. This was the first scientific controlled therapeutic trial of any kind in man since James Lind's study of lemon juice in scurvy in the eighteenth century.

When streptomycin was used alone, although there was usually rapid initial response, the trial showed that many patients later relapsed. It was then found that their tubercle bacilli had become resistant to the drug. With the introduction of PAS in 1948 and isoniazid in 1952, later MRC controlled trials showed that resistance could usually be prevented by the right combinations of drugs. The criteria for successful treatment were, of course, clinical improvement and for pulmonary tuberculosis, radiological evidence of improvement. But by far the most important criterion was the conversion of the patient's sputum from positive to negative for tubercle bacilli, both by smear and culture. Equally important was the detailed testing of positive cultures for drug resistance.

Dr Archie Wallace[144] was the consultant bacteriologist at the City Hospital laboratory. Already carrying an enormous load of routine bacteriology, tuberculous and non-tuberculous, he applied all his talents for meticulous, painstaking and devoted work to these new challenges, giving wonderful support to his clinical colleagues and working very long hours. He inspired his own team with equal enthusiasm. Later he supplied the bacteriological back-up for the Edinburgh component of successive co-operative controlled trials, conducted through the Scottish Tuberculosis (later Scottish Thoracic) Society. These were the first to show that, with good chemotherapy, bed rest was unnecessary in milder forms of tuberculosis; that chemotherapy could prevent breakdown of doubtfully active lesions; that high dosage isoniazid (as claimed by some American workers) was unnecessary; and that, although corticosteroids plus chemotherapy produced initial improvement in well-being and X-ray changes, they had no effect on the rate of sputum conversion and, as assessed after a year, patients treated with chemotherapy alone had made just as good progress.

Probably the most important contribution of the Edinburgh group was the detailed in-depth study of apparent failures of chemotherapy. At that time, when knowledge was only being slowly gleaned, much previous chemotherapy had been

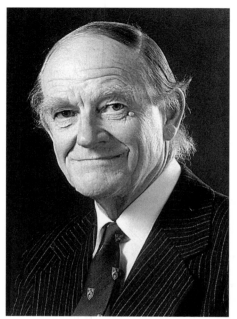

143. *Emeritus Professor Sir John Crofton*

144. *Dr Archie Wallace*

145. *Dr Sheila Stewart*

146. *William Webber*

poor by later standards. There had been many failures. Clinicians and bacteriologists of the Edinburgh group held detailed weekly sessions on such patients. At these sessions, clinical, X-ray and bacteriological progress was meticulously reviewed and further bacteriological work carried out if necessary. From these joint studies it became clear that virtually all failures to arrest pulmonary tuberculosis by chemotherapy were due to drug resistance. But it was also found that careful use of correct combinations of drugs could prevent this acquired resistance. It was also discovered that a few patients had been infected with primarily resistant bacilli. Treating these with only two drugs could be equivalent to giving one drug alone and could result in additional resistance to a second drug. Primary resistance to two or more drugs was very rare. Consequently, to prevent failure due to primary resistance, it became routine in Edinburgh always to initiate treatment with at least three drugs. Eventually, this practice was accepted worldwide.

Up to that time tuberculosis had been notoriously a relapsing disease. It was soon found that chemotherapy could prevent the disastrous local spread of infection which had led surgeons to abandon resection of lung lesions. Subsequently, resectional surgery was widely practised in an attempt to prevent relapse. Because of the large numbers of patients in Edinburgh, they often had to wait many months for surgery. This gave the opportunity to determine the viability and drug resistance of residual tubercle bacilli in lesions resected after various periods of chemotherapy. Meticulous studies by Dr Sheila Stewart[145] and Dr Derrick Turnbull demonstrated a steady decrease in culture positivity with duration of chemotherapy. They found a very low positivity rate in patients who had received a year or more of treatment and no positives in those who had received therapy for eighteen months or more. No resistant bacilli were isolated from patients whose organisms had been initially sensitive and who had received reliable drug combinations. Simultaneous analysis of the relapse rates after various periods of chemotherapy showed remarkable accord with the positivity rates in resected lungs. Eighteen months' chemotherapy therefore became the standard practice. (The development of newer antimycobacterial drugs has enabled this period to be shortened.)

These studies laid the foundation for the claims by the Edinburgh group that 100% arrest of disease was a reasonable aim in patients with pulmonary tuberculosis caused by initially sensitive organisms. It was further claimed that treatment for eighteen months or more should prevent relapse in virtually all cases. For a number of years the claims were disbelieved, both internationally and in the UK. Indeed the Edinburgh group were sometimes accused of fiddling their figures! Eventually the group, with the close support of two French bacteriologists, Drs Noel Rist and Georges Canetti of the Pasteur Institute in Paris, persuaded the International Union Against Tuberculosis to test the claims by a co-operative trial in twenty-two countries. To avoid accusations of bias the trial was carefully co-ordinated by Dr Regi Bignall at the Brompton Hospital in London. The report in 1964 fully confirmed the Edinburgh claims which thereafter were generally accepted.

Effect of the Research on Services for Tuberculosis

One of the exciting aspects of this combined clinical and bacteriological research was that its results could be immediately applied in practice. From 1954 the group became responsible for all tuberculosis in Edinburgh, in-patient and out-patient. In the city at that time there were almost 1,000 new notifications a year, 600 beds for tuberculosis and 400 patients on the waiting list, many with a positive sputum and probably infecting others while they waited. By good organisation and by applying research results rapidly in practice, the waiting list disappeared within a year. To everyone's astonishment, a previously steadily increasing notification rate was more than halved within three years, a rapidity of improvement which has never been exceeded anywhere. Thereafter there was a steady decrease to a negligible rate, mainly due to breakdowns in elderly patients infected during the high prevalence era.

The group inherited many multiresistant patients. Many others were referred from elsewhere. Even with the very limited reserve drugs then available, the careful bacteriological studies of Drs Wallace and Stewart, together with surgery when indicated, enabled the group to salvage about half the patients. And of course, Edinburgh clinicians had by then learned how to prevent new drug resistance. So drug resistance soon ceased to be a local problem (though sadly, it is still a major problem in many countries).

The City Hospital laboratory did much reference work for others, as the Edinburgh group were consulted about patients at home and abroad and were training clinicians from many countries. For a number of years Dr Wallace's laboratory did all the drug resistance tests for Libya. When he retired he spent three years in Libya setting up an excellent tuberculosis laboratory there. His influence led to a high standard of treatment of the disease in that country.

Conclusion

Dr Archie Wallace and Dr Sheila Stewart made major contributions both to the classical initial trials of antituberculosis chemotherapy by the British Medical Research Council, and to the subsequent trials by the Scottish Tuberculosis (later Thoracic) Society and, above all, to the detailed studies by the Edinburgh group* which helped to establish the best methods of achieving virtually 100% cure without relapse in newly diagnosed patients with pulmonary tuberculosis. They also helped to establish the best methods of carrying out the often very tricky tests for drug resistance. Their influence was worldwide. At the time of writing, the City Hospital laboratory includes the Mycobacteria Reference Laboratory for Scotland.

---

* Our photographs show some of the key workers concerned in the laboratory aspects of these studies[143,144,145,146].

STAFF AND ASSOCIATES OF THE UNIVERSITY DEPARTMENT OF MEDICAL MICROBIOLOGY

1. Robert Irvine Chair of Bacteriology

Professor James Ritchie: Appointed 1913. Died in office 1923.

Born at Duns on 5 August 1864. Graduated MA Edinburgh University 1884. MBChB (Honours) 1888. House Surgeon to Professor John Chiene who established early bacteriology laboratory in the Department of Surgery. Gained BSc in Public Health 1889. In 1889 took post in surgical practice in Oxford with Mr Horatio Symonds, FRCS (Edin.). After working and teaching in Radcliffe Infirmary Pathology and Bacteriology laboratories, appointed Professor of Pathology in Oxford 1902. He was awarded MD (Gold Medal) by Edinburgh University in 1895.

Appointed in 1907 to post of Superintendent of the Royal College of Physicians' Laboratory, Edinburgh. In 1913 appointed to Chair of Bacteriology. For a further seven years during World War I he retained the RCP post, while also occupying the Chair. From 1914 to 1922, Bacteriologist to The Royal Hospital for Sick Children. Co-author with Professor Robert Muir, the University's first formal lecturer in Pathological Bacteriology, of *A Manual of Bacteriology,* 1897. Died 28 January 1923.

Inaugural Address

"The Development of Bacteriology and the Place it Occupies amongst the Sciences".. Delivered 7 October 1913. Published in *Edin Med J* 1913; **11**: 388-394.

Professor Thomas Jones Mackie: Appointed 1923. Died in office 1955.

Born at Hamilton 5 June 1888. Graduated MBChB (Honours) 1910, at Glasgow University and gained DPH in 1913 at Oxford. Held research posts in Pathology Department of Glasgow University and Western Infirmary under Professor Robert Muir. In 1914 he joined staff of Bland Sutton Institute of the Middlesex Hospital as assistant bacteriologist. During World War I served as Officer in Charge of various military laboratories notably at Gallipoli and Alexandria. Awarded MD, with Bellahouston and Straits Settlement Gold Medal by Glasgow University in 1921. In 1917 appointed first Wernher-Beit Professor of Bacteriology, University of Cape Town. For short period also acted as Professor of Pathology there.

Upon the death of Professor James Ritchie in 1923, in the same year was appointed his successor. Co-author of Mackie & McCartney's *An Introduction to Practical Bacteriology* published in 1925. The book ran to nine editions in his lifetime. With C.H. Browning, T.J. Mackie also revised the 8th edition of Muir & Ritchie's *Manual of Bacteriology* in 1927 and this text went on to be known in its 11th edition in 1949 as "Browning & Mackie". In 1942, Professor Mackie received the honour of CBE and in 1947, Glasgow University conferred on him the honorary degree of LL.D. He died on 6 October 1955.

Inaugural Address

"An address on the present position of Medical Bacteriology". Delivered 11 October 1923, Published in *Br Med J* 1923; **2**: 1241-1246.

Professor Robert Cruickshank: Appointed 1958. Retired 1966.

Born near Aberdeen on 26 September 1899. Graduated MBChB (Honours) Aberdeen University 1922. As postgraduate spent two years at Pathology Department, Glasgow University and Western Infirmary with Professor Robert Muir and Professor

Carl Browning. In 1923 graduated MD with Honours and worked at Royal Hospital for Sick Children and Belvedere Hospital, Glasgow. Gained DPH at Glasgow in 1926. After one year as a Cancer Research Fellow in Aberdeen, was appointed lecturer in Bacteriology at Glasgow University and Bacteriologist to Glasgow Royal Infirmary in 1928. In 1936 appointed to the London County Council group laboratory at the North Western Fever Hospital. When the Central Public Health Laboratory was established at Colindale in 1946, appointed Director, remaining there for three years. In 1949 invited to succeed Sir Alexander Fleming in Chair of Bacteriology, St. Mary's Hospital Medical School and in 1955 became Principal of the Wright-Fleming Institute of Microbiology.

When Professor Mackie died in 1955, after an inter-regnum of three years, Professor Cruickshank was appointed to the Chair. He was honoured by the award of the CBE in 1966 and was awarded an Honorary LL.D. by Aberdeen University in 1968. He was editor of *Modern Trends in Immunology I* in 1963 and co-editor, with D.M. Weir, of *Modern Trends in Immunology II*, Butterworths, London, 1967. He was editor-in-chief of the 10th edition of Mackie & McCartney's *Handbook of Bacteriology* published by Livingstone, Edinburgh & London, in 1960. This book appeared as Cruickshank's *Medical Microbiology* in its 11th edition in 1965 with reprints that endorsed its success in 1968, 1969, 1970 and 1972. The 12th edition, edited by R. Cruickshank, J.P. Duguid, B.P. Marmion and R.H.A. Swain, appeared in two volumes: Vol. 1 in 1973 and Vol. II in 1975, just after Professor Cruickshank's death. When Professor Cruickshank retired in 1966 he set up a new Department of Social and Preventive Medicine in Kingston, Jamaica. While holding this post he travelled widely in the West Indies and South America advising on the setting up of public health laboratories. Professor Cruickshank died on 16 August, 1974.

Inaugural Address

"New Horizons in Microbiology". Delivered 17 January 1958. Published in *Univ Edin J* 1958-60; **19**: 93-102.

Professor Barrie P. Marmion: Appointed 1968. Resigned 1978.

Born 1920 in Alverstone, Hants. Graduated University College and Hospital, London: MBBS; MD 1947, DSc 1963. FRCPath 1962, FRCP(A) 1964, FRCP(E) 1970, FRACP 1984, FRSE. Bacteriologist, Public Health Laboratory Service, Leeds, 1943-62. Rockefeller Travelling Fellow, Walter and Eliza Institute, Melbourne, Australia 1951-52. Foundation Professor of Microbiology, Monash University, Melbourne, 1962-68.

When Professor Cruickshank retired in 1966 there was a second inter-regnum until 1968 when Professor Marmion was appointed to the Chair and as Chief Bacteriologist, Royal Infirmary of Edinburgh. He was co-editor of Cruickshank's *Medical Microbiology* (12th edition) and co-editor of Mackie & McCartney's *Medical Microbiology* (13th edition), Vols. I and II.

On his resignation in 1978 he retired to Australia to become Director of Division of Virology, Institute of Medical and Veterinary Science, Adelaide, 1978-85 and Clinical Professor (Virology) in the Department of Microbiology and Immunology. He was honoured by Special Election to the Fellowship of the Royal Australasian College of Physicians in 1984. Appointed Visiting Professor in the Department of Pathology, 1985. On May 1 1990, the degree of Doctor of the University, University of Adelaide, Australia, was conferred on him in recognition of his distinguished service to the University.

Inaugural Address

"What Kind of Microbiology?". Delivered 17 February 1969. Inaugural Lecture No. 60 lodged in Erskine Medical Library, George Square, Edinburgh.

Professor J. Gerald Collee: Appointed 1978. Retired 1991.

Born Bo'ness, West Lothian, 10 May 1929. Graduated University of Edinburgh. MBChB 1951; MD (Gold Medal) 1962; FRCPath, FRCP(E). During National Service was RAMC officer with 5th Royal Northumberland Fusiliers at Newcastle. After assistantship in general practice in Shropshire, joined University Bacteriology Department staff as lecturer in 1955. In 1963/64 was WHO Visiting Professor of Bacteriology, Baroda Medical College, India. On his return in 1964 appointed Senior Lecturer and subsequently Consultant Bacteriologist, S.E. Scotland Regional Hospital Board (now Lothian Health Board). Professor Collee was awarded a Personal Chair (Bacteriology) in 1974.

In 1979 he became the Robert Irvine Professor of Bacteriology; Chief Bacteriologist, Royal Infirmary of Edinburgh; Consultant Adviser in Microbiology, Scottish Home and Health Department; first Convener University Safety Committee. Formerly Senior Editor and Chairman of Editorial Board, *Journal of Medical Microbiology*. Member of Editorial Board of *A Companion to Medical Studies* (Blackwell); Co-editor of Mackie and McCartney's *Practical Medical Microbiology* (13th edition, Vol. II) 1989. Awarded CBE 1991. Retired 1991. Elected FRS(E) 1993.

Inaugural Address

"Medical Microbiology: Opportunities, Challenges and Degrees of Freedom". Delivered 24 April 1975. (Then Personal Chair). Inaugural Lecture No. 59 lodged in Erskine Medical Library, George Square, Edinburgh.

Personal Chair: Professor Donald M. Weir: Appointed 1983.

Born in Edinburgh, 16 September 1928. Graduated University of Edinburgh MBChB 1955; MD (Gold Medal) 1962; FRCP(E) 1981. Research Fellow, MRC Rheumatic Research Unit, Taplow. Joined University Bacteriology Department staff as Lecturer in 1961; Senior Lecturer 1967; Reader 1978; appointed to Personal Chair of Microbial Immunology, 1983; Honorary Consultant, Lothian Health Board. Editor of *Handbook of Experimental Immunology*, 4th edition (1986); Author of *Immunology: Student Notes,* 6th edition (1988); *Aids to Immunology,* 1st edition (1986); *Principles of Infection and Immunity in Patient Care* (with C.C. Blackwell).

Inaugural Address

"Friends, Foes and Phagocytes". Delivered 8 May 1984. Lodged as a mimeographed typescript in Erskine Medical Library, George Square, Edinburgh.

2. Biographical Details of Former Staff of the University Department of Medical Microbiology, and Certain Staff of Other Edinburgh Microbiological Laboratories

Key to Abbreviations and Layout

BORN	:	Place/date, if known.
GRAD.	:	University of original graduation: degrees: later degrees: learned societies.
P.G.	:	Postgraduate appointments.
J.D.	:	Joined the University Department, etc.
SUB.	:	Subsequent appointments after leaving Department.
S.I.	:	Special interests.
AUTH.	:	Authorship of books or editorship of textbooks/journals.
HONOURS	:	viz. CBE, Knighthood, etc.
RETIRED	:	Date, if known.
DIED	:	Date, if known.

ALEXANDER, Dr William A.

GRAD.	:	1912: University of Edinburgh MBChB.
		1927: FRCP(E).
P.G.	:	1920-24: Assistant Pathologist, RIE.
J.D.	:	1926-27: Lecturer.
SUB.	:	1925-32: Physician RHSC. Later, Edinburgh physician of note.
		1951-53: President, RCP(E).

ALLAN, Mrs Margaret (née Kelly)

GRAD	:	1948: University of Edinburgh, BSc (Hons.).
P.G.	:	Assistant in Fife District Bacteriological Laboratory, Cameron Bridge.
J.D.	:	1950-52: Demonstrator/Research Assistant.
		1961: Moved to Wolverhampton when her husband, Dr W.A. Allan, was appointed Consultant Haematologist to the Royal Hospital.
DIED	:	1988.

ALLAN, Dr. William S.A.

GRAD.	:	1947: University of Edinburgh MBChB
		1974: FRCP(E)
J.D.	:	1953: Lecturer, Research Assistant, Bacteriology Department, RIE.
S.I.	:	In collaboration with Dr J.C. Gould, carried out studies on prevention of staphylococcal infections, treatment of carriers and staphylococcal cross-infection.
SUB.	:	Pathology Department, Western General Hospital, Edinburgh, and Medical School.
		1961: Consultant Haematologist, Royal Hospital, Wolverhampton.

ALSTON, Dr James Maxwell

BORN	:	London
EDUC.	:	George Watson's College, Edinburgh, After leaving school, during First World War joined Royal Flying Corps.
GRAD.	:	1924: University of Edinburgh, MBChB (Hons.).

	1948: MD (Gold Medal)
	1952: FRCP(E).
	1966: FCPath.

J.D.   : 1924: Vans Dunlop-Scholar. Assistant.

SUB.   : 1927: Commonwealth Fund scholarship, Harvard Medical School.
1933: Head of Archway Group Laboratory, London County Council.

S.I.   : At Edinburgh, studies on leptospirosis and filterability of tubercle bacillus. At Archway Group Laboratory, notable for his studies of leptospirosis which he had continued since 1930. With J.C. Broom became an authority on this disease.

AUTH.   : *Leptospirosis in Man and Animals* with J.C. Broom, E. & S. Livingstone, 1959. *A New Look at Infectious Disease,* Pitman, 1967.

DIED   : 1990.

AMOS, William McG.G.

J.D.   : 1959: Trained in enteric and food bacteriology, shigella typing and immunology. In course of food examination, involved in the isolation of *S. typhi* strain from canned corned beef that confirmed the findings concerning the source of the serious Aberdeen typhoid outbreak in 1964.
1964-76: Worked in Immunology Laboratory.
1967: Awarded Fellowship of IMLS for thesis on "The extraction of mycological antigens and their use in serological techniques as an aid to the diagnosis of bronchial disorders caused by fungi".
1967-76: Senior MLSO in Immunology Lab. Assisted in undergraduate and Honours teaching.
1968: Accepted as postgraduate student at Edinburgh University. This was the first occasion when the University approved of the entry of a full-time member of the technical staff who had neither formal and existing entrance qualifications nor a degree from another University. This was a precedent for other UK Universities.
1972: Awarded MSc for thesis on "Immunological aspects of *Aspergillus fumigatus*".

SUB.   : 1976: Chief, then Senior Chief MLSO, Immunology Department, Raigmore Hospital, Inverness. Served on various educational bodies and member of professional societies. Primarily responsible for establishment of Special Examination in Immunology for the IMLS.
1975-83: Chief IMLS Examiner in Immunology.
Experienced mountaineer – deputy leader of Dundonell Mountain Rescue Team.

AUTH.   : *Basic Immunology,* Butterworth, 1982.

ANDERSON, Dr Cameron G.

BORN   : 1904

GRAD.   : 1926: University of Birmingham, BSc (Hons).
1929: University of Birmingham, PhD.
1930: Diploma in Bacteriology (London).

P.G.   : 1928: McGill University, Montreal, Research Fellowship.
1929: London School of Hygiene and Tropical Medicine (Diploma

in Bacteriology).

1930: Lecturer in Biochemistry Department, London School of Hygiene and Tropical Medicine.

J.D.   : 1935: First Lewis Cameron Teaching Fellow: Developed course in Bacteriological Chemistry.

SUB.   : 1938: Wellcome Physiological Research Laboratory, Bacteriology Department.

1947: South African Institute of Medical Research, Johannesburg, Biochemistry Department Serum and Vaccine Laboratories.

S.I.   : London School of Hygiene and Tropical Medicine. Worked with Professor Raistrick on fungal and bacterial carbohydrates.

Edinburgh University. Chemistry and Immunity; Gastric mucin and pathogenicity of meningococcus and other organisms; cataphoresis and erythrocytes.

AUTH.   : *Introduction to Bacteriological Chemistry*. E. & S. Livingstone, 1938.

RETIRED   : 1976.

ANDERSON, Miss Nan P.H.

BORN   : 1934.

J.D.   : 1950: General training.

1955: virology laboratory, eventually Senior MLSO there until joining staff of Department of Microbiology, Faculty of Medicine, University of Toronto, becoming a Senior Tutor in this department.

S.I.   : Electron microscopy. Diagnostic virology and virology research.

AUTH.   : *Electron Microscopy in Diagnostic Virology*, with Frances W. Doane. Cambridge University Press, 1987.

ANNAT, Douglas, FIMLS

BORN   : 1921

J.D.   : 1936: General training.

1939: World War II, RAMC Scottish Command Laboratory, University Bacteriology Department, District Laboratory, Lahore, India, Bengal, Assam.

1946: Returned to Department. Research Assistant with Dr A.J. McCabe; in charge of Preparation Room.

1953: Senior Medical Laboratory Technologist, Municipal Hospitals Laboratory at Northern General Hospital.

1961: Appointed Senior Chief Medical Laboratory Scientific Officer, General Microbiological Laboratories, Western General Hospital.

DIED   : In post, November 1981.

ARMSTRONG, Douglas, FIMLS

BORN   : 1925, Edinburgh.

J.D.   : 1940: Worked with Dr S.W. Challinor on bacteriological chemistry. General bacteriological training.

SUB.   : 1942: Assistant Chemist, Dr A. Scott-Dodd, Edinburgh City Analyst.

1945: Laboratory Assistant, Royal Navy.

1947: Blood Transfusion Service, Edinburgh; Analytical Chemist with Truman's Brewery, London; Senior Research Technician, BTS

Edinburgh; Stirling Area Laboratory Services; Assistant Chief Technologist, Hamilton General Hospital, Hamilton, Ontario; and other Canadian and USA appointments; Coulter Electronics Inc., Hialeah, Florida, Tech. Met. Path. Inc., Florida.

ATACK, William Norman

BORN : 10 June 1944.

Norman Atack was trained as a technician in the University Pathology Department from 1960 to 1966. He passed the Intermediate Examination of the Institute of Medical Laboratory Technology in 1966. Breaking off to spend two years as Assistant Manager of "The Old Howgate Inn" near Penicuik, he returned to laboratory work as a senior Medical Laboratory Technician in the Nuffield Unit for Animal Pathology, Royal (Dick) Veterinary College, Edinburgh.

In 1970, Norman joined the staff of the University Bacteriology Department. Following general experience in various techniques he was appointed in charge of thin section cutting and the cutting and viewing of bacterial and viral preparations for electron microscopy; the production of EM micrographs for publication; and the training of technicians and also medical and science graduates in EM techniques. He also served as a senior MLSO in the Diagnostic Virology Laboratory, gaining experience in virus isolation, serology by complement fixation tests, and hepatitis testing. From 1972 to 1978, he lectured and demonstrated in microbiology evening classes at Napier College of Science and Technology.

In 1982, Norman took up the post of Head Technician in the Virology Department, Public Health Laboratories, Kuwait. He trained and supervised staff in clinical virology. He was for a period in charge of the virology laboratory, supervised by a visiting medical consultant. In 1986 he had total responsibility for hepatitis and AIDS testing. He was a lecturer and demonstrator in Virology and Allied Sciences, Faculty of Medicine, Kuwait University. Norman contributed to several publications on hepatitis; rabies, rubella and hepatitis A.

In July 1990, shortly after returning to Kuwait from leave in Scotland, Iraq invaded Kuwait. Norman spent two months in hiding. On September 30 1990, he died of spontaneous gastro-intestinal haemorrhage due to peptic ulceration. His body was brought home to be interred in Mount Vernon Cemetery, Edinburgh.

BAILLIE, Andrew

BORN : Edinburgh.

J.D. : 1930: After general training, in charge of medium preparation room.

1938: Resigned to take up post with Sudan Medical Service in Khartoum.

1942: Appointed Senior Technical Officer in charge of routine Diagnostic Laboratory of Biological Institute of Evans Medical Supplies, Runcorn.

1945: Bacteriologist and mycologist in Research and Development section of ICI, Nobel Division, Stevenson, Ayrshire.

RETIRED : 1975: Consultant bacteriologist with small firm at Ledbury specialising in toxicology.

BARCLAY, Dr. Grizel (née Borthwick)

GRAD. : 1932: Edinburgh University, BSc.
         1935: PhD, (studies for this degree carried out mainly in Berlin).
P.G.   : Short period on departmental staff working on anaerobes.
SUB.   : Posts in Bristol and Leeds. World War II: emergency Medical Service Laboratory, Birmingham. After several years interval: Regional Virus Laboratory, East Birmingham Hospital. Member of influenza research team. Dr Barclay's father was Captain A.E. Borthwick, RSA. Amongst his many portraits was one of Professor T.J. Mackie.

BARR, Robert

BORN   : 1890, Edinburgh.
         1904: Began as "lab. boy" in Royal College of Physicians' Laboratory, Forrest Road with Willie Watson.
         1913: Appointed Senior Laboratory Assistant in Royal Infirmary of Edinburgh Bacteriology Laboratory, under Dr W. Logan. During World War I, served in RAMC at Guy's Hospital, London. In RIE laboratory, responsible for routine diagnostic bacteriological and serological techniques. Taught in PBLAA evening classes. Participated in various research projects. Appointed Senior Chief Medical Laboratory Technologist. Awarded Life Membership of the Institute of Medical Laboratory Technology.
RETIRED : 1955.
DIED   : 1964.

BEATTIE, Professor Colin P.

BORN   : 1902: Oban
GRAD. : 1922: University of Edinburgh, MA.
         1928: MBChB.
         1930: FRC Path.
J.D.   : 1930: Lecturer in charge of Bacteriology Diagnostic Laboratory. Scholarship, Rockefeller Institute, USA.
SUB.   : 1937: Professor of Bacteriology, Royal Faculty of Medicine, Iraq, and Director of Government Bacteriology Laboratory, Baghdad.
         1946: Professor of Bacteriology, Sheffield: Retired.
S.I.   : Brucellosis; typhus (with J.H. Bowie on British troops in Baghdad during World War II); toxoplasmosis (leading authority); early virology laboratory (Sheffield); pioneering work on influenza.
AUTH. : *Toxoplasmosis of Animals and Man,* Joint author with J.P. Dubey. CAB International, 1988.
DIED   : July, 1987.

BEATTIE, Dr May (née Christison)

BORN   : Edinburgh, 1908.
GRAD. : 1929 University of British Columbia, BA.
         1929-30: Part-time, Bacteriology Department, University, British Columbia, Vancouver.
J.D.   : 1932: PhD. Then nine months at Reichsgesundheitsamt, Berlin.

Returned to Edinburgh University Bacteriology Department, Assistant in Diagnostic Laboratory. Two year course in anatomy prior to studying medicine. Discontinued.

SUB. : 1937: Married Dr C.P. Beattie who was appointed to Chair of Bacteriology, Royal Faculty of Medicine, Iraq, and Director, Government Bacteriology Laboratory, Baghdad. During World War II Mrs Beattie was evacuated to India. Served as bacteriologist to Mission Hospital in Miraj.

1946: Returned with Professor Beattie.

S.I. : In University Bacteriology Department carried out many studies, some in collaboration with Dr Helen Wright, on diphtheria types and carriers. See "Extramural Activities" below.

BEGBIE, Dr Ralph S.

GRAD. : University of Edinburgh, MBChB.
1923: DPH.
1931: MD.
J.D. : 1928-29.
1929: Early studies on BCG.
DIED : In China.

BERTRAM, William

BORN : 1922, Edinburgh.
J.D. : 1937: General basic training.
1939: World War II, RAMC, general laboratory studies.
1945: Returned to University department.
SUB. : 1947: Appointed to post as Medical Laboratory Technician in hospital attached to a copper mine in Mufilira, then N. Rhodesia.
1951: Peel Hospital laboratory for six months. Appointed Chief Medical Laboratory Technician, Falkirk Royal Infirmary.
1976: Appointed Principal MLSO at Monklands Hospital, Lanarkshire. Played important part in the work of the Institute of Medical Laboratory Technology (later IML Sciences) and was member of Council, 1963-74.
HONOURS : 1981: Awarded MBE.
RETIRED : 1984.
DIED : 1985.

BEVERIDGE, Dr William J. (1940-42)

GRAD. : 1932: BA (Cantab); LRCP/LRCS (Edin); DPH (Glasg.).
J.D. : Briefly Assistant Bacteriologist, Royal Infirmary of Edinburgh.
S.I. : Syphilis serology, in particular early studies on the Kahn Verification Test.

BISSET, Dr Kenneth A.

GRAD. : 1937: University of Edinburgh BSc (Bact. Hons).
1939: PhD.
1950: DSc.
J.D. : 1937: Demonstrator. Bacteriologist to Salmon Fishery Board, Scotland. World War II, Royal Marines, Africa, Sicily, W. Europe.

SUB.	: 1946: Bacteriology Department, University of Birmingham. 1966: Head of above Department.
S.I.	: Smooth – rough colony variation; bacterial morphology and life cycles; oral flora; immunology of fish.
AUTH.	: *The Cytology and Life History of Bacteria,* E. & S. Livingstone. 1949, 1955, 1970). *Bacteria: An Elementary Text Book,* Livingstone, 1952. *The Microbial Flora of the Mouth,* with G.H.G. Davis, Heywood & Co., 1960. Broadcaster and writer for non-medical publications.
HONS.	: 1970: Gold Medal of Merit by President of Italy for services to Italian medicine.
RETIRED	: 1979.

BOISSARD, Dr Guy P.B.

GRAD.	: University College, London. 1938: BSc (Hons) Physiology. 1951: MB, BS. 1954: Dip. Bact.
P.G.	: On the outbreak of World War II in 1939, Boissard was working in Brisbane, Australia, and joined the Australian Navy. On account of his qualification in physiology he was detailed by the naval authorities to study the physiological effects on submarine and gunboat personnel of the firing of torpedoes, viz. consequences of "kick back" etc.; and relation of distance of submarine to the ship which was the target. After the war, Boissard entered upon the study of medicine. Following graduation, he worked in the London School of Hygiene and he worked in London later in the Virus Reference Laboratory at Colindale. His special interest was in poliomyelitis.
J.D.	: 1959: Lecturer, Virus Laboratory.
SUB.	: 1961: In charge of Wellcome Virus Research Laboratory, Edinburgh City Hospital. Later, in the same year, resigned to take up post with Burroughs Wellcome.
DIED	: 1978.

BOOG-WATSON, Dr William N.

GRAD.	: 1923: University of Edinburgh, MBChB.
J.D.	: 1924.
SUB.	: Studied tuberculosis at Lausanne and Tor-na-Dee Sanatorium, Aberdeenshire. 1942: Joined Edinburgh School Health Service, becoming Chief Executive School Medical Officer from 1950-62.
DIED	: 1973, April.

BOTT, Henry

1920-29: After service in the First World War in West Yorkshire Rifles, joined Royal Army Medical Corps working in bacteriology, serology and parasitology.

1929: Appointed technician in Usher Institute, working with Professor Lelean, and with some contact with Professor T.J. Mackie. Duties included bacteriology,

involving preparation of teaching material etc.; research included work on dysentery phage typing. Assistant to Colonel Langrishe and Colonel Morrison. Worked with Professor Sir John Brotherstone.
1963: Retired officially, but continued in post until 1968.
DIED   : 1972.

BOWIE, Dr John H.

BORN   : 1909, Edinburgh.
GRAD.   : 1934: Edinburgh University MBChB.
P.G.   : 1936: Indian Medical Service, MO 20th Lancers and 1/3 Gurkhas.
                1940: Senior Pathologist, Military Hospital, Dehra Dun, and adviser in pathology Eastern Command, India; formed Army in India penicillin research team; developed Secunderabad apparatus for small volume injections of penicillin.
                1948: Lecturer in bacteriology, University of Sheffield.
J.D.   : 1949: Senior Lecturer and Consultant Bacteriologist to RIE under Professor T.J. Mackie.
S.I.   : Typhus in India with Professor C.P. Beattie; with Dr J.C. Gould, pioneering controls for antibiotic sensitivity testing; world authority on hospital sterilisation practice and design, introduced new processes; with J. Dick pioneered Bowie-Dick Test for monitoring high prevacuum steriliser performance; developed Edinburgh Tray System for supply of sterile instruments to operating theatres; awarded Fellowship, RCS(E) and RCP(E), FRCPath.
HONOURS : Kaiser-i-Hind Silver Medal from Indian Government for penicillin work.
RETIRED   : 1976 to live in Zimbabwe.
DIED   : 1984, April

BRENNAN, John

BORN   : 1925, Edinburgh.
J.D.   : 1940: General training. In charge of various sections of the department. Also in virology, gaining FIMLS in this subject.
                1963-64: Worked on Baroda project. Latterly technician in charge of the GP Diagnostic Laboratory until this was transferred to the RIE Bacteriology Laboratory. Technical charge of Research and Development Laboratory Chief MLSO.
DIED   : 1976, as a result of a car accident.

BROWN, Dr Peter P.

BORN   : 1925: October.
GRAD.   : 1951: University of London, MBBS.
                1951: MRCS(Lond.).
                1961: Diploma in Bacteriology.
                1975: FRCPath.
P.G.   : 1956-57: Medical Registrar, University Cottage Hospital, Ibadan.
                1957-61: Research Officer, West African Council for Medical Research.
J.D.   : 1961: Lecturer.
SUB.   : 1963: Consultant in Clinical Pathology, Regional Thoracic Centre,

Papworth Hospital.

1966: Consultant Microbiologist, Queen Elizabeth Medical Centre, Birmingham Area Health Authority.

1977-78: Visiting Professor of Microbiology, Medical Schools of Baghdad and Accra.

S.I.   : Pulmonary tuberculosis; bacterial resistance; ethylene oxide sterilisation; on-line computer system for hospital bacteriology.

RETIRED   : 1989, June.

BROWN, Dr T. Gow

BORN   : 1902.

GRAD.   : 1927: University of Edinburgh, MBChB.

1929: DPH.

1944: MD.

1965: FRCP(Glas.).

J.D.   : 1929.

SUB.   : 1930: Bacteriologist, County of Lanark.

DIED   : 1985, November.

See "Extra Mural Activities" below.

BUCHANAN, Dr George

GRAD.   : 1918: University of Edinburgh MBChB.

1924: DPH.

1925: MD.

J.D.   : 1925-26.

SUB   : Assistant Clinical Pathologist, Royal Infirmary of Edinburgh.

Assistant in Edinburgh University Pathology Department and Assistant Bacteriologist, Royal Infirmary of Edinburgh laboratory (no date).

House Physician, Crichton Royal Infirmary, Dumfries.

Subsequently Superintendent, South African Institute for Medical Research, Johannesburg.

BURRELL, Professor Christopher J.

BORN   : 1941, November.

GRAD.   : 1962: University of Sydney, BSc(Med).

1964: MBBS.

1977: PhD, Department of Microbiology, John Curtin School for Medical Research, Australian National University, MRCPath (UK).

1980: FRCP(A).

J.D.   : 1971.

1973: Lecturer.

1973-79: Honorary Registrar in Bacteriology, RIE.

SUB.   : 1979: Medical Specialist, Division of Medical Virology, Institute of Medical and Veterinary Sciences, Adelaide.

1984: Consultant Specialist in Virology, Royal Adelaide Hospital, Adelaide Children's Hospital and Queen Victoria Hospital.

1985: Senior Director, Division of Medical Virology, Institute of Medical and Veterinary Sciences, Adelaide.

1986: Clinical Professor, Virology, University of Adelaide.

S.I.   : Diagnostic virology and virus serology; molecular biology of viruses of man; virus epidemiology; nucleic acid hybridisation; Hepatitis B vaccination studies and surveys.
1984: Recipient Wellcome Australia Award for distinguished scientific achievement.

CALDER, Dr Margaret

GRAD.   : 1945: University of Edinburgh, MBChB.
1962: MD with commendation – "A Study of Non-tuberculous Respiratory Infections".

P.G.   : 1946-57: Department of Genito-urinary Medicine, RIE; Simpson Memorial Maternity Pavilion.

SUB.   : 1957-1981: Assistant Bacteriologist, City Hospital.
1981-86: Consultant in charge of Bacteriology Laboratory, City Hospital. Director, Scottish Mycobacteria Reference Laboratory, City Hospital.

S.I.   : Participated in number of long-term clinical-bacteriological studies of aetiology of pneumonia in hospital practice; extensive study of pneumococcal types (first in UK following the introduction of antibiotics); long-term clinical-laboratory studies of chronic bronchitis; studies of *H. influenzae* and *H. parainfluenzae* in bronchitis; whooping cough; pathogenicity of *B. catarrhalis;* detection of pneumococcal capsular antigen; member of Scottish Working Party on tuberculosis; in Bombay in joint City Hospital/Bombay King Edward Hospital study of respiratory disease related to pollution. Author of several papers.

RETIRED   : 1981.

CAMPBELL-RENTON, Miss Margaret

BORN   : Berwickshire 1897.
GRAD.   : St Hugh's College, Oxford, BSc.
J.D.   : 1943. Part-time demonstrator; assistant in RIE laboratory.

No documentation could be obtained from St. Hugh's College or the laboratories in which Miss Campbell-Renton worked before joining the University Department staff. These notes are prepared from information supplied by her contemporaries in the department, her housekeeper/companion and the book cited below. She began her studies at a relatively late age. It is believed that soon after graduating at Oxford, she worked for a short time in Paris, possibly in the Pasteur Institute, and also (and perhaps there) it is believed, with Frederick Twort and D'Herelle, on bacterial phages. This belief would link up with Miss Campbell-Renton's later work which is documented. Trevor I. Williams in his *Howard Florey: Penicillin and After* (1984) has two references to her. Firstly, it appears that she was a part-time research worker on the staff of the Department of Pathology in Oxford in 1935, during the last years of Georges Dreyer's professorship in the Sir William Dunn School of Pathology. Dreyer had been interested in the work of Twort and D'Herelle on phages and thought that Fleming's penicillin might be a type of bacteriophage. He obtained a culture from Fleming of his *P. notatum* mould and this was maintained in Dreyer's Oxford lab. by Miss Campbell-Renton. When Professor Mackie appointed

Miss Campbell-Renton a part-time demonstrator and research worker (voluntary) in 1943, she worked on penicillinase. Miss Campbell-Renton died in 1981.

CHALLINOR, Dr Sydney W.

GRAD.   : 1931: University of Birmingham, PhD.
            1948: DSc (Edin).

P.G.   : London School of Hygiene and Tropical Medicine (Professor Raistrick). Isolation, composition and chemical properties of bacterial (salmonella) antigens.

J.D.   : 1938: Research on microbiological chemistry (succeeded Dr C.G. Anderson); early preparation of penicillin; air disinfectants.

SUB.   : 1946: Research Station, Long Ashton, Bristol, Principal Scientific Officer; Microbiologist/biochemist in charge of fermentation studies. 1951: Senior Lecturer, Department of Biochemistry, University of Birmingham. Studies of chemical composition of the cell and cell wall.

S.I.   : As above.

RETIRED   : 1967.

DIED   : 1991, June.

CHEYNE, Alexander B.

BORN   : 1896, 6 November.

Commenced as "lab. boy" in University Pathology Department in 1911. Trained by Richard Muir under departmental headship of Professor Greenfield, later Professor Lorrain Smith. On outbreak of World War I joined 2nd Battalion Black Watch. Served in France and Mesopotamia as Sergeant Major. After the war, worked in Bellahouston Hospital, Glasgow. In November 1923 returned to Edinburgh when appointed Bacteriology Department's first Senior Laboratory Assistant. After various designations, eventually Senior Chief Medical Laboratory Technologist. Sandy Cheyne's special responsibilities and his forte for his whole career in the department was preparation of first-class laboratory material, *viz.* cultures, stained films, various tests and demonstrations for large practical classes in various courses. During World War II worked with Professor Mackie in establishing and equipping various emergency medical service hospital laboratories at Bangour, Peel Hospital and other locations. From his initial appointment until well into his career, taught voluntarily (often twice per week) in evening classes for junior medical laboratory technicians, first in the PBLAA and then in the IMLT. For long was Vice-President of former organisation and was awarded Life Membership of the IMLT.

RETIRED   : 1964.

DIED   : 1979, 15 June. Honoured by University in memorial service in Greyfriars Kirk.

CHEYNE, Sir William Watson

Sir William Watson Cheyne was Joseph Lister's house-surgeon and close colleague at Edinburgh Royal Infirmary from 1876 to 1877. He was a native of Shetland. Graduating in medicine at Edinburgh University in 1875, he carried out further studies at Vienna and Strasbourg. Possessed of a deep admiration of Lister – whose lectures he had attended, and whose new antiseptic surgical techniques he fully supported – Cheyne became Lister's house-surgeon and was given the task of operating a small bacteriological laboratory to monitor Lister's work. He may be regarded as Edinburgh's first bacteriologist. His original techniques are described earlier in this book.

When Lister was appointed to the Chair of Surgery specially created for him at King's College Hospital, London in 1877, he invited Cheyne to accompany him there as his house surgeon. He shared in and suffered with Lister the latter's cold and cynical reception in London medical circles on account of his advocacy and practice of antiseptic surgery. He continued to provide bacteriological monitoring of Lister's work. Cheyne in his own lectures was a pioneer in the use of "lantern slides". In recognition of his distinguished career he was elected President of the Royal College of Surgeons (England) in 1914. He was amongst the last of surgeons to give up antiseptic surgery for surgery with aseptic technique. As an indication of his deep admiration for the great master, his son was named Joseph Lister Cheyne. Cheyne died in April 1932.

AUTH.   : See Bibliography.

CHIENE, Professor John

This pioneer of bacteriology in Edinburgh who continued the laboratory work begun by Lister and Watson Cheyne and, it is claimed, was the first to teach practical bacteriology in Britain, graduated in medicine at Edinburgh University in 1865. He became James Syme's house surgeon and a colleague of Lister's who influenced him greatly as regards bacteriology. After considerable experience in anatomy and the teaching of surgery in the Edinburgh Extra-Mural School, Chiene was appointed to the Chair of Surgery in 1882.

Chiene was a highly effective teacher. He devoted a substantial amount of his class fees to the establishment and maintenance of his bacteriological laboratory. The clinical material for the laboratory investigation was obtained from his wards in the Royal Infirmary. He was much concerned with the physical fitness of his students and encouraged sporting activities and athletics. He himself was the first President of the Scottish Rugby Union and excelled at golf and curling. Amongst his world-wide friends was Lowenstein of the tuberculosis culture medium.

One-time President of the Royal College of Surgeons of Edinburgh, Chiene received many honours. He was known to staff and students as "Honest John". He retired in 1909 and died in May 1923.

AUTH.   : See Bibliography.

COGHLAN, Dr Joyce (née Cranfield)

At Dr Coghlan's personal request, no *curriculum vitae* appears here.

COLQUHOUN, Duncan B.

Joined Pathology Department as "lab. boy" under Richard Muir 1919. Later transferred to Bacteriology Department. Resigned in 1925 to take up post as first medical laboratory assistant employed in Bacteriology Laboratory, Glasgow Royal Infirmary. Moved to post in West of Scotland Neuro-Psychiatric Research Institute. In 1954 joined staff of Bacteriology Department, Glasgow Western Infirmary, until retiral from there in 1969. Winner of Greenfield Memorial Prize. Played important part in the early development of the PBLAA and in this organisation's change to become IMLT in 1940. Early lecturer in PBLAA classes, Glasgow. Authority on discovery of penicillin by Sir Alexander Fleming and controversies *re* the antibiotic's early development.

DIED : September, 1990.

CONN, Dr Nancy

GRAD. : 1940: University of St. Andrews, MA.
1945: MBChB.
1956: MD.

SUB. : 1948-52: Registrar in Infectious Diseases, City Hospital, Edinburgh.
1952-56: Junior Hospital MO in Bacteriology, City Hospital, Assistant to Dr A.T. Wallace.
1956-57: Locum Senior House MO in Bacteriology, Ayrshire Central Hospital, Irvine.
1957-61: Senior House Medical Officer in Bacteriology, Northern General Hospital, Edinburgh, Assistant to Dr A.F. McCabe.
1961-72: Senior Hospital Medical Officer in Bacteriology, Central Microbiological Laboratories, Edinburgh; Hon. Lecturer, Edinburgh University, Bacteriology Department.
1972-80: Consultant Bacteriologist and Deputy Director of City Laboratory, Glasgow.

S.I. : General diagnostic bacteriology; research associated with infectious diseases, hospital cross infection and tuberculosis; investigation of typhoid fever outbreak caused by *S. typhi*, Vi-phage type Kl; studies in shellfish toxicity.

AUTH. : Papers on various bacteriological studies.
RETIRED : 1980.

CONSTABLE, Dr Frank Leonard

BORN : 1920, May.
GRAD. : 1942: University of Durham, BSc(Hons).
1951: MBBS.
1960: MD.
1973: FRCPath.

P.G. : 1952-53: Registrar, Microbiology, Royal Victoria Infirmary, Newcastle upon Tyne.

J.D. : 1953: Lecturer, Bacteriology and Virology.
1961: Honorary Senior Registrar, RIE

SUB. : 1961: Lecturer, University of Newcastle then Consultant Microbiologist, Newcastle Area Authority.

S.I. : Wide variety in microbiology and virology; established electron microscopy laboratory, Royal Victoria Infirmary, Newcastle. Associated in many studies with Professor Y. Ibata, Department of Anatomy, Kyoto University of Medicine, Japan. As Consultant Pathologist to the Army, many visits to Army hospitals abroad.
1975: Honorary Physician to HM The Queen.

RETIRED : 1985.

CRANSTON-LOW, Dr Robert

BORN	: 1879, Edinburgh.
GRAD.	: 1900: University of Edinburgh, MBChB (Hons).
	1924: MD (Gold Medal).
P.G.	: Dermatologist in Neisser's clinic, Breslau and also worked in Hamburg.
	1945-49: Superintendent and Curator of Royal College of Physicians' Laboratory in Forrest Road.
J.D.	: 1942-45: Mycologist and demonstrator.
S.I.	: Anaphylaxis. Fungi. Staphylococcal pigmentation on solid medium. He was a skilled artist. In Paris, Dr Low learned to make plaster casts of skin conditions under the expert, Baretta, and he himself subsequently produced a series of such casts for use in teaching in the Bacteriology Department.
AUTH.	: *The Common Diseases of the Skin,* with George A.G. Peterkin. Oliver & Boyd, 1927.
	Atlas of Bacteriology, with T.C. Dodds, E. & S. Livingstone, 1947.
DIED	: 1949.

CREW, Dr Helen C.

GRAD.	: 1912: MBChB.
P.G.	: Assistant Medical Officer of Health, Oxford.
J.D.	: 1944: EMS (World War II).
	Resident Medical Officer and Bacteriologist, Killearn and Peel Hospitals. Part-time assistant in department.

CUBIE, Dr Heather A.

BORN	: 1946, 8 December.
GRAD.	: 1968: University of Edinburgh BSc (Hons) Bacteriology.
	1972: MSc.
	1972: Teaching Certificate, Secondary Education Biology, Moray House.
	1989: PhD.
	1991: MRCPath.
P.G.	: 1968-69: Physicist, Department of Paediatric Pathology, Royal Hospital for Sick Children, Edinburgh.
J.D.	: 1969-72: Postgraduate student; research studies in virology, class demonstrator.
SUB.	: 1974-75: Part-time Research Associate on human papilloma virus, Department of Dermatology, University of Edinburgh (RIE).
	1975: Part-time virologist, Regional Virus Laboratory, City Hospital.
	1978-83: Diagnostic virology, Regional Virus Laboratory, City Hospital, specialising in rubella.
	1983-89: Part-time Senior Grade virologist, Regional Virus Laboratory, City Hospital – research and diagnostic virology; research project, molecular probes in respiratory virus infections; during 1985-88 also part-time Research Associate, University Bacteriology Department, on human papilloma virus.
S.I.	: Considerable studies on human papilloma virus; studies on rubella.

CUNNINGHAM, Lt.-Col. John

Lt.-Colonel John Cunningham, who was the eldest son of the noted anatomist, Professor J.D. Cunningham, graduated at Edinburgh University, BA in 1903, MBChB in 1904 and MD in 1906. In 1905 Lt.-Col. Cunningham obtained a commission in the Indian Medical Service. He was given a research appointment with the Indian Government. After working for several years in provincial laboratories, he was appointed Assistant Director of the Bombay Bacteriological Laboratory in 1910. Two years later he became Assistant Director and later Director of the Central Research Institute of India at Kasauli. During the First World War, he organised the production of large amounts of typhoid and cholera vaccine for the troops in the Middle East and Mediterranean zones. In 1919, he was appointed Director of the King Institute of Preventive Medicine in Madras and seven years later, Director of the Pasteur Institute at Kasauli, the first such Institute to be established in India concerned with the suppression of rabies. Cunningham was appointed Companion of the Order of the Indian Empire in 1928.

In 1929 Lt.-Col. Cunningham became Medical Superintendent of the Astley Ainslie Hospital in Edinburgh. He was instrumental in re-orientating the hospital from a "convalescent institution" to an important centre for the positive concept of rehabilitation. In this latter context, he did much to establish the hospital as an internationally renowned School of Occupational Therapy. He had published many papers on the prevention of various diseases in India. At the Astley Ainslie he opened a bacteriology laboratory which, apart from its routine diagnostic and monitoring function, carried out considerable research related to the types of cases admitted to the hospital especially of tuberculosis and rheumatoid arthritis. He worked in close collaboration with Professor T.J. Mackie who acted as adviser and who provided various forms of assistance as regards laboratory staff and materials. Lt.-Col. Cunningham died in 1968.

DAVIDSON, Professor Sir Stanley, K.T.

BORN	: 1894, Ceylon.
GRAD.	: BA (Cantab). 1919: University of Edinburgh MBChB (following studies interrupted by World War I).
P.G.	: Brief period in Pathology Department, University of Cambridge under Professor H.R. Dean. Experience gained in serology.
J.D.	: 1923: One of Professor T.J. Mackie's original three academic staff. 1925: MD (Gold Medal) for thesis "Immunisation and antibody reactions – a series of experimental studies". This work evoked considerable interest in the early days of immunology and is regarded as of relevance 65 years later.
S.I.	: Bacteriology of intestinal tract which Sir Stanley sought to relate to *Cl. welchii* as the cause of pernicious anaemia. Also worked on early typing of pneumococci and production of antisera; later on leptospirosis in Aberdeen.
SUB.	: 1930: Regius Professor of Medicine, University of Aberdeen. Collaborated with Sir John Boyd Orr on studying relationship of nutrition and disease. 1938: Appointed Professor of Medicine, University of Edinburgh.

Distinguished clinician. Important contribution to Medical School developments.

1946: Reorganised Edinburgh's Municipal Hospitals. Noted for policy of "shoestring" research from Professor T.J. Mackie's influence. With Lady Davidson, very generous benefactors to Edinburgh University Medical School, Royal College of Physicians and Aberdeen University. 1953: Elected President Royal College of Physicians of Edinburgh.

DIED   : 1981, September.
HONOURS : 1955: Knight of the Order of the Thistle (K.T.).

DAVIES, Dr Benjamin I.

BORN   : 1932, Cheshire.
GRAD.   : 1955: University of London, London Hospital Medical College, MBBS.
           1972: MD.
           1977: FRCP.
P.G.   : 1958-60: Registrar in Pathology, Edgware General Hospital, London.
J.D.   : 1960: Lecturer.
SUB.   : 1971: Consultant Microbiologist, Edgware General Hospital.
           1975: Specialist in Microbiology and Head of Regional Public Health Laboratory, De Wever Ziekenhuis, Heerlen, The Netherlands; Part-time Senior Lecturer in Microbiology, State University of Limburg, Maastricht, NL.
S.I   : Role of new antimicrobial agents in treatment of purulent lower respiratory tract infections; modern methods for management of urinary tract infections, especially in domiciliary practice; evaluation of role of inducible and non-inducible beta-lactamases in the results of antimicrobial chemotherapy.

DEMPSTER, Professor George

BORN   : 1917, June.
GRAD.   : 1940: University of Edinburgh, MBChB.
           1941: BSc (Bact. Hons)
           1953: MD.
J.D.   : 1941: Assistant in Bacteriology Diagnostic Laboratory.
           1942: Lecturer in charge of Diagnostic Laboratory; Laboratory Consultant in Peel Hospital.
           1946-48: RAMC Pathologist on Gold Coast, Sierra Leone and Nigeria.
           1948: Returned as Lecturer, Bacteriology Department.
SUB.   : 1950: Research Associate Virus Diseases with Professor C.E. Van Rooyen, Connaught Medical Research Laboratories, Toronto. Professor (part time) Virus Diseases, Ontario Veterinary College and Lecturer in School of Hygiene, Toronto. 1953: Professor of Bacteriology and Director of Bacteriology, Medical College, Saskatoon.
S.I   : Infectious mononucleosis; influenza virus; Coxsackie virus; fimbriae, etc.

AUTH.   : Collaborated with Rhodes and Van Rooyen in 5th edn of *Textbook of Virology*.
RETIRED   : 1980.

De WAAL, Dr Hermanus L.

GRAD.   : 1935: University of Edinburgh, MBChB.
             1937: DPH.
             1939: MD (Gold Medal).
             1939: DTM&H (Cape Town and Edinburgh).
P.G.   : 1942-45: Emergency Medical Service.
             1945-46: Royal Army Medical Corps.
J.D.   : 1947-49: Lewis Cameron Lecturer. Assistant in VD Clinic, Royal Infirmary of Edinburgh.
S.I.   : *Streptococcus pyogenes* and scarlet fever; Griffith's streptococcal typing in relation to epidemiology of scarlet fever. Wilkie Research Scholar: investigation of wounds. Author of many papers on anaemia and asthma.
             Awarded Wellcome Prize History of Medicine in 1938 and 1939.
SUB.   : Returned to South Africa, 1949.
DIED   : 1950.

DICK, James

BORN   : 1911, Edinburgh.

Joined technical staff of Royal Infirmary Bacteriology Laboratory, 1926. In addition to wide experience in and responsibility for diagnostic bacteriological techniques, with his "Chief", Dr J.H. Bowie, made an important contribution to the development of hospital steam sterilisation. One of the RIE team associated with development of first high pre-vacuum steam steriliser in 1957, also water spray rapid cooling device. Name commemorated by Bowie-Dick Autoclave Tape test used worldwide for monitoring efficient sterilisation of dressings and other materials. Also involved in originating pre-set tray system (surgical instruments) and establishment of Theatre Service Centre in the RIE. With Dr Bowie worked on monitoring of sterility level of operating theatre instruments. One of the pioneers of voluntarily teaching evening classes for junior medical laboratory technicians, and tutor for the IMLS Special Examination. Much involved in committees of PBLAA and IMLT, later IMLS. Appointed by Scottish Secretary of State a member of the Medical Laboratory Technicians' Board at its inception. Succeeded R. Barr as Chief, then Senior Chief, Medical Laboratory Technologist in 1955. A most meticulous and conscientious man, Mr Dick was also a highly respected officer in the Boys' Brigade.

DIED   : In post 1972.

DICKSON, Dr William E. Carnegie

GRAD.   : 1901: University of Edinburgh, BSc (Distinction) Anatomy. 1901: MBChB (Hons). 1905: MD (Gold Medal).
             1908: FRCP(E).
J.D.   : 1906-14: Originally Lecturer in Pathological Bacteriology in the Edinburgh University Pathology Department (succeeding Dr Robert Muir); Pathologist and Bacteriologist to the Royal Hospital for Sick

Children, Edinburgh.

1913: Lecturer in Bacteriology Department after Professor James Ritchie's appointment.

SUB. : Held posts in a number of military hospitals in England. 1919: Established a practice in Harley Street.

AUTH. : Co-author with Professor J.M. Beattie of various text books of pathology (subsequently revised by Professor J.A. Murray Drennan).

Author of *Bacteriology* in People's Books Series (1914).

DILL, Dr Alfred V.

GRAD. : 1916: University of Edinburgh, MBChB (Hons).
1920: DPH.
1921: MD.

J.D. : 1917-18: Following service in RAMC, World War I.

SUB. : Pathologist, Royal Hospital for Sick Children, Edinburgh. House Physician, City Fever Hospital, Edinburgh.

DOUGLAS, Dr Andrew C.

GRAD. : 1946: University of Edinburgh, MBChB.
1965: FRCP(E).

J.D. : 1951-53: Assistant Bacteriologist; post combined with lectureship in University Bacteriology Department.

SUB. : Reader in Medicine and Reader in Respiratory Medicine in the University. Consultant Physician, City Hospital and Royal Infirmary, Edinburgh.

S.I. : Bronchial physiology. Granulomatous disorders, especially tuberculosis, sarcoidosis, granulomatous vasculitis. General respiratory conditions.

AUTH. : Co-author postgraduate textbook *Respiratory Diseases,* with Crofton and Douglas, Blackwell, 1969, 1981. "Diseases of Respiratory System" in *A Companion to Medical Studies,* Blackwell, 1974.

RETIRED : 1988

DOW, John

In 1929 Mr Dow succeeded James Smith, the Royal Hospital for Sick Children's first technician in pathology and bacteriology. He was the only technician to work with Dr Agnes McGregor. After eleven years service at the hospital laboratory for a period working in both disciplines then latterly as senior medical laboratory technologist in the bacteriology laboratory, Mr Dow took up an appointment with the Animal Diseases Research Association at the Moredun Institute, Edinburgh.

DUERDEN, Professor Brian Ion

BORN : 1948, Nelson, Lancashire.

GRAD. : 1970: University of Edinburgh, BSc (Medical Science), (Hons Bact.).
1972: MBChB.
1979: MD, FRCPath.

J.D. : 1973: Lecturer; GP Diagnostic Laboratory.

SUB. : 1976: Lecturer in Department of Medical Microbiology, University of Sheffield Medical School.
1979: Senior Lecturer.

1983: Professor of Medical Microbiology and Head of Department, University of Sheffield Medical School.

1991: Professor of Medical Microbiology, University of Wales College of Medicine, Director of the Cardiff PHLS and Manager, Medical Microbiological Services of South Glamorgan Health Authority.

S.I.   : Bacteroides; clinically important anaerobes; continuous culture.

AUTH.   : Joint Author of *Short Textbook of Medical Microbiology* and *Parasitic Infection,* Hodder & Stoughton, 1987; Contributor to and co-editor of Vol. 2 of Topley and Wilson's *Principles of Bacteriology, Virology and Immunity,* Edward Arnold, 8th edn. 1990. Chairman, Editorial Board of *Journal of Medical Microbiology.*

DUGUID, Professor James P.

BORN   : 1919, Bo'ness, West Lothian.

GRAD.   : 1942: University of Edinburgh, MBChB (Hons).

1943: BSc (Bact. Hons).

1949: MD (Gold Medal) FRCPE; received special exemption from World War II service to continue research and early work on penicillin.

J.D.   : 1944: Lecturer.

1954: Senior Lecturer.

1960: Reader.

SUB.   : 1963: Professor of Bacteriology, University of St. Andrews. 1967: Professor of Bacteriology, University of Dundee.

HON.APP : Member/Chairman many national Committees in a wide range of bacterial and medical subjects. 1958-62: Honorary Consultant in Bacteriology, S.E. Scotland Regional Hospital Board. 1963-84: Honorary Consultant in Bacteriology, Scottish Eastern Regional Hospital Board, later Tayside Health Board. 1968-71: Director Postgraduate Medical Education, University of Dundee. 1971-74: Dean of Faculty of Medicine, University of Dundee. 1967-85: Consultant Adviser in Microbiology, Scottish Home and Health Department.

EDIT.   : Co-editor of the following: *Journal of Pathology and Bacteriology,* 1959-68, *Journal of Medical Microbiology,* 1968-71, *Medical Microbiology,* Churchill Livingstone, 11th edn, 1968, *Medical Microbiology* 12th edn, Vol. I, 1973, *Medical Microbiology* 12th edn, Vol. II, 1975, Mackie & McCartney *Medical Microbiology* 13th edn, Vol. I, 1978; and Mackie & McCartney Practical *Medical Microbiology,* 13th edn, 1989.

S.I.   : Airborne and droplet infection and disinfection; early work on preparation, administration and mechanism of action of penicillin; pioneering work on fimbriae; whooping cough; laboratory use of dangerous pathogens; biotyping of salmonellae; adhesive properties of bacteria.

HONOURS : 1979: Commander of the Order of the British Empire (CBE).

RETIRED : 1984.

DURIE, Dr Thomas B.M.

BORN   : 1919, 23 September.

GRAD.   : 1943: University of Edinburgh MBChB.

	1974: FRCPath.
	1979: FRCP(Edin.).
	1944-47: World War II: Normandy to Germany with Field Ambulance units of the 51st (Highland) and 49th (WR) Divisions; and principally as Regimental Medical Officer, 79th (Scottish Horse) Medium Regiment, Royal Artillery.
J.RIE.	: 1948: Assistant Bacteriologist.
	1952: RIE post combined with Lectureship in Bacteriology Department, University of Edinburgh.
	1963: Senior Lecturer in Bacteriology Department and Honorary Consultant in Bacteriology until 1984.
S.I.	: Application of bacteriology to clinical medicine, particularly with regard to rapid reporting systems. Sterilisation and disinfection. Antimicrobial therapy.
	1949-84: teaching commitments to nurses.
RETIRED	: 1984.

EDMOND, Dr Elizabeth

BORN	: 1936, Gretna, 25 April.
GRAD.	: 1960: University of Edinburgh, MBChB.
	1979: FRCPath.
P.G.	: 1963: Registrar in Microbiology, Central Microbiology Laboratories, Western General Hospital, Edinburgh.
	1968: Registrar in Virology, Regional Virus Laboratory, City Hospital. Visited USA laboratories with special interest in infectious mononucleosis, rubella and hepatitis.
	1974: Consultant Virologist, Regional Virus Laboratory, City Hospital.
J.D.	: 1979: University Bacteriology Department as Senior Lecturer in Virology.
S.I.	: Infectious mononucleosis; hepatitis; Epstein-Barr virus infection; diagnosis and control of virus infection in transplant surgery. Involved in national programme of rubella immunisation with Dr Helen Zealley which was of international importance.
DIED	: 1986, in post.

EDMUNDS, Dr Patrick N.

BORN	: 1922, Swatow, China.
GRAD.	: 1947: University of Edinburgh, MBChB. 1950: BSc (Hons Bact.).
	1959: MD.
	1972: FRCP(E).
J.D.	: 1950: Lecturer.
SUB	: 1954: Senior Hospital Medical Officer in Bacteriology at Astley Ainslie Hospital.
	1960: Consultant Bacteriologist to Fife Hospitals.
S.I.	: Staphylococcal infections in the newborn; Haemophilus influenzae-like bacilli; leptospiral jaundice.
RETIRED	: 1979.
DIED	: 1983.

ELIAS-JONES, Dr Thomas F.

GRAD.   : 1945: University of Edinburgh MBChB.
                1968: FRCP.
                1981: FRCP (Glasgow).
J.D.   : 1948: Lecturer.
SUB.   : 1953-56: GP
                1956: Consultant in Clinical Pathology, Ilford and Barking Hospital Group.
                1962: Consultant Bacteriologist, Western Regional Hospital Board as Director of the Glasgow City Public Health Laboratory. Honorary Lecturer in Bacteriology, University of Glasgow.
                1967: One of the chief founders of the Communicable Diseases (Scotland) Unit, initially joint editor of *Communicable Diseases (Scotland) Weekly Report*.
S.I.   : Hospital staphylococcal infections; diphtheria; food poisoning; sexually transmitted diseases.
RETIRED   : 1981: Dr Elias Jones, a native of Wales, was well versed in Welsh culture, spoke the language, and was an entertaining speaker on this subject.
DIED   : 1990, November 4th.

FARMER, Robert K.

BORN   : Edinburgh.
J.D.   : 1929: After basic training became personal technical assistant to Professor T.J. Mackie, then Senior Medical Laboratory Technician in charge of Public Health diagnostic laboratory. Responsible for departmental administration and training of technical staff. Pioneered nationally adopted education and training scheme for IMLT.
SUB.   : 1946: Resigned. Senior Scientific Officer, Research Department, Boots Ltd., Nottingham; Laboratory Controller, Rentokil Research Laboratories; Technical Director, Rentokil. Author of many scientific papers and produced many award-winning scientific films.
DIED   : 1992, 28 January.

FERGUSON, John

Commenced as junior medical laboratory assistant in RCP Laboratory, Forrest Road, in November 1934. Trained in bacteriology. October 1939: following outbreak of World War II, joined Royal Navy as Sick Berth Attendant. Promoted to Petty Officer. Tour of duty included Simonstown, South Africa.

1946: returned to RCP Laboratory. Soon afterwards moved to Astley Ainslie Hospital laboratory as senior medical laboratory technician, successively with Dr Levinthal, Dr Edmunds and Dr Helen Wright. In 1961, when this laboratory closed, John Ferguson transferred to the bacteriology department at the Northern General Hospital. Soon afterwards he moved with the staff of this laboratory to the newly built Central Microbiological Laboratories at the Western General Hospital, officially opened in July 1962. John Ferguson gained the Fellowship of the IMLS. by thesis in 1962.

AUTH.   : Joint author of several papers.
DIED   : 1969, October.

FINKELSTEIN (FINLAYSON), Dr J.D. [also known as Morris Harris Finlayson]

J.D.	: 1925.
GRAD.	: 1930: MBChB (Edinburgh).
SUB	: 1933: Appointed Lister Institute, London.

GANGULI, Dr Leela A.

BORN	: 1938, Madras, India, 1938.
GRAD	: 1962: University of Madras MB BS.
	1966: University of Edinburgh, PhD.
	1974: City of Manchester, Diploma in Bacteriology.
J.D.	: 1963: Postgraduate Research Fellow. 1970: Lecturer.
SUB.	: 1971: Senior Registrar, Manchester Teaching Hospitals.
	1975: Senior Lecturer/Honorary Consultant Hope Hospital, Manchester Medical School.
	1980: Consultant in Microbiology, Head of Department of Microbiology, Hope and Associated Salford Hospitals. Honorary Associate Lecturer, Manchester Medical School.
S.I.	: Bacteriuria in pregnancy; serotyping of *E. coli;* T-strain mycoplasmas *(Ureaplasma urealyticum);* anaerobes; rapid detection of septicaemia.

GIBSON, Dr Hubert J.

GRAD.	: 1926: University of Edinburgh, MBChB, DPH.
J.D.	: 1928-1935.
SUB.	: Royal Hospital, Bath.
DIED	: In post.

GIEBEN (SINCLAIR-GIEBEN), Dr Abraham H.C.

Dr Abraham Gieben, MD; MRCP(E); DTM&H; and Dip.Psych. was born in 1923 in Java, son of a distinguished Dutch judge and administrator. After some years in the Dutch East Indies, he began the study of medicine at Amsterdam University. During the Second World War, while still a medical student, he was prominent in the Dutch Resistance movement. After the war, he was selected to continue his medical studies at Edinburgh. He thus had qualifications from Amsterdam and Edinburgh. For a short time he practised in the Dutch East Indies and in Singapore. While in Edinburgh in 1955, he gained his membership of the Royal College of Physicians and then decided to study psychiatry. He was deeply influenced by Professor Alexander Kennedy. He obtained a diploma in psychiatry and was appointed as a registrar at the Royal Edinburgh Hospital and subsequently became a lecturer in 1958, then Senior Lecturer at Aberdeen University in the Department of Mental Health. Dr Gieben specialised in psychosomatic medicine and hypnosis. A colleague at Aberdeen, speaking for the department, paying tribute said: "Brilliant is the only word to describe him".

Professor J.G. Collee has kindly contributed the following note:

> Brom Gieben came to the department in 1950 as a lecturer. We trained together in the diagnostic laboratory ("Lab. 4") under Dr Helen Wright's firm command. Brom and Dr Wright had several brushes. On one occasion, Dr Gieben complained about the excessive ventilation of the laboratory on a cold winter's morning. Helen Wright dismissed the plea and observed that there was snow on the end of her bed that morning "and a beautifully bright day lay ahead". Brom's riposte was in Dutch (which I understood).

He was a highly intelligent man of striking appearance. He was originally Dutch, but his English was perfect and his knowledge of language and words was remarkable. He loved good music and good company. He married Gay Sinclair and the family adopted the name of Sinclair-Gieben. Brom endeared himself to his colleagues in the department with his ready wit, his bright courtesy, and his friendly manner. In 1963, five years after his taking up an appointment as a lecturer in Mental Health at Aberdeen University, we were stunned to hear of the death of Brom in a remote part of Sutherland, and we mourned the untimely loss of such a gifted colleague who had enriched our lives in the short time that we had known him. He was 39.

GILLIES, Professor Robert R.

BORN   : 1924, Kelty, Fife.
GRAD.   : 1947: University of Edinburgh, MBChB.
           1952: DPH.
           1959: MD.
           1963: FRCP.
           1971: FRCP(E).
J.D.   : 1952: Lecturer.
           1960: Senior Lecturer.
           1962: Visiting Professor and Head of Department of Bacteriology, University of Ibadan, Nigeria.
           1972: Reader; Associate Dean, Faculty of Medicine for nine years.
SUB.   : 1976: Appointed to new Chair of Clinical Bacteriology, Queen's University, Belfast.
S.I.   : Bacillary dysentery; colicine typing; streptococcus and pneumococcus; bacterial fimbriae (subject of MD thesis) with J.P. Duguid; pseudomonas typing; special biochemical test media; hospital infection.
AUTH.   : *Bacteriology Illustrated,* with T.C. Dodds, Livingstone, 1965. *Lecture Notes in Medical Microbiology,* Blackwell, 1968. Contributor to various textbooks.
DIED   : In post, July 1983.

GOULD, Dr James Cameron

GRAD.   : 1945: University of Edinburgh, BSc (Bact. Hons), MBChB.
           1959: MD, FRS(E).
           1966: FIBiol, FRCP(E).
           1972: FRCPath.
           1975: FFCM.
           1975: FRS Edin.
           1942-44: During medical studies assisted Dr G. Ludlam, Dr R.K. Oag and Dr S. Challinor.
J.D.   : 1946: Vans Dunlop Fellow.
           1946-1948: RAMC.
           1948: Senior Bacteriologist, Bacteriology Laboratory, RIE, replacing Dr Logan.
           1950: Lecturer in Department, Senior Lecturer; Africa: Sabbatical year: 1960: returned to Department in 1961.
SUB.   : 1961: Director, Central Microbiological Laboratories, Western General Hospital. Member, Convener or Chairman of many senior

committees, he had significant professional links with London and with Europe.

S.I.   : Virulence enhancement factors with special reference to gastric mucin; staphylococci; antibiotics in the environment; development of antibiotic resistance; diagnosis and treatment of respiratory infections; quantitative bacteriology..

RETIRED   : 1988.

GOWANS, Dr Eric J.

BORN   : 1947, 16 September, Edinburgh.

GRAD.   : 1982: M.App. Sc. (SAIT).
1986: PhD, University of Adelaide.

J.D.   : 1964: General training.
1969-71: Scientific Officer wholly engaged on electron microscopy.
1972-75: Senior Scientific Officer, Department of Veterinary Pathology (virus research), Royal (Dick) Veterinary College. 1975: returned to the department as Chief MLSO in Hepatitis Reference Laboratory.

SUB.   : 1979-80: hospital scientist, Institute of Med. and Vet. Science, Adelaide, Australia. Responsible for management of Hepatitis Reference Laboratory. Senior Hospital Scientist there 1980-85; then Principal Hospital Scientist. Lecturer and demonstrator. All these posts in virology.

S.I.   : Virology: diagnostic and research and especially use of electron microscope in this work.
1987-88: Visiting Fellow, Division of Molecular Virology and Immunology, Georgetown University, Rockeville, MD, USA.

AUTH.   : Author and joint author of many papers, especially on Hepatitis B.

GRAY, Dr James D. Allan

BORN   : Edinburgh.

GRAD.   : 1926: University of Edinburgh, MBChB.
1927: BSc (Path. Hons).
1930: DPH (Liverpool).
1931: FRCP(E).
1963: FRCPath.
1969: MD.

J.D.   : 1926: Lecturer.

SUB   : 1929: Assistant City Bacteriologist, City of Liverpool, Lecturer, Liverpool University.
1934: Senior Bacteriologist, Department of Preventive Medicine, University of Bristol.
1938: Pathologist to Central Middlesex Hospital; World War II, Posted to China as Deputy Assistant Director of Pathology and Pathologist Specialist to the China Command.
1941: Japanese prisoner of war. During detention, his copies of MD manuscript lost. This had to be re-written and MD was awarded 43 years after original graduation.

S.I.   : Early work on Wilson and Blair's brilliant green tellurite medium; paratyphoid B; antibiotics.

RETIRED : 1967.
DIED   : 1993.

GREEN, Professor Cecil A.

BORN   : 1908: Davenport.
GRAD.   : 1932: University of Edinburgh, MBChB.
           1934: DPH 1934.
           1941: PhD, MD (Gold Medal), FRCP.
P.G.   : GP in Rhondda Valley; developed special interest in rheumatism.
J.D.   : 1933: Lecturer.
SUB   : 1938: Director of Naval Research Foundation of the Empire
           Rheumatism Council, Greenwich.
           1947: First Clinical Bacteriologist, Royal Victoria Infirmary, Newcastle.
           1959: Chair of Bacteriology (invited to succeed Professor E.M.
           Dunlop) at University of Durham, while retaining Newcastle post.
           Visiting Professor to Ghana, Nigeria and Jamaica.
S.I.   : Streptococci in relation to rheumatism; antibiotics; in World War II,
           Surgeon-Commander RNVR and later responsible for establishing
           penicillin production plant for use of the antibiotic by the Navy; close
           collaborator with Sir Alexander Fleming.
RETIRED : 1974: Acted as Consultant in Microbiology in Sunderland Royal
           Infirmary for some years.
DIED   : 1980.

GRIERSON, Dr Alexander M.M.

GRAD.   : 1923: University of Edinburgh, MBChB.
           1924: DPH.
           1928: MD.
J.D.   : 1925-1926: in charge of Department's early diagnostic laboratory.
S.I.   : Anthrax.
SUB.   : 1928: Became Assistant Medical Officer of Health and Port Medical
           Officer, City of Edinburgh.

HADDOW, Sir Alexander

BORN   : 1907, Leven, Fife.
GRAD.   : 1929: University of Edinburgh, MBChB.
           1937: PhD.
           1937: MD (Gold Medal).
           1938: DSc.
J.D.   : 1932: Assistant Lecturer.
SUB.   : 1936: Research Institute, Royal Cancer Hospital.
           1947: Director, Chester Beattie Research Institute.
S.I.   : All aspects of cancer research, especially chemical and genetic
           mechanisms of carcinogens. Began cancer research in University
           Bacteriology Department.
HONS.   : 1962: President of International Union against Cancer. Honoured
           by the Universities, Academies of Science, learned bodies of very
           many countries. Fellow of World Academy of Arts and Science.
           Chevalier of the Legion of Honour, France.

1958: Fellow of Royal Society.
1967: Honorary DSc, Edinburgh University.
1966: Awarded Knighthood.
DIED   : 1976.

HAYWARD, Dr Nancy J.

Dr Hayward, who was a graduate in microbiology and chemistry of Melbourne University, Australia, came to work in Edinburgh University Bacteriology Department, during two periods – 1963-64 and 1976. As a result of the former visit she re-wrote the culture medium section for Professor Robert Cruickshank's 13th edition of Mackie and McCartney's *Textbook of Medical Microbiology*. During her latter visit, Dr Hayward discussed new methods for gas chromatographic analysis of cultures and specimens; nitrosamines; carcinogenic agents and bacterial interactions with dietary constituents.

Dr Hayward's most notable work included the effect of sulphapyridine in meningococcal meningitis in children (the subject of her MSc degree); presumptive identification of *Cl. welchii* (perfringens); important studies on the Nagler test for *Cl. welchii,* leading her to convert Nagler's fluid medium method to the "Nagler" plate, really her own production. This was the first diagnostic method of its kind. Its importance was such as to persuade the Australian authorities, who in 1943 had interned Nagler as a German refugee, to release him to continue his laboratory work.

Work on anaerobic infection of war wounds gained Dr Hayward a PhD in 1946. In 1966 she joined Professor B.P. Marmion's new department at Monash University. She was one of the first to attempt identification of bacteria by chromatographic analysis of their products of metabolism. Dr Hayward died in Victoria, Australia, in June 1989.

HENDERSON, Miss Frances Lizars

Miss Henderson graduated MA at Edinburgh University in 1923 and then studied for a year at the College of Art. After experience as a freelance journalist, she was appointed in 1930 as part-time secretary to Professor T.J. Mackie and some months later was engaged part-time by Professor Drennan of the Pathology Department.

In 1937 Miss Henderson resigned her joint bacteriology/pathology appointments to return to journalism. She was then engaged by Dr C.E. Van Rooyen and Dr A.J. Rhodes, early virologists in the Bacteriology Department, to prepare for publication of their book *Virus Diseases of Man* (Oxford University Press, 1940).

Miss Henderson's brother, Sir William McGregor Henderson, FRS, FRSE, gained a BSc in the Bacteriology Department and the MRCVS and had a distinguished career, becoming secretary of the Agricultural Research Council and President of the London Zoogical Society. In addition to her work as a journalist, Miss Henderson was author of *Rambles Round Edinburgh* (W. & A.K. Johnston, 1927) well received by the critics of its time and becoming one of the classics of its kind.

HENRICHSEN, Clark

BORN   : 1946, 27 February.
J.D.   : 1964: Royal Infirmary Bacteriology Laboratory. He was one of the most productive and innovative MLSOs in the department with publications from his work in the microbiology of sexually transmitted

diseases and in bacterial identification, a subject in which he was particularly interested, producing many papers and lecturing widely on this topic. Some aspects of this latter work were taken up by a renowned commercial company.

In latter years he was involved in the management of the Fellowship examination of the Institute of Medical Laboratory Sciences. His enthusiasm for the professional image of MLSOs was exemplified in his effort to attain the highest standards for the profession.

He was an active member of the departmental squash team and a lover of the Scottish Highlands which he explored on many outings with his colleagues.

DIED : In post, 19 October 1985.

HOLBROOK, Dr Peter

GRAD. : 1976: University of Edinburgh, PhD.
SUB. : Member of Research team, Microbial Pathogenicity Research Laboratory, University Department.
1976-78: Lecturer, University of Manchester Department of Oral Medicine.
1978: FDS Glasgow.
1978-79: Registrar in Bacteriology, Western General Hospital (CML) Edinburgh.
1979-81: Lecturer in University Department and Senior Registrar, Western General Hospital, Central Microbiological Laboratory.
SUB. : 1981-88: Senior Lecturer in Microbiology, Faculty of Odontology, University of Iceland.
1989: Reader.
S.I. : Bacteroides and periodontal disease; candidiasis; penicillin tolerance: endocarditis; aetiology, prediction and prevention of caries.
AUTH. : Co-author with Dr Philip Ross of *Clinical and Oral Bacteriology*, Blackwell 1984.

IVES, Dr John C.J.

GRAD. : 1937: University of Edinburgh, MBChB.
J.D. : 1938: Assistant. World War II, RAMC. Specialist in Pathology, Kirkwall Hospital, Orkney, and Edinburgh, then Commanding Officer of mobile field laboratory in Rangoon.
1942: to India when Burma fell; mobile laboratory, Arakan; bacteriologist to 14th Army and directed penicillin research team.
1946: Invited to return as lecturer in Department.
SUB. : 1950: William Teacher Lecturer in Bacteriology, University of Glasgow; Honorary Consultant in Bacteriology, Glasgow Royal Infirmary. Member and Convener of many committees, Western Regional Hospital Board, Glasgow Royal Infirmary, including Chairman of Standing Advisory Committee for Laboratory Services (Scotland); Medical Laboratory Sciences State Registration Board.
S.I. : Hospital infection; leptospirosis in man and animals.
RETIRED : 1978.

JOE, Dr Alexander

BORN	: 1894, Brechin.
GRAD.	: 1919: University of Edinburgh, MBChB.
	1922: DPH
	1923: MD, DTM&H.
J.D.	: 1923: Assistant. One of Professor T.J. Mackie's original three assistants.
SUB.	: 1924: Assistant Medical Officer, City Hospital under Dr Claude Ker; Assistant Medical Officer of Health and Port Medical Officer, Edinburgh. 1937: Medical Superintendent, North Western Fever Hospital, Hampstead. Medical Superintendent, City Hospital, Edinburgh; Lecturer in Infectious Diseases, University.
S.I.	: Early work on diphtheria immunisation; scarlatina; wide range of infectious diseases; involvement in Edinburgh smallpox outbreak in 1942. Airborne infection.
AUTH.	: *The Acute Infectious Fevers,* Churchill, 1947.
DIED	: 1962.

KER, Dr Claude B.

Dr Claude Ker graduated in medicine at Edinburgh University in 1890. He then worked in Lock and Observation Wards in the Royal Infirmary in Infirmary Street. This prompted the beginning of his interest in infectious diseases. He was appointed assistant Medical Officer at the City's Fever Hospital which had been established in the Royal Infirmary's former surgical building in Drummond Street, vacated when the hospital moved to its new purpose-built premises in Lauriston Place in 1879. In 1896 the subject of Dr Ker's MD thesis, awarded a Gold Medal, was "The General Treatment of Enteric Fever". In the same year, Ker became Medical Superintendent of the early City Fever Hospital.

As the old RI Building in Drummond Street became increasingly unsuitable and overcrowded, Dr Ker collaborated with Edinburgh's distinguished first Medical Officer of Health in campaigning for the opening of a purpose-built infectious diseases hospital. In 1895, Edinburgh Town Council decided to build such a hospital at Colinton Mains. Ker also collaborated with Bailie Pollard in the detailed planning of the hospital which was duly opened in 1903. Dr Ker, who was appointed Medical Superintendent of the new City Fever Hospital, had already become regarded as a leading authority on infectious diseases. As noted in another chapter, as soon as the hospital was opened, he established a bacteriology laboratory with the primary object of confirming or excluding the clinical diagnosis of the large number and widely varied cases admitted to the hospital and of monitoring their treatment before discharge. After the outbreak of the First World War, Dr Ker became Medical Officer for the prisoners of war at Redford Barracks.

Appointed President of Edinburgh University Athletic Club, Dr Ker saw the club as an important means of encouraging physical fitness in students. He became president of many medical societies and a member of the Faculty of Medicine. A devotee of Napoleon, his room at the City Fever Hospital was adorned with portraits of the French Emperor. He ran the hospital on a strict regime, especially as regards the duties and "decorum" of the medical and nursing staff. Dr Ker died in March 1925 after nearly 35 years as a specialist in infectious diseases.

AUTH.　　　: *A Manual of Fevers,* Oxford Medical Publications 1911.

KERR, Eric J.C., FIMLS

BORN	: 1930
J.D.	: 1945: General training. (During National Service had worked at Porton Chemical Defence Experimental Establishment.) Returned to department: wide experience in routine bacteriology.
SUB.	: 1954: Bacteriology Laboratory for Municipal Hospitals at Northern General Hospital.
	1961: transferred to Central Microbiological Laboratories, Western General Hospital. Following death of Douglas Annat in 1982, succeeded to latter's post of Senior Chief MLSO.
RETIRED	: 1990.

KING, Professor Hugh K.

GRAD.	: 1941: University of Cambridge, PhD.
P.G.	: Lister Institute, London. Boots, Nottingham.
J.D.	: 1945: Teaching Fellow, then lecturer in bacteriological chemistry. Succeeded Dr S.W. Challinor.
SUB.	: 1949: Biochemistry Department, Liverpool University. Lecturer, then Reader.
	1966: Combined Chair Biochemistry and Agricultural Biochemistry, University College of Wales, Aberystwyth.
S.I.	: In Department, early work on mucin with Dr J.C. Gould. Further developed studies in microbiological chemistry in the Department.
RETIRED	: 1982.

LEES, Mrs Jessie (née Wallace)

J.D.	: 1950: General training. Worked on bacteriological chemistry with Dr H. King. Research on antibiotics.
SUB	: Technician in charge of general laboratory (Departments of Bacteriology, Biochemistry, Haematology and BTS) at Peel Hospital, Galashiels. Medical Laboratory Technician, Veterinary Research Station, Vom, Nigeria. Trained native technicians and conducted examinations for the IMLT. Attended Ruskin College, Oxford, gaining Diploma in Economics and Political Science; Dip. Educ., Moray House, Edinburgh. MA Maths and Nat. Phil., Edinburgh University. Left for Canada: took M.Educ., Dalhousie University, Halifax, Nova Scotia. Teacher, mathematics, Charlotte Town Rural High School, Prince Edward Island. Head of Mathematics Department, 1978. Specialised in computer science.
AUTH.	: Various publications on mathematics and computing.

LEES, Dr Robert.

GRAD.	: University of Edinburgh, MBChB 1925.
J.D.	: 1931: Assistant Bacteriologist in the Royal Infirmary of Edinburgh and Assistant in Venereal Diseases Department in the Royal Infirmary of Edinburgh.
SUB.	: Resident Medical Officer of Health at St. Bartholomew's Hospital, London.

LEVINTHAL, Dr Walter M.

Born in Berlin 1886. Studied medicine in Berlin, Freiburg and Munich, with specialisation in bacteriology and serology. Graduated in Berlin in 1909. Subsequently awarded MD.

1914: Appointed assistant to public health consultant, with responsibility for bacteriology laboratory. Specialised in studies on influenza. First produced "Levinthal agar" in 1919. Joined Robert Koch Institute, Berlin as deputy director of research. Trained medical laboratory technicians. 1924: three months study at Rockefeller Institute, New York. On return to Berlin continued important studies on pneumococci and the variability of the diphtheria bacillus. Developed technique for microscopic manipulation of single cells. From April 1928 was chief assistant to Neufeld. 1930: read paper on discovery of causative agent of psittacosis. Awarded Paul Ehrlich Prize. 1933: Levinthal, as a Jew, was arrested in the Robert Koch Institute by the Nazis. He escaped to London. He worked there and in Bath. May 1941: joined staff of RCP Laboratory, Forrest Road. Published several papers there. After the war, in recognition of research achievements in Berlin and to compensate, Dr Levinthal was granted title of Professor Emeritus of the Robert Koch Institute and awarded a pension.

1946: Dr Levinthal was appointed bacteriologist at the Astley Ainslie Hospital, joined by John Ferguson, also from the RCP Laboratory, who then served as his senior technician. Dr Levinthal retired in 1954 and he died in Edinburgh in 1963. An important contribution to the discovery of DNA may be attributed to Dr Levinthal, in collaboration with F. Neufeld (see Note by Professor J.P. Duguid, Appendix B7).

LINDSAY, Robert P.J.

BORN	: 1926
J.D.	: 1941: General training. Salmonella identification; virology laboratory. World War II: service in India and Egypt.
	1948: Rejoined Department. Research assistance; diagnostic bacteriology.
SUB.	: 1956: Stirling Royal Infirmary bacteriology laboratory.
	1957: Bangour Hospital, West Lothian, bacteriology laboratory; examination of milk and water samples for West Lothian; syphilis serology, also pregnancy diagnostic tests. Gained FIMLS in Haematology and Blood Transfusion procedures.
RETIRED	: 1991.

LOGAN, Dr William Robertson

BORN	: 1888, Kelso.
GRAD.	: 1909: University of Edinburgh, MBChB.
	1913: M.D.
	1919: FRCP(E).
	1925: DPH.
P.G.	: Assistant in Pathology Department, University of Edinburgh, with Professor J. Lorrain Smith.
	1913: period of study in Paris. Clinical Pathologist for brief period at RIE. World War I: RAMC: Bacteriologist in East Madras with Middle

East Forces, later in charge of laboratory at 42nd General Hospital at Salonika.

J.RIE. : c. 1919. Clinical Pathologist/Bacteriologist. After appointment of Professor T.J. Mackie as Consultant Bacteriologist to the RIE Bacteriology Laboratory in 1923, Dr Logan was designated as Senior Bacteriologist in this laboratory.

S.I. : Dr Logan's MD thesis was "A Study of the Normal and Pathological Intestinal Flora of Infants and Very Young Children", dated March 1913. His clinical work for this thesis was carried out on patients in Edinburgh's Royal Hospital for Sick Children and the laboratory facilities were provided by Professor James Ritchie in the Royal College of Physicians' Laboratory, of which Professor Ritchie was Superintendent. Dr Logan published a number of papers. He played a prominent part in BMA scientific meetings.

DIED : 1948.

LUDLAM, Dr Gilbert B.

BORN : 1911, Heidelberg.
GRAD. : 1933: University of Edinburgh MBChB.
 1935: DLO.
 1937: DTM&H.
 1953: MD.
P.G. : 1937-39: Junior Research Fellow in Tropical Medicine, Sierra Leone.
J.D. : 1939: Lecturer. In charge of Diagnostic Laboratory. Research.
SUB. : 1948: Consultant Bacteriologist, PHLS, Nottingham.
 1954: Director, Leeds Public Health Laboratory.
S.I. : Toxoplasmosis, making a contribution on this subject of international importance.
DIED : 1976, December.

LUDLAM, Dr Martin

GRAD. : 1937: University of Edinburgh, MBChB.
J.D. : 1938: Demonstrator. Assistant in department's Diagnostic Laboratory. Research: repeated and followed up work of Twort and D'Herelle of the Pasteur Institute, Paris, on bacteriophage with special reference to the city water supplies; studies in bacteriostatic effect of sulphonamides in vitro and in bile fluid; experimented with tellurite medium in the diagnosis of diphtheria.
SUB. : Period of laboratory work Quaker Hospital in central India.
 1948: General practice in Carlisle.
RETIRED : 1976.

LUMSDEN, Professor William H.R.

BORN : 1914, Forfar.
GRAD. : 1935: University of Glasgow, BSc (Hons Zoology).
 1938: MBChB.
 1956: DSc.
 1975: MD (Hons).
 1939: University of Liverpool, DTM&H.

P.G.	: 1938-41: Medical Research Council, Research Fellow. 1941-46: Active service. Lt.-Col. (CO) Malaria Field Laboratories, RAMC, Eastern Mediterranean; N. Africa, Italy, India. 1947-57: Entomologist, Epidemiologist; Assistant Director, East African Virus Research Institute. 1957-63: Director, East African Trypanosomiasis Research Organisation.
J.D.	: 1963-65: Lecturer, Department of Bacteriology, Edinburgh University.
SUB.	: 1965-68: Senior Lecturer, Royal (Dick) School of Veterinary Studies, Edinburgh University. 1968: Visiting Professor, University of Toronto. 1968-79: Professor of Medical Protozoology, London School of Hygiene and Tropical Medicine, University of London.
RETIRED	: 1979. 1979-81: Honorary Research Fellow, University of Dundee. 1981-89: Senior Research Fellow, University of Edinburgh, Department of Genito-urinary Medicine, Royal Infirmary.

McBRIDE, Professor William H.

BORN	: 1944, Worcester, 14 April.
GRAD.	: 1965: University of Edinburgh, BSc (Zoology). 1971: PhD. 1987: University of Edinburgh, DSc.
J.D.	: 1971: Lecturer. 1982: Senior Lecturer.
SUB.	: 1984: Adjunct Professor, Department of Radiation Oncology, University of California, Los Angeles.
S.I.	: In Department: while lecturing in immunology also included cancer biology; effect of adjuvants in immune response; effect of *C. parvum* in anti-tumour responses; mycoplasma and diphtheroids in rheumatoid arthritis. Special interest in teaching methods. At University of California, LA, various aspects of cancer research, especially biology and oncology in relation to radiotherapy.
AUTH	: *The Macrophage and Cancer,* with K. James and A. Stuart, editors, Edinburgh 1977. Contributor to several textbooks. Many scientific papers.

McCABE, Dr Andrew T.

GRAD.	: 1936: University of Edinburgh MBChB. 1940: DPH. 1949: MD. 1963: FRCPath.
P.G.	: RAMC, Pathologist, World War II. EMS Law Junction Hospital.
J.D.	: 1946: Lecturer. 1953: Senior Lecturer.
SUB.	: 1953: Bacteriologist to newly established laboratory at Northern General Hospital. 1961: Consultant Bacteriologist, Central Microbiological Laboratories, Western General Hospital.

RETIRED   : 1976.
DIED   : 1991, November.

McCARTNEY, Dr James E.

BORN   : 1891, Whithorn, Wigtownshire.
GRAD.   : 1915: University of Edinburgh MBChB.
               1922: MD Edin. (Gold Medal).
               1924: DSc.
J.D.   : 1919: Under Professor J. Ritchie, lecturer, following service in RAMC laboratory units in World War I.
               1922: Rockefeller Research Fellow.
               1923: Returned to department.
               1924: Began preparation with Professor T.J. Mackie of first edition of "Mackie and McCartney", *Handbook of Practical Bacteriology* (1925).
SUB.   : 1925: Appointed Director of Metropolitan Asylums Board Research and Pathology Service, London County Council. Became head of laboratory and culture media supply division at Southern Group Laboratory. This service to London hospitals became unique. Of inventive mind, McCartney devised and organised manufacture of many items of laboratory equipment, notably screw cap bottles, the "Universal container" coming to bear his name, also range of prepared culture media. Equipment included a microscope lamp and, in pre-disposable syringe era, an early type of syringe container. In World War II, Southern Group Laboratories supplied culture media, etc. not only to the Emergency Medical Service, but also to British Forces laboratory units and those of allies.
               1949: Dr McCartney acted as consultant to the W.H.O. in connection with a survey of the Italian public health services.
               1952: After 25 years in charge of above service, retired to Adelaide where he became Medical Bacteriologist to Institute of Medical and Veterinary Sciences and Adviser to Southern Australia government hospitals.
DIED   : 1969.

McDONALD, Dr Sheila

BORN   : 1931, Edinburgh.
GRAD.   : 1954: University of Edinburgh: MBChB.
               1966: MD.
               1970: Fellow, Royal College of Physicians of Canada.
P.G.   : 1959-61: Fellowship in Bacteriology, Research Institute, Hospital for Sick Children, Toronto.
               1961-63: Senior Registrar Bacteriology, Western Infirmary, Glasgow.
J.D.   : 1963-67: Lecturer.
SUB.   : Associate Professor of Microbiology, University of Toronto; Associate Professor, Sunnybrook Medical Centre, Toronto.
S.I.   : Transduction in staphylococci. Hospital cross infection.

McGREGOR, Dr Agnes R.

Graduated MBChB at Edinburgh University in 1922 and joined the staff of the

Pathology Department. Four years earlier, while she was still a medical student in the pathology class, Professor J. Lorrain Smith of that department had asked her to undertake part-time work in his department, carrying out biopsies, post-mortems and certain bacteriological examinations. After joining the Pathology Department following graduation, Dr McGregor had been appointed part-time pathologist and bacteriologist to the Royal Hospital for Sick Children in 1922. Prior to this date, Professor James Ritchie, the first incumbent of the new Chair of Bacteriology, had acted as visiting bacteriologist to the hospital.

Dr McGregor's MD thesis was on an aspect of perinatal pathology, and in 1938 she published an important paper on pneumonia in the newborn. Her studies were carried out in collaboration with Dr W.A. Alexander, who for a short period was a member of staff of the University Bacteriology Department and who, in later years, was elected President of the Royal College of Physicians of Edinburgh. In 1938 Dr McGregor was also acting as part-time pathologist to the Simpson Memorial Maternity Pavilion and this work, combined with that in the RHSC, greatly influenced her to develop a special interest in infections of the newborn.

The bacteriological laboratory work required for Sir Harold Stiles' important studies on tuberculosis of children in the RHSC had been carried out in the RCP Laboratory in Forrest Road. Dr McGregor was the first resident bacteriologist at the hospital when appointed in 1922, and although part-time, she began to develop the laboratory and its service. Dr McGregor collaborated closely with Sir Robert Philip, distinguished pioneer and expert on tuberculosis and subsequently with Sir John Crofton. Sir Robert Philip's worldwide reputation maintained Edinburgh's pre-eminence in this field. Herself an internationally recognised authority on the subject, Dr McGregor established at the RHSC a school of paediatric pathology that gained great renown. Indeed, in *Perspectives in Paediatric Pathology* (1987), she was honoured as a founder of this branch of medicine.

Dr McGregor for some time was a close part-time colleague at the hospital of another of Edinburgh's noted lady laboratory workers, Dr Helen Wright of the University Bacteriology department. They were also close friends. Dr McGregor was the first lady elder of the Church of Scotland. In her retirement she became a well known and much loved figure at her cottage in Glen Lyon in Perthshire. She attended the 150th Anniversary Celebrations of the University Department of Pathology in 1981. She died in 1982.

MACGREGOR, Alexander

BORN   : 1930.
J.D.   : 1946: General training. National Service period at Bacteriological Warfare School, Porton.
SUB.   : 1954: BTS Course at RIE, Peel Hospital laboratory, Galashiels.
1956-59: Research technician East Africa Vet. Res. Organisation, Nairobi, Kenya. Technician in charge of clinical laboratory, Aga Khan Hospital, Nairobi.
1961: Technician in charge of Haematology section Pathology Department, Port Moresby General Hospital, Papua, New Guinea.
1969: For three months technician in charge of BTS service in King Edward VII Hospital.

1969: Senior Executive Officer, Laboratory and Field Services, Papua, New Guinea Institute for Medical Research.

1976: Officer in charge of Pathology Department, Warwick Base Hospital, Queensland, Australia.

1979: Sen. Scientist, Gladstone District Hospital.

S.I. : Various haematology studies in New Guinea.

MACKAY, Dr John M.K.

BORN	: 1929, Fife.
GRAD.	: 1951: MRCVS, PhD. (Glasgow).
P.G.	: Assistant in animal practice, Devon. Department of Veterinary Pathology, Glasgow. Lecturer in Veterinary Pathology, Liverpool. Moredun Institute, 1957.
J.D.	: 1971: Senior Lecturer in Virology.
S.I.	: Liver diseases of animals (PhD thesis); at Moredun, early application of cell culture techniques to virology and animal diseases; adenomatosis; scrapie; aetiology of jaagsiekte; alveolar macrophages and herpes virus; viruses in rheumatoid arthritis.
DIED	: 1976, 10 August.

MACKAY, Dr Patricia (Telfer Brunton)

BORN	: 1951, 12 November.
GRAD.	: University of Edinburgh, BSc (Bact. Hons). 1977: PhD.
J.D.	: 1978: Research Fellow.
S.I.	: Structure and antigenic components of hepatitis B surface antigen (PhD thesis); detection of specific viral nucleic acid sequences in liver tissue for patients infected with hepatitis B; Hepatitis Reference Laboratory, diagnostic techniques; many studies on hepatitis B.
RESIGNED	: 1980, October.

McLACHLAN, Dr Donald G.S.

BORN	: 1900.
PRE-UNIV.	: Leaving school at 17, gained commission in Royal Scots. For two years, served in India and Mesopotamia as infantry officer. 1919: Returned to Edinburgh.
GRAD.	: 1924: University of Edinburgh, MBChB (1st class Hons).
J.D.	: 1924: Assistant Lecturer in 1926 and Extra-Bacteriologist to RIE. 1930: Contracted tuberculosis. 1934: While patient in Southfield Sanatorium awarded research fellowship by the RCP(E) and in the Southfield laboratory carried out work on tuberculous allergies.
S.I.	: Toxigenic and serological properties of scarlatinal streptococci; post-operative tetanus.
DIED	: 1935: Professor T.J. Mackie in obituary described Dr McLachlan as "a scientific worker of outstanding ability".

McLEOD, James A.

BORN	: 1922.
J.D.	: 1937: Personal technician to Dr C.E. Van Rooyen and Dr A.J. Rhodes,

in virology. General bacteriological training. Specialised in salmonella identification; leptospiral diagnostic tests.

SUB : 1945: Bacteriology Department, Western Infirmary, Glasgow.
1948: Returned to Edinburgh University Bacteriology Department.
1950: Woodilee Hospital for Mental Disorders, Lenzie.
1962: Bangour Hospital, Haematology and BTS.
1974: Protein Fractionation Centre, BTS, Edinburgh, Processor Controller.

RETIRED : 1982.

McNAUGHTON, Dr Jean (née Wiseman)

BORN : Edinburgh.
GRAD. : 1934: St. Andrews, BSc.
1936: University of Edinburgh BSc (Hons Bact.).
P.G. : 1936: Bristol University. Bacteriology and Pathology Laboratories.
J.D. : 1941: Routine bacteriology of water and milk samples; diphtheria studies with Dr H. Wright. Early preparation of penicillin with Duguid, Challinor, *et al.*, for use in RIE cases.
RESIGNED : 1946.
DIED : April 1990.

MACRAE, Dr Alastair D.

Dr A.D. Macrae graduated from Aberdeen University, MBChB in 1940 and MD in 1950. He became FRCPath in 1969. After war service in the RAMC when he was attached to 51st (H) Division, from Alamein to Germany, he joined the Public Health Laboratory Service as a trainee in 1946 and took the London University Diploma in Bacteriology in 1948. This was followed by a year at Liverpool University Department of Bacteriology studying chlamydial infections, then transfer to the Virus Reference Laboratory, Colindale in 1949. On a US fellowship in 1952-53 at Yale University School of Medicine, New Haven, he took part in the investigation of enteroviruses newly discovered by the cell culture methods introduced by Enders and colleagues. Over the years at Colindale the work included surveys of poliovirus immunity and the prevalence of other enteroviruses, and assessments of the efficacy in the UK of both Salk and Sabin vaccines. Other investigations involved smallpox and chlamydia diagnosis, together with studies of hepatitis B, rabies and rubella, particularly in pregnancy. He was appointed Laboratory Director of the Virus Reference Laboratory at Colindale in 1961 and also contributed virological revision for the 5th and 6th editions of Topley and Wilson's *Principles of Bacteriology, Virology and Immunity*.

From 1970 to 1974 Dr Macrae was Consultant Virologist, City Hospital, Edinburgh and Honorary Senior Lecturer, Department of Bacteriology, Edinburgh University. He enlarged the scope of viral investigations. He then returned to the PHLS as Consultant Virologist and Senior Lecturer, Department of Microbiology, Nottingham University; an outbreak of Legionnaires' disease during this period led to investigations including the development of procedures for diagnosis. He retired in 1983.

McWILLIAM, Dr Joan M.

GRAD. : 1941: University of Edinburgh, MBChB.
1950: DPH

	1964: MRCPath.
	1973: MFCM.
P.G.	: 1944-46: UK and India. Resident Medical Officer, Edinburgh City Hospital; General Practice.
J.D.	: 1957-66: Honorary Registrar, S.E. Scotland Regional Hospital Board; Assistant Bacteriologist, R.I.E. While in the department, Dr McWilliam developed interests in the laboratory diagnosis of pertussis and in general diagnostic bacteriology.
SUB	: 1966-72: Assistant Medical Officer, Communicable Diseases, Edinburgh Health Department. 1972-74: Senior Clinical MO, Edinburgh Health Department. 1978-81: Senior Clinical MO, Edinburgh Community Health Service and Environmental Health CMS, Lothian Health Board.
RETIRED	: 1981.

MESSER, Dr J.D.

J.D.	: 1926.
SUB.	: 1927: Appointed Assistant Medical Officer of Health, Northumberland.

MOFFAT, Dr Margaret A.J.

BORN	: 1934, 12 July.
GRAD.	: 1956: University of Edinburgh, BSc (Hons) Bacteriology. 1960: PhD.
J.D.	: 1956: Research Assistant, Departments of Bacteriology and Pathology. Virology: time-lapse cinematography; Newcastle Disease virus.
SUB.	: 1958: Carnegie Research Scholar. State Serum Institute, Copenhagen. Common Cold Research Unit, Salisbury. 1960: Virologist, Wellcome Research Laboratory, Edinburgh City Hospital. 1967: Lecturer, Department of Bacteriology, University of Aberdeen. 1970: Senior Lecturer, later department (Medical Microbiology), of diagnostic virology service, Grampian area, Orkney and Shetland; HIV screening, testing for rubella immunity and hepatitis B antigen.
S.I.	: At Aberdeen: rubella and influenza vaccine studies; psittacosis; human Q fever; CMV infection in renal transplants; MMR vaccine monitoring.

MUIR, Richard

Richard Muir was born in 1862 and began as a "lab. boy" *c.*1876 in the Pathology Department of Edinburgh University with Professor William R. Sanders who had set out to establish the study and teaching of pathology in Great Britain. Muir was probably the first such "lab. boy" to be employed in an Edinburgh medical laboratory and possibly amongst the first in Great Britain. He rapidly gained great proficiency in pathological techniques, notably staining and microscopy, including the microscopic identification of pathological conditions. He became an internationally recognised authority on his branch of laboratory medicine and was consulted by medicals not only in Edinburgh but from abroad. Muir's distinction was recognised by the University and he was designated as Demonstrator in Pathological and Bacteriological Methods. He was a talented artist and produced a large collection of finely illustrated wall diagrams of pathological conditions and bacteriological subjects as seen microscopically. With the encouragement of Professor T.J. Mackie, whom he assisted technically for some time after his appointment to the Chair of Bacteriology in 1923, he published his famous *Muir's Atlas* in 1927. At that time, he collaborated to produce the section on pathology with Professor James Hamilton of Aberdeen in the *Encyclopaedia Brittanica*, 11th edition, 1920-11. With the active support of his departmental colleague, Dr (later Sir) G. Sims Woodhead, Richard pioneered the founding of the first educational and qualifying body for medical laboratory technicians, with a few English colleagues, establishing the Pathological and Bacteriological Laboratory Assistants' Association. He personally guaranteed the cost of founding the Association and was the body's first Vice-President. He died in February 1931.

MUIR, Professor Sir Robert

GRAD.   : 1881: University of Edinburgh, MA.
             1888: MB.CM.
             1890: MD.
             1895: FRCP(E).
             1901: FRCP (Glas.).
             1911: FRS.
             Awarded other honorary degrees.

P.G.   : After graduating in medicine, awarded a Vans Dunlop Scholarship for research in pathology, carried out under Professor W. Greenfield. MD thesis on study of leucocytes in infectious disease. In 1894 he was appointed to the newly created Edinburgh University Lectureship (within Pathology Department) in Pathological Bacteriology. In 1898, appointed Professor of Pathology in the newly created Chair of Pathology, Glasgow University. In 1897, Muir had published jointly with Dr James Ritchie (then in Oxford, but 16 years later to become first Professor of Bacteriology at Edinburgh) his *Manual of Bacteriology* (1897) which quickly became a standard work, reaching its 11th edition in 1949. Muir's *Textbook of Pathology*, 1924, was also widely acclaimed. In his early years in the Glasgow Chair, Muir wrote an important series of studies on immunity, later published in book form. He later specialised in the study of haemolytic agents in vivo. Muir was knighted in 1934. He retired in 1936 and died in 1959 at the age of 95. A proper account and assessment of Sir Robert Muir's most substantial contribution to the development of pathology is outwith the scope of this work.

NORVAL, John

Mr Norval, as Veterinary Inspector for the City of Edinburgh and later Deputy Director of Environmental Health (Veterinary Services), with responsibility for meat and other food inspection in the city, had a very close association with the University Department of Bacteriology until his retiral in 1979. His important collaboration with Dr Joyce Coghlan on leptospirosis in piggery workers is referred to elsewhere. John Norval qualified as a veterinary surgeon from Edinburgh's Royal (Dick) Veterinary College in 1937, gaining many honours and distinctions. He joined Edinburgh Corporation as an Assistant Veterinary Inspector in 1940, and four years later he was appointed Veterinary Inspector for the city, in charge of veterinary services in the Public Health Department. Throughout his career Mr Norval was closely involved in supervising the inspection of foodstuffs in Edinburgh. While this responsibility was unusual for a veterinary inspector, such was common practice in many other countries.

In the 1950s, much dried egg and bulk frozen egg was imported from China and Australia, etc., and this was frequently contaminated with salmonellae. Mr Norval campaigned for a pasteurisation process to be enforced, which led to appropriate legislation. He influenced new legislation in several other spheres, thus ensuring good food standards and the prevention of food poisoning. Supervision of the school meals service was a special responsibility as was the advising of kitchen supervisors.

Amongst the many research projects Mr Norval carried out, one was the consequence of the Aberdeen typhoid outbreak of 1964. In experiments carried out in the University Bacteriology Department with the co-operation of Dr R.H.A. Swain, Mr Norval was able to report that bacteria of the salmonella group could be present and reproduce in a sealed tin of corned beef without causing blowing of the tin. This was relevant to the Aberdeen outbreak when *S. typhi* occurred in such a sealed tin. Another study was carried out on the dangers of serving pre-cooked meat in canteens when the meat had not been rapidly cooled. Other work with Dr (later Professor) J.G. Collee was concerned with safety precautions in large-scale pie production.

Mr Norval lectured to veterinary students and published and read many papers. His commitment and thoroughness and his great experience were admired. He regularly visited the department and gained much enthusiastic co-operation in investigations and teaching of real practical importance. The excellence of his own instruction at Gorgie Abattoir, where there was a small bacteriology laboratory, was widely acknowledged. Mr Norval was awarded the OBE in 1977. He retired in 1979.

OAG, Dr Robert K.

GRAD. : 1937: University of Edinburgh, MBChB.
J.D.   : 1937: Lecturer.
S.I.   : Worked with C.G. Anderson on effect of gastric mucin on meningococcus and other bacteria, with special reference to virulence. Bactericidal tests with early May and Baker (M & B) chemotherapeutic agents. Sterilisation by dry heat with special reference to resistance of spores.
DIED   : 1944: In September from a laboratory acquired infection (see note by Professor Duguid in Appendix B6).
       Dr Oag was a skilled marksman and shot for the King's Cup at Bisley.

OGMUNDSDOTTIR, Dr Helga M. (Mrs H. Holbrook)

BORN   : 14 December 1948, Iceland.
GRAD. : University of Iceland, Cand. med. et chir.
       1975: First-class Degree with Honours.
       1979: University of Edinburgh PhD in immunology.

P.G.   : 1975: House Officer, Department of Medicine, University Hospital, Reykjavik, Iceland.
J.D.   : 1975: Research Associate.
              1976: Awarded Gunning Research Scholarship.
              1979: Appointed lecturer.
SUB.   : 1981-86: Returned to Iceland to take up appointment in Virus Laboratory, National University Hospital of Iceland, Reykjavik and as part-time Senior Lecturer in Immunology and Virology.
              1982: Icelandic specialist recognition in immunology.
              1986: Reader in cell biology at Faculty of Medicine, University of Iceland.
              1987: Director of the Molecular and Cell Biology Research Laboratory at the Icelandic Cancer Society.
S.I.   : Macrophage function; chlamydia; natural killer cells in relation to haematological malignancies; cell biology of human breast cancer with particular reference to familial risk factors.

POOLE, William S.H.

BORN   : 1927, Edinburgh.
J.D.   : 1949: Graded Medical Laboratory Technician in view of military service (1946-48) in various disciplines in medical laboratories of the RAMC. Tropical experience in Malaya and Singapore. Trained in Public Health Diagnostic Laboratory; also in preparation of teaching material and was assistant to various research workers. Gained Associateship of IMLT.
SUB.   : 1958: Took up an appointment with Ministry of Agriculture and Fisheries, New Zealand.
              1958-70: Poultry diagnostic officer with wide range of experience; responsible for management of Silverstream Isolation Unit and Wallaceville Poultry Unit, Upper Hutt.
AUTH.   : Co-author of wide range of papers on veterinary laboratory diagnosis, research and control.
RETIRED   : 1989.

PURDIE, Dr Isabella A.

GRAD.   : 1935: University of Edinburgh MBChB.
              1938: DPH.
              1963: FRCP.
J.D.   : 1940: Part-time lecturer/demonstrator. EMS laboratories, World War II.
SUB.   : Consultant Bacteriologist, Bangour Hospital, West Lothian.
RETIRED   : 1965.
DIED   : 1989.

RATTRIE, Dr Robert J.G.

BORN   : 1919.
GRAD.   : 1943: University of Edinburgh MBChB.
              1946: MD.

J. RIE.   : 1946: Assistant Bacteriologist. 1948: Resigned to enter general practice in Maryport, Cumberland.
DIED   : 1966: Killed in car accident.

RHODES, Professor Andrew J.

BORN   : 1911, Inverness.
GRAD.   : 1934: University of Edinburgh, MBChB.
           1941: MD, FRCP(Edin).
           1972: FRCP(Canada).
P.G.   : Assistant Bacteriologist, Royal Infirmary of Edinburgh.
J.D.   : 1935: Lecturer.
SUB.   : 1941: Pathologist, EMS, Shrewsbury; Bacteriologist, Shropshire County Council.
           1945: Lecturer in Department of Bacteriology and Immunology, London School of Hygiene and Tropical Medicine, University of London.
           1947: Research Associate, Connaught Medical Research Labs., University of Toronto.
           1953: Director of Research Institute, Hospital for Sick Children, Toronto.
           1956: Director of School of Hygiene, University of Toronto.
           1970: Professor of Microbiology, Department of Microbiology, University of Toronto.
           1972: Medical Director of Laboratory Services Branch, Ontario Ministry of Health. In addition, several international appointments.
S.I.   : In Edinburgh: bacteriophage; dysentery in water supply; other studies on dysentery. Pioneered virology in Edinburgh University Bacteriology Department with Dr C.E. Van Rooyen in the 1930s. In Canada, wide-ranging interests in virology.
AUTH   : *Virus Diseases of Man* with C.E. Van Rooyen, Oxford University Press, 1940; *Textbook of Virology for Students and Practitioners of Medicine* with C.E. Van Rooyen, Williams and Wilkins, Toronto, 1949.
HONOURS : Fellow of Royal Society of Canada. Several medical honours.

ROBB, Iain

Mr Robb spent two years as a trainee technician in the University department. 1952-54. He subsequently began studies in the Faculty of Science in 1959 and graduated BSc (Hons) in Ecology in 1966. After teaching posts at Knox Academy, Haddington, and the then Napier College, he joined the University administration and became Assistant Secretary at the Old College in 1983. His special duties have included responsibility for Royal visits to the University and other ceremonial occasions.

ROBERTSON, James

BORN   : 1926, Edinburgh.

Jim Robertson's earliest association with Edinburgh Royal Infirmary to which he was to give such valuable and lengthy service in its Bacteriology Laboratory, began in 1940 when he was first employed as a "lift boy" in the busy surgical corridor. His other duties included delivering specimens to the laboratory at Westgate and such visits prompted him to seek a post as a junior laboratory assistant there. In 1941 therefore he changed over from delivering to receiving the specimens, in due course being trained to process them which he continued to do for 46 years. His training was at the hands of one of Edinburgh's most notable Chief Technicians, Bobby Barr.

Jim Robertson's career ranged widely in diagnostic bacteriology, but not until he had first been "broken in" by washing up duties and delivering reports and specimen containers to the wards. He had obtained a useful groundwork in laboratory methods when he was called to the Royal Army Medical Corps in 1945 for three years' service. Returning to the laboratory, Jim Robertson, having first taken the Institute of Medical Laboratory Technology Associateship in Bacteriology, subsequently gained the Fellowship by the examination in histopathology. After Jimmy Dick's death, Jim Robertson acted as Senior Technician until the appointment of Ian Samuel from Moredun Institute, then continued as Chief Technician. For several years he was a part-time Demonstrator in the Ordinary National Certificate (Microbiology) course at Napier College.

Amongst Jim Robertson's specialised experience in the laboratory was work with one of the hospital surgeons on wound infections; collaboration with Dr Joan McWilliam on work for the Renal Unit; involvement with Dr Ralph Tonkin on *Staphylococcus aureus* monitoring in the Simpson Memorial Maternity Pavilion and in renal transplants. Latterly he was responsible for special containment work on potentially dangerous pathogens including legionella and tubercle bacilli in the Category B and Containment Laboratory in the Clinical Microbiology Department after the Royal Infirmary Laboratory had transferred to the Medical School.

RETIRED : 1987.

ROBERTSON, Dr Matthew H.

GRAD.   : 1951: University of St. Andrews, MBChB.
             1976: FRCPath.
P.G.   : 1952-53: Assistant in Pathology and Bacteriology, University of St. Andrews.
             1954-56: RAF (National Service), pathologist, Squadron Leader.
             1957: assistant in pathology, University of St. Andrews.
J.D.   : 1958-63: Lecturer in Edinburgh University Bacteriology Department, working mainly in Bacteriology Laboratory, RIE
SUB.   : 1963: Consultant microbiologist, Epping Group of Hospitals serving general practitioners and Community Services.
S.I.   : Epidemiology, especially food poisoning investigations and leptospirosis in fish farm workers; hospital infection control; urinary infections; listeriosis. Member of many medical and laboratory committees in area.
AUTH   : Author and co-author of very many papers especially concerning typhoid fever outbreaks; haemolytic streptocci and tetracycline resistance; urinary tract infections; survival of *S. typhimurium* in floor dust, etc.

RYLAND-WHITTAKER, Dr Joseph (subsequently Rev. Fr. Whittaker, S.J.)

BORN   : 1896, Edinburgh.

PRE-UNIV. : 1916: World War I, 2nd Lieutenant Royal Field Artillery.
Awarded Military Cross for bravery in the field.
GRAD. : 1923: Licentiate Royal Colleges of Physicians and Surgeons (Edinburgh).
1926: MB, University of London.
J.D. : 1928: Lecturer.
S.I. : Bactericidal power of blood in pregnancy.
SUB. : 1936: Ordained Catholic priest (Society of Jesus). Eventually served at Lerwick where he restored the fine small chapel there built by Italian prisoners-of-war in World War II. Later at Stornoway.
DIED : 1963, Stornoway.

SAMUEL, John Ian McA.
BORN : 1920.
1935-62: Senior Experimental Officer at Animal Diseases Research Association laboratories (Moredun Institute).
J.D. : 1962: Chief MLSO, Royal Infirmary of Edinburgh Bacteriology Laboratory.
1972: On James Dick's death, promoted to Senior Chief MLSO. Wide experience of animal diseases and preparation of vaccines and antisera for these. On joining RIE staff responsible for technician training and the work of the technical staff in the various diagnostic groups. Collaborated with Dr J. Bowie in monitoring of hospital sterilisers, etc. Taught voluntarily in IMLS courses for 20 years. Member of various IMLS committees responsible for training and examinations.
A special feature of the Royal Infirmary Bacteriology Department has been its team system: the various bacteriologists and MLSOs working in groups or teams with each of these responsible for a particular section of the laboratory's diagnostic work and each team also associated with groups of wards and specialised units in the hospital. In turn, these teams are integrated and collaborate in the work of the laboratory as a whole. Such an approach demands careful organisation, planning and most essential, motivation and detailed application stemming from leadership. For long, all of this was made possible by the strong influence and driving force of Ian Samuel.
RETIRED : 1982.

SELWYN, Professor Sydney
BORN : 1934, Leeds.
GRAD. : 1958: University of Edinburgh, BSc (Bact. Hons).
1959: MBChB.
1966: MD.
1968: FRCPath.
1972: FIBiol.
J.D. : 1960: Research Fellow in Bacteriology, Research Fellow in Virology.
1962: Lecturer.
1966: Senior Lecturer.
1966: WHO visiting Professor S.E. Asia, based in Baroda, India.

SUB. : 1967: Senior Lecturer in Bacteriology, Westminster Medical School and Honorary Consultant in Bacteriology, Westminster Hospital.
1974: Reader, Medical Microbiology, London University, Westminster Medical School.
1979: Professor of Medical Microbiology, London University, Westminster Medical School; also in 1983 Professor Medical Microbiology, Charing Cross Hospital Medical School (this and Westminster Medical School Chairs combined in 1984).

S.I. : Early work in virology in Edinburgh University. In the bacteriology section, he was interested in epidemiology and prevalence of hospital acquired infections; microflora of skin and mucous membranes. Antimicrobial therapy. Broadcaster and writer. Authority on the history of medicine and medical microbiology in the UK and abroad.

SEMPLE, Dr Stuart M.

GRAD. : 1962: University of Edinburgh MBChB.
1974: MRCGP.
1979: MFHom.

J.D. : 1966: Registrar post, University and RIE in bacteriology and pathology; clinical chemistry and haematology.
1968-72: Lecturer, Bacteriology Department.

SUB. : 1972-75: General practice, Livingston. 1975-78: General practice, Bo'ness. 1977-88: General practice, Winchburgh. 1989: Private practice, Edinburgh and West Lothian.

S.I. : Chairman, British Homoeopathy Research Group.

SHENNAN, Dr Theodore

GRAD. : 1890: University of Edinburgh, MBCM.
1895: MD
1808: FRCS(E).

Dr Shennan was appointed Senior Pathologist, Edinburgh Royal Infirmary in 1906. He lectured on bacteriology in the University Pathology Department and to the R.I.E. nursing staff. He carried out work in the Royal College of Physicians' Laboratory in Forrest Road. He lectured on tuberculosis in the USA and he published papers on this subject and also on *Spirochaeta pallidum* in syphilis and the bacteriology of epidemic cerebro-spinal meningitis. Dr Shennan was one of the earliest to carry out bacteriology work, within the Pathology Department, at the Royal Infirmary. He was appointed Professor of Pathology at Aberdeen University in 1914.

AUTH. : Publications include "Koch and His Work". Health Lectures for the People. No. 6. MacNiven & Wallace, 1899.

SINCLAIR, Dr Robin

GRAD. : 1959: University of Edinburgh, MBChB.

SUB. : Junior Assistant, Departments of Bacteriology and Pathology, Southern General Hospital, Glasgow.
1972: Consultant Bacteriologist, Mansefield and Chesterfield Hospitals.

J.D.	: 1962: Assistant bacteriologist, RIE Bacteriology Laboratory; Lecturer, University Bacteriology Department.
S.I.	: Extensive development work on sterilisation of heat-sensitive materials, especially use of ethylene oxide.
DIED	: 1981. Dr Sinclair is warmly remembered for his good fellowship, his conscientious work and his enduring courtesy.

SLEIGH, Professor James Douglas

BORN	: 1930.
GRAD.	: 1953: University of Glasgow, MBChB (Hons).
	1976: FRCPE.
	1982: FRCP(Glas.).
P.G.	: 1954: Pathologist, Royal Army Medical Corps.
	1956: Registrar in Bacteriology, Western Infirmary, Glasgow.
J.D.	: 1958: Lecturer. Honorary Senior Registrar, South-East Scotland Regional Hospital Board.
SUB.	: 1965: Consultant in Clinical Pathology, Dunbartonshire Area Laboratory; Consultant in Bacteriology, Killearn Hospital.
	1969: Senior Lecturer, Department of Bacteriology and Immunology, Western Infirmary and University of Glasgow; Honorary Consultant in Bacteriology, Western Infirmary, Glasgow.
	1984: Reader, Department of Bacteriology, Royal Infirmary of Glasgow and Honorary Consultant in Bacteriology, Royal Infirmary, Glasgow.
	1989: Awarded Personal Chair of Bacteriology, University of Glasgow.
	1990: Acting Head of Department.
S.I.	: Urinary tract infections; antibiotic administration, especially in surgical cases; *Shigella; E. coli; Klebsiella;* enteric fevers; Hepatitis B and laboratory staff; diminished immune response.
AUTH.	: *Notes on Medical Bacteriology,* with M.C. Timbury, Churchill Livingstone, 1982.
RETIRED	: 1994.

SMEALL, Dr John T.

BORN	: Jedburgh.
ARMY SERVICE	: 1900: Joined London Scottish Regiment, then Gordon Highlanders and served during Boer War in the South Africa Campaign. Awarded Military Cross.
	Trained as an accountant, then studied medicine.
GRAD.	: 1912: University of Edinburgh, MBChB.
J.D.	: 1930: RIE staff. Assistant Bacteriologist.
RETIRED	: 1946.

SMITH, Charles J.

BORN	: 1920, Edinburgh.
J.D.	: 1934.
	1965: Senior Chief MLSO. FIMLS.
S.I.	: Syphilis serology (including TPI.); fish examination.
	1940-55: Professor T.J. Mackie's personal technician.

Monitoring of sterility of surgical sutures.

Writer and lecturer on aspects of Edinburgh's history. (See also the Foreword to this volume).

RETIRED   : 1982.

SMITH, James H.T.

Began as laboratory assistant in Pathology Laboratory in RIE in 1918 with pathologist Dr W.A. Alexander, then worked in University Pathology Department in the Medical School, followed by a spell in the Pathology Laboratory in the RHSC. Subsequently, he worked with Dr Agnes McGregor, carrying out bacteriological procedures in addition to pathology. After six years at the RHSC, James Smith became technical assistant to the Conservator of the museum of the Royal College of Surgeons in Nicolson Street.

Mr Smith was appointed a member of the City of Edinburgh Special Constables.

STEWART, Professor Charles Hunter

Professor Hunter Stewart graduated at Edinburgh University: BSc in 1882, and MBChB in 1884, specialising in chemistry and, to gain experience during his vacations, worked in laboratories in Munich, Amsterdam and Paris, in the latter studying under Louis Pasteur. Professor Stewart was appointed assistant to Professor Sir Douglas Maclagan in the Department of Medical Jurisprudence (subsequently Forensic Medicine) and was placed in charge of the "public health laboratory" that Professor Maclagan had established in his department. No details of the work of this early laboratory could be traced, apart from its use in teaching public health.

When the new Bruce and John Usher Chair of Public Health was created in 1898, Stewart was the first incumbent. Four years later, when the Usher Institute was opened, Professor Stewart transferred there and he was responsible for the teaching of bacteriology and the establishment of a large bacteriology laboratory which, in 1902, took over from the Royal College of Physicians' Laboratory the provision of a bacteriological diagnostic service for general practitioners, under the aegis of Edinburgh Corporation. Professor Stewart delegated the actual equipping of this laboratory and its day-to-day supervision to his assistant, Dr James B. Young (see biographical notes). He published many papers on bacteriological subjects, notably in the study of air in schools and public buildings and the ventilation of the wards of the Royal Infirmary.

Professor Stewart died in June 1924.

STEWART, Dr Donald

GRAD.   : 1925: University of Edinburgh MBChB.
             1927: MD.
J.D.   : 1928-32: Assistant to Edinburgh University Professor of Tuberculosis.
             Medical Officer, Southfield Sanatorium, Edinburgh.
S.I.   : Studies on tuberculosis; tuberculous meningitis.

STEWART, Dr Sheila M.

BORN   : 1923.
GRAD.   : 1945: University of London, BSc (Hons).
             1957: University of Edinburgh.

P.G.   : 1945-46: Assistant Bacteriologist, Express Dairy Processing Laboratory, London.

1946-48: Assistant, Chemotherapy Department, Wellcome Physiological Research Laboratories.

1948-52: Bacteriologist, Children's Hospital, Sheffield and Honorary Demonstrator, Department of Bacteriology, University of Sheffield.

1952-67: Royal Victoria Hospital Tuberculosis Trust, Bacteriology Research Fellow, Department of Respiratory Diseases and Tuberculosis, University of Edinburgh.

J.D.   : 1967-68: MRC Assistant, Edinburgh University Department of Bacteriology, Honorary Lecturer.

1968-75: Lecturer.

S.I.   : 1952-60: With Professor Sir John Crofton and Dr A.T. Wallace (City Hospital and Southfield Hospital), investigations into optimal drug regimens in treatment of tuberculosis, along with the laboratory detection of and clinical significance of all degrees of drug resistance in *M. tuberculosis;* research into non-tubercular respiratory diseases, including mycoplasma pneumonia and rheumatoid arthritis (see Note by Professor Sir John Crofton in the Appendix C).

AUTH.   : Many research papers on bacteriology of bronchitis and pneumonia, role of *Mycoplasma pneumoniae* in respiratory infection, antibiotic studies on *Mycobacterium tuberculosis,* antibiotic sensitivity patterns of respiratory isolates.

RETIRED   : 1975.

STILES, Professor Sir Harold

Sir Harold Stiles was one of Edinburgh's earliest bacteriologists. He graduated MBChB in 1885, the most distinguished graduate of the year. His postgraduate appointment to Professor John Chiene led to his acquiring the latter's keen and practical interest in bacteriology and also in his new pathological techniques. Stiles was Chiene's "carbolic spray clerk" for some time. It is claimed that he introduced aseptic surgery into Scotland. When appointed surgeon to the Royal Hospital for Sick Children in 1898, Stiles persuaded the directors to install a steam steriliser. The Royal Infirmary adopted this practice soon afterwards.

As a result of his work with children suffering from tuberculosis, Stiles along with the distinguished surgeon Sir John Fraser, contended against Robert Koch's thesis that "the bovine tubercle bacillus was not responsible for the development of human tuberculosis" and that "the risk of human infection from milk from tuberculous cows was negligible". In 1910 a Royal Commission disproved Koch's statements. The laboratory investigations on bovine and human tuberculosis by Stiles, Fraser and J.P. McGowan were carried out in the Royal College of Physicians' Laboratory. McGowan was a bacteriologist on the staff of this laboratory. Stiles eventually set up a small bacteriology laboratory in the RHSC. Sir Harold Stiles was appointed to the Chair of Clinical Surgery in Edinburgh in 1910. He died in 1946.

SUTHERLAND, Professor Ian W.

GRAD.   : 1960: University of Edinburgh, BSc., PhD., DSc.

J.D.   : 1961: Lecturer in Microbial Physiology. Worked with (the then) Dr J.F. Wilkinson on proteins of *Bordetella pertussis* and chemical structure of Klebsiella type-specific capsular polysaccharides.

SUB. : Visitor to Karolinski Institute, Stockholm, during studies for PhD, two sabbatical periods at Max Planck Institut fur Immunobiologie, Freiburg, working on bacterial lipo-polysaccharides and exopolysaccharides. There developed interest in microbial extracellular and wall polysaccharides leading to widespread co-operation with laboratories in Europe and North America; also to collaboration in industrial aspects of these effects and UK Department of Energy.

1966: One of the founder members of the then new Department of Microbiology at King's Buildings.

1975: Became a Senior Lecturer.

1979: Reader.

1991: In October he was appointed to a Personal Chair in Microbial Physiology.

Member, Convener or Chairman of various senior professional committees.

AUTH. : Many research papers in scientific journals and contributor to several textbooks.

SUTHERLAND, James A.W.

BORN : 1920.

J.D. : 1937: General training. Assistant to Dr Alexander Haddow, worked on studies of induction of tumours in rats; virology laboratory; Public Health Diagnostic Laboratory, Salmonella identification.

SUB : 1960: University Hospital, Saskatchewan, with Professor Dempster. 1962: returned to Edinburgh, appointment in Regional Virus Laboratory, City Hospital, Edinburgh as Senior MLSO. Routine virology.

RETIRED : 1985.

SWAIN, Dr Richard H.A.

BORN : 1910, Wimbledon.

GRAD. : Downing College, Cambridge, MA.

1937: St. Bartholomew's Medical School, MBBS.

1943: MD (Cantab), FRCP(E), FRCPath, FRSE.

P.G. : Trained as pathologist under Professor L.P. Garrod, St. Bartholomew's; Senior Demonstrator in Morbid Anatomy and Histology, St. Bartholomew's 1942; Pathologist in charge of Clinical Pathology, EMS, Hillend Hospital, St. Albans; World War II Specialist Pathologist in RAMC, Middle East, Sicily, Italy and Austria where he directed the main laboratory for Central Mediterranean Forces. Returned to Hillend Hospital (under auspices of St. Bartholomew's Hospital) in charge of bacteriology, pathology and Public Health laboratories.

J.D. : 1947: Appointed lecturer in Edinburgh University Bacteriology Department, but sent for six months to study virology with Professor S. Bedson at the London Hospital. 1948: Senior Lecturer with special responsibility for virology.

1951: Established first electron microscopy unit in Scotland.

1957: Reader in Virology, Honorary Consultant Virologist to RIE and City Hospital.

1955-58 and 1966-68: Acting Head of Department during the interregnum periods

S.I. : Myxoviruses, electron microscope studies of cells and tissues infected with viruses, and structure of spirochaetes.

AUTH. : *Clinical Virology* with T.C. Dodds, Livingstone, 1967. Co-editor of Mackie and McCartney *Handbook of Practical Bacteriology*. Dr Swain edited revised reprints of the 9th edn of Mackie and McCartney's *Handbook of Practical Bacteriology* (1956, 1959), Livingstone. He contributed to the 10th edn (1960) and was an Assistant Editor of the 11th and 12th edns (1965, 1973-75). He was co-editor, with J.P. Duguid and B.P. Marmion, of Vol. I of the 13th edn, (1978).

RETIRED : 1975.

DIED : 1981, May.

TELFER BRUNTON, Dr William Andrew

BORN : 1948, 20 February.

GRAD. : 1970: University of Edinburgh, BSc (Bact. Hons).
1973: MBChB.
1980: MRC.Path.

P.G. : 1974: Lecturer, Department of Clinical Chemistry, Edinburgh University; Royal Infirmary of Edinburgh then Senior House Officer and Registrar.

J.D. : 1976: Lecturer.

SUB. : 1980: Director/Consultant Microbiologist, Public Health, Royal Cornwall Hospital, Truro.

S.I. : Clinical chemistry studies; campylobacters; urinary tract infection; mycoplasmas; computerisation of laboratory records.

THOMSON, Professor Scott

GRAD. : 1933: Edinburgh University, MBChB.
1936: DPH.
1940: MD (Gold Medal).
1954: FRCP(E).
1964: FRCPath.

J.D. : 1934: Crichton Scholarship then Lewis Cameron lecturer. World War II: RAMC. Important work with Penicillin Control Unit as Bacteriologist to the Penicillin Research Team in the Central Mediterranean Force, 1943-45.

SUB. : Bacteriologist, Dumfries; Professor of Bacteriology, Welsh National School of Medicine, Cardiff; Consultant Bacteriologist, Public Health Laboratory, Cardiff and Cardiff Royal Infirmary; Consultant Adviser in Bacteriology, Welsh Health Board with special reference to intestinal infections, tuberculosis, staphyloccal infections.

S.I. : Immunology; scarlatina; early research on penicillin; Public Health diagnostic methods.

DIED : 1992, March.

TINNE, Dr John E.

BORN	: 1913.
GRAD.	: 1941: University of Edinburgh, MBChB.
	1948: DPH.
	1951: BSc. (Bact. Hons).
	1964: MD, MRCP.
	1941-42: Bacteriologist, City Hospital.
P.G.	: World War II, Medical Officer to General Montgomery's HQ Staff, S.E. England; then Arakan Front, Burma; in charge of laboratories at Jalna and Ahmednagar in India, responsible for local public health control and military hospitals.
J.D.	: 1948: Lecturer, short period teaching.
SUB.	: January 1952: City Hospital, Edinburgh, Assistant Bacteriologist.
	October 1952: Assistant Bacteriologist, Public Health Laboratory, Taunton.
	December 1953: Honorary Assistant Bacteriologist, Glasgow Royal Infirmary, and Lecturer, Glasgow University.
	September 1958: Consultant Bacteriologist, Glasgow Royal Infirmary, and Honorary Clinical Lecturer in Bacteriology, Glasgow University.
S.I.	: Tuberculosis, many aspects, and related chemotherapy; infantile gastroenteritis; surgical disinfectants; establishment of museum of microbiology at Glasgow Royal Infirmary.
RETIRED	: 1978.

TONKIN, Dr Ralph W.

BORN	: 1922.
GRAD.	: 1945: University of Edinburgh MBChB.
	1974: FRCPath.
	1979: FRCP(E).
	1946-48: Surgeon-Lieutenant RNVR with Destroyer Flotilla, British Pacific Fleet.
J.D.	: RIE staff.
	1948: Assistant Bacteriologist.
	1952: RIE post combined with lectureship, Bacteriology Department, University of Edinburgh.
	1953: Honorary Senior Hospital Medical Officer in Bacteriology to the Royal Infirmary of Edinburgh.
	1968: Senior Lecturer, University Bacteriology Department and Honorary Consultant in Bacteriology.
S.I.	: *E. coli* in infants; neonatal staphylococcal infections; procedures to prevent spread of such staphylococcal infections; monitoring bacteriologically of Renal Transplantation Unit and other operating theatres. Hepatitis Advisory Group 1970; risks to hospital personnel.
RETIRED	: 1983.

TULLOCH, Dr Nina (née Verity)

GRAD.	: 1937: University of Edinburgh MBChB (Hons).
P.G.	: House Surgeon, Minehead and West Somerset Hospital. Resident

House Surgeon, Simpson Memorial Maternity Pavilion, Edinburgh.
J.D.   : 1940-64: Part-time lecturer and demonstrator.
             See "Extra Mural Activities" below.

VALENTINE, William A.B.

Mr Valentine was educated at George Heriot's School and began work as a junior clerk in the former Edinburgh Public Health Department in Johnston Terrace. His duties included the investigation of cases and outbreaks of infectious diseases such as diphtheria, scarlet fever, food poisoning, etc. He qualified as a member of the Royal Sanitary Institute. For some time he lectured on building construction at the Heriot-Watt College. Eventually, in the course of his duties as Epidemics Inquiry Officer, Mr Valentine became closely associated with the University Bacteriology Department. Following an outbreak of food poisoning Mr Valentine would obtain samples of suspected food which he brought to the department's public health laboratory for bacteriological examination. He recalled being involved in endeavouring to trace the source of an epidemic of meningococcal meningitis during World War II. During the serious outbreak of smallpox in Edinburgh in 1942, Mr Valentine, with his colleagues, were on call "night and day", visiting the affected households. Houses in which a case had occurred were disinfected by Dr Jack of the Public Health Department. Mr Valentine served under six successive Edinburgh Medical Officers of Health. He would now have been designated an Environmental Health Officer. He died in February 1991.

VAN ROOYEN, Professor Clennel E.

BORN   : 1907, Ceylon
GRAD.   : 1931: University of Edinburgh, MBChB.
             1934: MD (Gold Medal), FRCP, FRCP(E), FRS Canada.
             Member of many Canadian learned societies.
J.D.   : 1932: Lecturer. Pioneered establishment of virology in the department with Dr (later Professor) A.J. Rhodes. Early studies in department on Hodgkin's Disease; then influenza, poliomyelitis and vaccinia. Treatment of GPI in selected Craighouse Mental Hospital patients by inducement of malaria. Appointed extra-bacteriologist to Royal Infirmary of Edinburgh. In World War II was initially pathologist at Military Hospital in Peebles Hydropathic. Subsequently pathologist at 1st General Hospital, RAMC, British Expeditionary Forces, Dieppe. Dealt with outbreaks of meningitis. Was appointed officer with specialist knowledge of virus diseases to Central Laboratory, Middle East Forces, Egypt. There investigated typhus, plague and smallpox. Awarded Order of Ismail by Egyptian government for important work on typhus and smallpox. Also important studies on infectious hepatitis in British and other Middle East troops (10,000 cases in 1943). Proved experimentally on prisoners in USA penitentiary that infectious hepatitis (as hepatitis A was then called) was transmitted by faeces.
SUB   : 1946: Appointed Professor of Virus Diseases, University of Toronto School of Hygiene and research work in Connaught Medical laboratories.

1956	: Appointed Professor of Microbiology at University of Dalhousie, occupying this post for 20 years. After retiral, remained consultant to Canadian government bodies. Awarded many Canadian civil and medical honours.
AUTH.	: Published revised edition of *Muir's Bacteriological Atlas* in 1937. *Virus Diseases of Man* with A.J. Rhodes, Oxford University Press, 1940. *Textbook of Virology for Students and Practitioners of Medicine*, Williams & Wilkins, Baltimore, 1962.
DIED	: February 1989.

WALLACE, Dr Archibald T.

GRAD.	: 1931: University of Edinburgh MBChB. 1936: DPH. 1951: MD. 1963: MRCP(E). 1979: FRCP(E).
P.G.	: General practice, Dingwall. 1937-39: Assistant Bacteriologist, Royal Infirmary of Edinburgh. 1939-40: Junior TB Officer, Edinburgh Corporation Public Health Department. World War II. 1941: RAMC Medical Officer and Pathologist 42nd and 59th Gordon Highlanders and later other companies of this regiment. Served in Ethiopia, Egypt, Sudan and Italy. MO, Military General Hospital, Peebles.
J.D.	: 1946: Lecturer. 1946-74: Senior Lecturer.
SUB.	: 1948-74: Bacteriologist, City Hospital. 1974-78: Bacteriologist, Tuberculosis Service in Libya.
S.I.	: Hospital infection; bacteriological studies of air; very many aspects of tuberculosis and sensitivity of tubercle bacilli to chemotherapy; participation in trials with Professor Crofton in association with MRC and International Union Against Tuberculosis; general diagnostic bacteriology.
RETIRED	: 1978.
DIED	: 1992, August.

WATSON, Dr Hugh F.

GRAD.	: 1911: University of Glasgow MBChB (Dist. Pathology and Bacteriology). 1913: MD (Glas., Hons), and Bellahouston Gold Medal. 1916: DPH (Edin.), FRS(E).
J.D.	: 1923-24.
S.I.	: Syphilis in relation to mental disorders.

WATT, Dr Brian

| BORN | : 1941, Edinburgh. |
| GRAD. | : 1965: University of Edinburgh, MBChB.
1972: MD (high commendation). MI Biol. |

1984: FRCPath.
1988: FI Biol.

J.D.   : 1968-73: Lecturer, Honorary Registrar South Eastern Regional Hospital Board, then Senior Registrar, Honorary Senior Lecturer 1974.

SUB.   : 1982: Consultant Microbiologist, City Hospital, Edinburgh. Head of Department from 1986. Appointed Director, Scottish Mycobacteria Reference Laboratory from 1986.
Area Director, Medical Microbiology Services, Lothian Health Board, from 1991, and Director, Scottish National Anaerobe Reference Laboratory, in addition to his other duties.

S.I.   : Anaerobic bacteria; recovery of these on solid media; antibiotics; wide range of diagnostic bacteriology procedures; mycobacteria and mycobacterial disease in man.

WEIR, Robert H.

J.D.   : 1934: Junior technician, general training.
1939: World War II, RAMC 23rd (Scottish) General Hospital.
1944: Sergeant in technical charge of hospital laboratories in Middle East, gaining wide experience in bacteriology and other related disciplines. Subsequently sergeant in charge of certain hospital laboratories in France, Belgium and Germany.
1946: Returned to University Department, in charge of preparation of culture media.
1948: Appointed Chief Medical Laboratory Technician, Ards Hospital, Newtonards, Northern Ireland.

RETIRED   : 1978.

WILKINSON, Professor John

GRAD.   : 1946: University of Cambridge, BA (Biochemistry).
1949: PhD.

P.G.   : In Cambridge, carried out postgraduate studies in Ernest Gale's Sub-Department of Microbial Biochemistry.

J.D.   : 1949: Lecturer in bacteriology, specialising in microbial biochemistry.

S.I.   : Soon after appointment collaborated closely with Dr (later Professor) J.P. Duguid in investigating various aspects of the physiology of enterobacteria. These studies provided basis for later developments in bacterial continuous culture and the production of extracellular polysaccharides. Research on storage of polymers followed. This work had practical industrial applications. Promoted to Reader in 1963.

SUB.   : 1963: Dr Wilkinson was appointed head of the new Department of Microbiology at King's Buildings which shared staff with the East of Scotland College of Agriculture. In this department, Dr Wilkinson's interests changed to studies of methane-utilising bacteria associated with possible commercial development of single cell protein. This work also had important implications for the production of cheap protein for the undernourished in the developing countries. These studies involved collaboration with British Petroleum at Grangemouth in a large research group financed in part by BP and SERC. Dr Wilkinson's researches led to many visits to universities in the USA, Europe and the Far East. He was awarded a Personal Chair in Microbiology in 1968.

AUTH. : Many scientific papers. Contributor to many textbooks.
RETIRED : 1989.

WILSON, Dr Alastair M.M.

GRAD. : 1939: University of Oxford, BA (Hons) Animal Physiology.
1942: BMBCh.
1959: Dip.Bact. London.
1966: FRCP.

P.G. : 1943 (Apr.-Nov.): Resident Medical Officer, Tuberculosis Department, Radcliffe Infirmary, Oxford.
1943: World War II. GD Medical Officer, RAF, UK and N.W. Europe.
1946: In charge of Nutrition Survey Team, British Zone, Germany.
1947: Registrar in Medicine and Pathology, Postgraduate Medical School, Hammersmith.
1948: Registrar in Pathology, Radcliffe Infirmary, Oxford.
1949: Senior Registrar in Pathology, Stoke Mandeville Hospital.
1960: Reader and Head of Department, Department of Medical Microbiology, Makerere University College Medical School.
1962: Professor and Head of Department, Department of Bacteriology, University of Ibadan, Nigeria.

J.D. : 1965: Senior Lecturer in Tropical Microbiology and Immunology; Honorary Consultant to Lothian Area Health Board.

SUB : 1973: Professor and Head of Department, Department of Medical Microbiology, University of Malaya.
1974: Consultant Microbiologist, City Hospital; Part-time Senior Lecturer, University Bacteriology Department.

S.I. : Recognition of the specific causes, prevalence of and geographical distribution of a wide range of locally important infectious diseases; whooping cough: laboratory diagnosis and vaccination (for PHLS); campylobacter infections; brucellosis.

RETIRED : 1980, 15 June.

WILSON, George

BORN : 1920, Edinburgh.
J.D. : 1951: December. Previous experience: A.H. Baird, Laboratory Supplies; Heriot-Watt College, Department of Physics, gained HNC Electrical Engineering.
1940: Served in Royal Navy.
1951: Responsible for maintenance of electron microscope; maintenance of departmental equipment and in charge of workshop.

S.I. : Attended three international conferences on electron microscopy at Rome, Prague and Philadelphia. Trained several visiting technicians in electron microscopy.

| RETIRED | : 1976. |
| DIED | : 1991, 6 June. |

WINTON, Dr Fred W.

GRAD.	: 1954: University of London (Barts), MB BS.
P.G.	: 1962: Central Microbiological Laboratories, Western General Hospital.
	1965: Lecturer, University Bacteriology Department.
	1970: Assistant then Consultant Bacteriologist, Vale of Leven Hospital, Dunbartonshire.
AUTH.	: Contributor to the bacteriological section of *A Companion to Medical Studies,* Blackwell, Vol. 2, 1970 and 2nd Ed., 1980.
DIED	: 1984: In post.

WRIGHT, Dr Helen A.

BORN	: 1895, Leith.
GRAD.	: 1926: University of Edinburgh MBChB.
	1930: DPH.
P.G.	: Medical Officer to Jeanes School, Kebete, Kenya.
J.D.	: 1930: Part-time research worker.
	1932: Appointed Bacteriologist and assistant Pathologist to Edinburgh Royal Hospital for Sick Children, holding this post for 11 years. During this period, had a close association with the University Bacteriology Department and with Dr Agnes McGregor, RHSC pathologist.
	1939: On outbreak of World War II, established Regional Laboratory of Emergency Medical Services at Ayr.
	1940: Transferred to Bangour Hospital to establish bacteriological service for this newly opened EMS hospital. Very many of the University Bacteriology Department's staff were on war service and Dr Wright's experienced services were made available in 1943 when she joined the full-time staff as lecturer. She took charge of much of the diagnostic laboratory work for Edinburgh Public Health Department and South East Scotland.
	1950: Senior Lecturer and Honorary Consultant Bacteriologist to the then South East of Scotland Regional Hospital Board.
S.I.	: From early 1930s was a recognised authority on diphtheria biotypes, collaborating with the then City Fever Hospital. Responsible for wide range of post-World War II diagnostic bacteriology and epidemiology studies with Edinburgh Public Health Department and Health Authorities of the three Lothian counties.
RETIRED	: 1960: Short period as bacteriologist at Astley Ainslie Hospital, Edinburgh.
DIED	: 1972, 27 August.

YOUNG, Dr James B.

Dr Young graduated in medicine at Edinburgh University in 1890, and later gained a DSc in Public Health and specialised in this subject. He was an assistant to Professor Sir Douglas Maclagen and later to Dr Henry Littlejohn, Edinburgh's first

Medical Officer of Health when the latter became Professor of the joint subjects of Forensic Medicine (earlier referred to as Medical Jurisprudence) and Public Health in 1892. When a separate Chair of Public Health was established in 1902 at the then newly opened Usher Institute, with Professor Charles Hunter Stewart as the first incumbent, Dr Young became his assistant and was given the task of organising a bacteriological laboratory in the Institute and subsequently a bacteriological diagnostic laboratory by arrangement with the Edinburgh Corporation Public Health Department as a service to the city's general practitioners. This was transferred in 1926 to the University Bacteriology Department.

Dr Young published many studies in bacteriology. Two of his contributions to the *Proceedings of the Royal Society of Edinburgh,* of which he was a Fellow, were: "A New Apparatus for Counting Bacteriological Colonies in Roll Cultures" (1893) and "Chemical and Bacteriological Examination of Soil", with special reference to graveyards. Dr Young died in March 1928.

ZEALLEY, Dr Helen Elizabeth

BORN	: 1940, 10 June.
GRAD.	: 1964: University of Edinburgh, MBChB.
	1968: MD (high commendation).
	1973: Dip. Soc. Med.
	1974: MFCM/MFPHM, by examination.
	1980: FFCM/FFPHM, by election.
	1987: FRCP(E), by election.
P.G.	: 1964-65: House physician/House surgeon, Northern General Hospital and Western General Hospital, Edinburgh.
	1965-72: SHO/Registrar, Regional Virus Laboratory, City Hospital, Edinburgh.
	1969-70: Lecturer, part-time. Department of Orthopaedics, Genetic Research Unit, University of Edinburgh.
	1970-72: Medical Adviser, Scottish Television.
	1972-75: Fellow in Community Medicine, Common Services Agency of the Scottish Health Service.
J.D.	: 1972-88: Research Fellow, Department of Bacteriology, University of Edinburgh.
SUB.	: 1975-77: Community Medicine Specialist, Lothian Health Board.
	1977-79: Community Medicine Specialist jointly with the Scottish Council for Postgraduate Medical Education and Lothian Health Board.
	1979-88: Honorary Member of Clinical Teaching Staff, Department of Community Medicine, University of Medicine.
	1979-88: Community Medicine Specialist, Child Health Services, Lothian Health Board.
	1988: Chief Administrative Medical Officer and Director of Public Health, Lothian Health Board. Honorary Senior Lecturer, Department of Public Health Sciences, University of Edinburgh.
S.I.	: Rubella and its prevention by immunisation; health needs and how these are identified; the impact of deprivation and disadvantage on community health, and the role of health care staff in identifying

these factors and determining possible action; the planning, organisation and management of health services.

DIST.   : 1989: Honeyman Gillespie Lectureship, Edinburgh.
1991: Wilfrid Harding Prize, Faculty of Public Health Medicine.

---

3. Untraceable Early Members of Staff

The following appear in the records of the Medical Microbiology Department, University of Edinburgh, as having worked briefly in the department, some perhaps as staff, others on brief research studies and possibly some as members of staff of other departments.

Chesser, Dr	1926-27
Chisholm, Dr	1926
Fraser, Dr	1928
Gardner, Dr	1939
Glazebrook, Dr A.J.	1939
Jones, Dr	1950
Kirkpatrick, Dr	1933-34
Krishnan, Dr G.K.V.	1924-29
Lawson, Dr A.W.B.	1953-56
McDermott, Dr G.G.	1926
Mackenzie, Dr	1934
Nimmo-Smith, Dr	1949
Osman, Dr	1926
Ruebner, Dr	1950-51
Seles, Dr Jessie	1924-25
Sproat, Dr T.	1923-24
Vogt, Dr	1928
Williams, Dr Bryan	1928-34
Williamson, Dr I.J.F.	1929
Wilson, Dr F.F.	1955

4. Senior Staff of the Department of Medical Microbiology, University of Edinburgh in 1992

Peutherer, Dr J.F.	Head of Department and Hon. Consultant
Weir, Professor D.M.	DMLSO
Anderson, Dr Felicity M.	Senior Lecturer and Consultant
Blackwell, Dr Cecelia C.	Senior Lecturer
Fraser, Dr A.G.	Senior Lecturer and Hon. Consultant
Gibb, Dr A.P.	Lecturer and Hon. Senior Registrar
Govan, Dr J.R.W.	Reader
Miles, Dr R.S.	Senior Lecturer and Hon. Consultant
Norval, Dr Mary	Senior Lecturer
Ogilvie, Dr Marie M.	Senior Lecturer and Hon. Consultant
Poxton, Dr I.R.	Senior Lecturer
Ross, Dr P.W.	Reader and Hon. Consultant
Simmonds, Dr P.N.	Lecturer and Hon. Senior Registrar
Smith, Dr Isabel W.	Senior Lecturer
Stewart, Dr J.	Lecturer
Young, Dr H.	Senior Lecturer
Brown, Dr Morag I.	Honorary Senior Lecturer
Emmanuel, Dr F.X.S.	Honorary Senior Lecturer
Guy, Dr K.	Honorary Fellow
Scott, Dr A.C.	Honorary Senior Lecturer
Watson, Dr K.C.	Honorary Senior Lecturer
Watt, Dr B.	Honorary Senior Lecturer
Wiseman, Dr R.	Honorary Senior Lecturer
Dickson, J.D.	Senior Chief MLSO
McInnes, G.J.	Senior Chief MLSO
Marr, W.	Senior Chief MLSO
Collins, Mrs J.	Senior Secretary
Combe, Mrs I.	Senior Clerical Officer
Newbigging, Mrs H.	Senior Secretary

5. Extra-mural Activities of Members of Staff and Students

In view of the variety and number of those who have served the University department – academic, technical, secretarial and other staff – and considering the innumerable succession of undergraduate and postgraduate students, it is not surprising that several who have passed through have had interesting extramural associations and quite notable talents. Some of these have achieved distinction in spheres outwith the department – in the church, in the arts, music and sport. In this chapter, we illustrate the rich versatility of many members of staff, some of whom continued their departmental duties while "making a name for themselves" elsewhere, whilst others chose to pursue their other interests full-time. As Professor T.J. Mackie's notably lengthy term of office extended to thirty-two years, most of the references are to staff of that period. The sequence is chronological.

Dr Thomas Gow Brown[147], who joined the staff in 1931, was a former pupil of George Heriot's School and a member of its notable F.P. Rugby Club. He was chosen to play for Scotland in 1929. Gow Brown also distinguished himself in athletic circles.

In the Scottish, English and international soccer world, the department may claim a little reflected glory from the achievements of Tommy Pearson[148] who was a junior technician in the department for a short period from 1931, and Sandy Cheyne, who in his younger days, played for Murrayfield Amateurs. In 1933, Pearson aged 19, signed professionally for Newcastle United, receiving a "signing on" fee of £20.00. While at Newcastle, Pearson, who played outside-left, was selected to play for Scotland which he did on several future occasions. He was to earn for himself a place in the *Guinness Book of Records*. On one occasion when the left-winger of the English international team was not available, the English manager asked Tommy to help out at the last minute. So a Scot trod the English left-wing! Alf Ramsay, the one-time English manager paid tribute to Tommy Pearson as the master of the "double shuffle". In 1948, Pearson signed for Aberdeen, and he later became manager of this club. He went on to be a sports writer for the *Daily Mail*. Perhaps football was in young Tommy Pearson's blood: his father had played for Heart of Midlothian and Tommy himself would have begun his career at Tynecastle had Newcastle not been ahead of Hearts in their offer. In the golfing world, Pearson won the Edinburgh Coronation Trophy twice and took part as a scratch player in the Open at Muirfield.

In a very different sphere were the interests and activities of a remarkable man who came to the department as a science student in about 1935. This was the 20th Earl of Suffolk and Berkshire[149,150]. He would be driven up to the Medical School each day by his chauffeur-batman who then spent the day in the department stoppering test tubes and otherwise assisting until His Grace was ready to go home! After about a year in the department, the Earl transferred his studies to the Pharmacology Department where he took a First Class Honours BSc in 1937. As a postgraduate, the Earl of Suffolk obtained a post as a research chemist in the Nuffield Laboratory in Oxford. In 1939, with the prospect of the Second World War, the Earl was appointed liaison officer in Paris between the British Ministry of Supply and the French Armaments Ministry. Following the collapse of the French Government in 1940, he returned to London and, not without great danger, secretly brought out with him valuable machinery plans and a huge and valuable collection of diamonds. At Bordeaux, he hid some of his precious cargo in a secluded place and then, with great difficulty, persuaded the Admiralty to send a destroyer to retrieve the diamonds. In his appearance, the Earl of Suffolk displayed the qualities historically attributed to his ancient and famous English family, often described as "those mad Howards". On account of his many adventures before coming to Edinburgh University, it was thought by some that his decision to study was a passing whim. His acquiring a First Class Honours degree certainly dispersed this view.

The Earl's daring, however, was to put a tragic end to his career. He had formed a Bomb Rescue Organisation to study methods of disposing of unexploded bombs. This dangerous task required not only courage but some scientific knowledge and expertise. The Earl recruited three volunteers and a lady secretary for the team. During the many London air raids, they were to be seen attired in old clothes and overalls in the restaurants and underground shelters. Alas, on 12 May, 1941, the team tackled a large German bomb that had lain in the open for some months, roped off. The Earl, a witness said, was measuring the bomb "like a Saville Row tailor attending a customer" when a gigantic explosion killed him and his several assistants and secretary. The George Cross was awarded posthumously for Conspicuous Bravery. A memorial window in the Church of St John the Baptist in Charlton, Wiltshire, commemorates one of "those mad Howards" who was fearless against danger. Charles Henry George Howard, the 20th Earl of Suffolk, was married to Mimi Crawford, a leading actress of the London West End theatre world.

Amongst the many anecdotes of Professor Mackie's "reign", another related to the world of the titled or distinguished. The Professor felt compelled to inquire of a female medical student around 1929 why she had rather a number of absences from his lectures (then virtually compulsory) and why she was missing on other occasions. What was the explanation? Apparently Mackie remarked to the girl that he understood she was frequently away opening garden fêtes and sales of work. Just who was she to be in such demand? The student's reply must have taken him aback. She told him she found herself involved at times in various public engagements since her father was the Prime Minister! One can perhaps imagine Professor Mackie's look of incredulity; hear the rattle of his keys, the light rapid cough! "Come, come . . !" On the cover of her examination books she had entered her address as No. 10 Downing Street. It was no hoax. It was all perfectly true. The female medical student was Joan Margaret MacDonald[151], younger daughter of Ramsay MacDonald, Prime Minister. Yes, her home address was indeed 10 Downing Street. Joan MacDonald was born in 1908 and matriculated at Edinburgh University in 1926. She graduated MBChB in 1932. In September of the same year, she married a fellow Edinburgh medical student of two years earlier, Dr Alastair McKinnon. Dr Joan McKinnon died as a result of a car accident in 1990.

In 1937 Dr Colin P. Beattie was appointed Professor of Bacteriology in the Royal Faculty of Medicine of Iraq University and Director of the Government Bacteriology Laboratory in Baghdad and also of the Pasteur Institute there. In the same year Professor Beattie and Dr May Christison, a member of the Edinburgh University staff, were married and set up home in Baghdad. In 1941 during the Second World War, Mrs Beattie[152] was evacuated to Miraj in India where she worked as a bacteriologist in the mission hospital. On returning in due course to Baghdad she worked at the British Embassy there. Searching in the markets for furnishings to replace those looted during wartime from their Baghdad home, Mrs Beattie began buying rugs and carpets of various kinds. She was eventually to become an expert on Oriental carpets. On their return to Britain, following Professor Beattie's appointment to the Chair of Bacteriology in Sheffield in 1946, Mrs Beattie further developed her interest and expertise in what she had begun as a hobby. By library studies and then travelling throughout Europe, North America, the Middle East and Africa, where she examined very many carpets and rugs, Mrs Beattie became an authority. She lectured and wrote widely on her subject. Thus, in 1987, in a special issue of the international journal dealing with Oriental carpets and rugs, tribute was paid: "It is our greatest pleasure to honour a distinguished colleague, friend and wonderful human being, May H. Beattie, PhD., on the approach of her 80th birthday. Internationally recognised as one of the great authorities on Oriental carpets, she has contributed a corpus of scholarship resounding with exemplary standards . . . Her infectious enthusiasm has probably left few rugs unturned!"

Enter stage left, Mr Andrew Downie[153] who made his mark in music, the theatre and television. Andrew, in a letter to the present writer outlining his career, began: "I really was never suited to the work in the lab . . ." Some former members of staff will still recall Andrew, his day's work in Lab. 4 over, fastening on his bicycle clips and losing no time in setting off for Methven Simpson's music shop then in Princes Street, for a rehearsal of the Edinburgh Bach Society Choir, of which he was principal tenor, under its distinguished conductor, Dr Mary Grierson; or on other occasions, singing with St Mary's Episcopal Cathedral Choir or that of St John's at the West End. The father of a departmental contemporary of Andrew Downie was to play an important part in encouraging and enabling him to become a professional singer and actor. This was Dr Herbert Wiseman, father of Dr Jean McNaughton, a member of the pioneer team with Dr J.P. Duguid and Dr S.W. Challinor and others who produced penicillin used in the Royal Infirmary. Dr Wiseman engaged Andrew to broadcast as a solo tenor in highly popular BBC music programmes for schools. For these performances, Andrew now admits slipping away from the laboratory for an hour or two – with or without the knowledge of technical "bosses" Sandy Cheyne and Robert Farmer – he doesn't quite remember!

The "crunch" had to come: the choice to be made. Remain as a technician or risk his fortune in the world of music and the theatre? In the same year as he passed his final examination for the Associate-ship of the then IMLT, Andrew was awarded a place at the Royal College of Music Opera School in London. Rather wondering how Professor Mackie would react to his resigning and launching out in the deep he was amazed at T.J.'s enthusiastic encouragement and praise for his initiative. In 1946, Downie won a Sir James Caird Travelling Scholarship for four years' study: three at the Royal College of Music, London. He subsequently won the Clara Butt award, recalling that with the prize-money he bought the ring for his engagement to Marion Studholme, who was to become one of Britain's leading operatic singers at Sadler's Wells. Other music awards followed, including a three-year bursary to study in Paris.

As regards his theatrical work, Andrew retains just pride in his appearance as one of the principal singers in Tyrone Guthrie's one and only Edinburgh Festival Production of Allan Ramsay's *The Gentle Shepherd*. Appearances in Guthrie's masterly productions of *The Thrie Estaites* followed, then tours with Marion in Canada, the USA and this country in Gilbert and Sullivan. Television work has included *The Sweeney, Dr Finlay's Case Book, Take the High Road,* along with advertising. Adviser in singing to the Royal Shakespeare Company, visiting professor of singing at Bergen, and for nineteen years Director of Opera at the Marley College, London, are amongst more recent work. Andrew's "sneaking away" to his early rehearsals was certainly to lead to rather more than he could ever have imagined!

The wide variety of extramural interests and activities of former members of departmental staff is further illustrated by Dr Nina Tulloch[154] who was a demonstrator and part-time lecturer in the department from 1940 until 1964. In 1962, quite by chance, Dr Tulloch's services – primarily her skills in house decorating – were enlisted by an Edinburgh minister who was pioneering the opening of the first Abbeyfield Home for the Elderly in Edinburgh. It was no passing "one-off" contribution. Dr Tulloch has remained heavily involved in the development of the Abbeyfield Society which now has twenty-seven houses in Edinburgh. She played an especially important part in the opening of the first Extra Care house in Ravelston Park for elderly people requiring special care but not full nursing. Dr Tulloch's medical training has proved particularly valuable in this new development. For her thirty years of service to the Society, Dr Tulloch, in September 1989, was presented with a Royal Patron's Award by the Duke of Westminster, the Abbeyfield President.

In this selection of former staff who have made names for themselves in other spheres, those who appear last in this account should perhaps have been referred to first – Divinity being traditionally "the queen of the sciences". Perhaps they may appropriately provide the Epilogue. Reference has been made in the main text of the department's history to Dr J. Ryland Whittaker[155], a lecturer who in the early 1930s became a Catholic priest of the Jesuit Order. Only one other member of staff has followed a religious vocation. This was a technician, John Caird[156]. John, who worked with Dr John Wilkinson and Dr Ian Sutherland in Lab. 3, married departmental technician colleague Anne Lodge in 1965. Soon afterwards they set off for Canada, John obtaining a post with a former departmental PhD student, Dr Gordon Wiseman, in the Department of Medical Microbiology in Winnipeg University. After ten years of service in this department, the work being mainly on staphylococcal toxins, John felt himself called to the Church and studied for a Master of Divinity degree, obtaining this in 1978. In the previous year he had been ordained to the Deaconate of the Anglican Church. In 1978 he was ordained priest. Two years later, he was appointed rector of a parish twenty-five miles north of Winnipeg. In 1983 he became rector of a large city parish. Outwith his clerical duties John upholds his Scottish heritage, being Bard of the St Andrew's Society of Winnipeg and Editor of a publication *The Saltire*. Teaching Scottish history is another of his activities at a School of Celtic Studies. Anne Caird was for some years a technician in the diagnostic bacteriology laboratory for the province of Manitoba.

147. *Dr T. Gow Brown*

148. *Tommy Pearson*

149. *The Earl and Countess of Suffolk*

150. *Earl of Suffolk (right) with bomb disposal colleague*

151. *Joan Margaret Macdonald with her Father, Ramsay Macdonald, Prime Minister*

152. *Dr May Beattie*

153. *Andrew Downie*

154. *Dr Nina Tulloch*

155. *Rev. Father J. Ryland-Whittaker*

156. *Rev. John Caird*

6. Obituaries

Early Bacteriology

Lord Joseph Lister. see Cheyne, W. Watson. *Lister and his achievement. First Lister Memorial Lecture.* Longmans Green, 1925.

Dr John B. Buist. *Br Med J* 1915; **1**: 274.

Sir William Watson Cheyne. *Lancet* 1932; **1**: 898 and 963. *Br Med J* 1932; **1**: 821-822.

Professor John Chiene. *Br Med J* 1923; **1**: 999-1002. *Edin Med J* 1923; **30**: 285-288.

Henry Duncan Littlejohn. *Br Med J* 1914; **2**: 648-650.

Professor German Sims Woodhead. *J Path Bact* 1922; **25**: 118-130.

Dr Claude B. Kerr. *Edin Med J* 1925; **32**: 265-269.

Sir Robert Muir. *Br Med J* 1959; **1**: 976 and 1050.

Sir Harold Stiles. *Lancet* 1946; **1**: 616 and 672. *Edin Med J* 1946; **53**: 458-461.

Departmental Professors

James Ritchie. *J Path Bact* 1923; **26**: 137-144. *Br Med J* 1923; **1**: 263-264. *Edin Med J* 1923; **30**: 124-127. *Lab Journal PBLAA* 1923; **5**: 86-88.

Thomas Jones Mackie. *J Path Bact* 1958; **76**: 605-620. *Br Med J* 1955; **2**: 973-974. Tribute by Sir Alexander Haddow, *Br Med J* 1955; **2**: 1092.

Robert Cruickshank. *J Med Microbiol* 1976; **9**: 503-512. *Br Med J* 1974; **3**: 582 and 633. *Lancet* 1974; **2**: 602-603. Portraits from memory, Professor Robert Cruickshank, by Sir James Howie. *Br Med J* 1988; **296**: 981-982.

Former Members of Staff or Referred to in Text

Mr. Robert Barr. *J Med Lab Tech* 1965; **22**: 241.

Professor Colin P. Beattie. *J Med Microbiol* 1988; **25**: 75-76. *Br Med J* 1987; **295**: 861. *Lancet* 1987; **2**: 753.

Dr John H. Bowie. *J Med Microbiol* 1985; **19-20**: 131-133.

Dr. Robert Cranston-Low. *Edin Med J* 1949; **56**: 163-164. *Roy Soc Edin Year Book* 1948-**49**; 26.

Mr Alexander Cheyne. Tribute by Professor J.G. Collee at University Memorial Service, Greyfriars Kirk, 14 November 1979; *Edin Univ Bulletin* October 1979. *Med Lab Sci* 1980; **37**: 97.

Lt.-Col. J. Cunningham. *Br Med J* 1968; : 503-504.

Professor Sir Stanley Davidson. *Br Med J* 1981; **283**: 993 and 1131. *Lancet* 1981; **2**: 819-820. The Scotsman 25 September 1981, Edinburgh.

Mr James Dick. *Med Lab Tech* 1972; **29**: 421.

Dr Elizabeth Edmond. *Br Med J* 1987; **294**: 452.

Dr Patrick N. Edmunds. *Br Med J* 1984; **288**: 249-250.

Dr T.F. Elias-Jones. *Br Med J* 1991; **32**: 405.

Professor Robert R. Gillies. *J Med Microbiol* 1984; **18**: 285-287.

Professor Cecil A. Green. *Br Med J* 1980; **280**: 802.

Professor Sir Alexander Haddow. *Br Med J* 1976; **1**: 287. *Lancet* 1976; **1**: 260-261.

Biographical memoirs of Fellows of the Royal Society

F. Bergel, *Proc Roy Soc* 1977; **23**: 133-191.

Dr Nancy Hayward. *J Med Microbiol* 1991; **34**: 239-240.

Dr. Alexander Joe. *Br Med J* 1962; **2**: 1620.

Dr Walter Levinthal. *Roy Soc Edin Year Book* 1963-64 (from *Zentralblat fur Bakteriologie* 1964; **193**: 137-139).

Dr William R. Logan. *Br Med J* 1948; **2**: 357.

Dr Gilbert Ludlam. *Br Med J* 1977; **1**: 517-518.

Dr James McCartney. *I.M.L.S. Gazette,* February 1980, 49-50. Obituaries in Australian publications not available. *Univ Edin J* 1969-1970; **24**: 208-209.

Dr John Mackay. *Vet Rec* 1976; **99**: 281.

Dr Joan M. McKinnon (née MacDonald). *Br Med J* 1989; **299**: 1026.

Dr Agnes Macgregor. *Br Med J* 1982; **284**: 590. Tribute by Dr Douglas Bain: Founders of Paediatric Pathology: Agnes Rose Macgregor, M.D., F.R.C.P.(E), F.R.C.O.G. In: *Perspectives in Paediatric Pathology* 1987; **2**: 1-5.

Dr Donald G.S. McLachlan. *J Path Bact* 1935; **41**: 571-572.

Mr Richard Muir. *Laboratory Journal PBLAA* 1931: **7**: 1-4.

Rev. Father J. Ryland-Whitaker, *S.J. Letters and Notices* 1965; **70**: No. 336, 49-56.

Professor Theodore Shennan. *J Path Bact* 1950; **62**: 461-467.

Dr A.H.C. Sinclair-Gieben. *Br Med J* 1963; **1**: 1351.

Dr Charles Hunter Stewart. *Edin Med J* 1924; **1**: 454.

Dr Richard H.A. Swain. *Br Med J* 1981; **283**: 1540-1541.

Professor Clennel E. van Rooyen. *Nova Scotia Med J* 1989; **68**: 74. (An Appreciation by Dr Alan J. MacLeod).

Dr W.N. Boog Watson. *Br Med J* 1973; **2**: 559.

Dr Helen A. Wright. *J Med Microbiol* 1973; **6**: 417-421.

Dr J.B. Young. *Br Med J* 1928; **1**: 614.

PORTRAITS

Dr W.A. Alexander

Dr Margaret Allan (née Kelly)

Dr W. Allan

Dr J. Alston

William Amos

Dr C.G. Anderson

Miss Nan Anderson

Douglas Annat

Douglas Armstrong

Norman Atack

Andrew Baillie

Dr G. Barclay (née Borthwick)

Sydney Barlow

Robert Barr

Professor C.P. Beattie

William Bertram

Dr K.A. Bisset

Dr G.P.B. Boissard

Dr W. Boog Watson

Henry Bott

Dr John H. Bowie

John Brennan

Dr T. Gow Brown

Dr Peter Brown

Professor C. Burrell

Dr Margaret Calder

Miss B. Campbell-Renton

Dr Sydney Challinor

Alexander B. Cheyne

Dr W. Watson Cheyne

Professor John Chiene

Duncan B. Colquhoun

Dr Nancy Conn

Dr Leonard Constable

Dr T. Cranston-Low

Dr Heather Cubie

Lieutenant Colonel John Cunningham

Professor Sir Stanley Davidson

Dr Ben Davies

Professor George Dempster

James Dick

Dr Andrew Douglas

John Dow

Professor Brian Duerden

Dr T.B.M. Durie

Dr Elizabeth Edmond

Dr Pat Edmunds

Dr T. Elias-Jones

John Ferguson

Dr J.C. Gould

Professor C.A. Green

Dr A. Sinclair-Gieben

Dr Eric Gowans

Dr J.D. Allan Gray

Sir Alexander Haddow

Dr Nancy Hayward

Miss Frances Henderson

Clark Henriksen

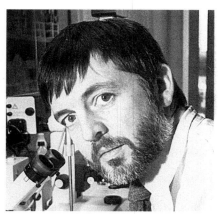

Dr Peter Holbrook

Dr John C.J. Ives

Dr Alexander Joe

Dr Claud Ker

Eric Kerr

Professor Hugh King

Mrs Jessie Lees (née Wallace)

Dr Walter Levinthal

Robert Lindsay

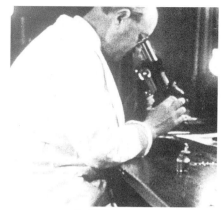

Dr William Logan

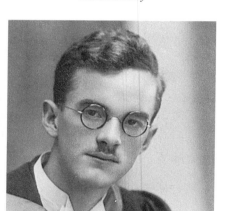

Dr Gilbert Ludlam

Dr Martin Ludlam

Professor W.H.R. Lumsden

Professor W.B. McBride

Dr Andrew McCabe

Dr J.E. McCartney

Dr Sheila McDonald

Dr Agnes McGregor

Sandy MacGregor

Dr John Mackay

Dr Pat Mackay

James A. McLeod

Dr Jean McNaughton (née Wiseman)

Dr Alastair Macrae

Dr Joan McWilliam

Dr Margaret Moffat

Richard Muir

Professor Sir Robert Muir

John Norval

Dr R.K. Oag

Dr Helga Ogmundsdottir

William Poole

Dr Isabella Purdie

Dr R. Rattrie

Professor A.J. Rhodes

Ian Robb

James Robertson

Dr M. Robertson

Rev. Father S.J. Ryland-Whittaker

Ian Samuel

Professor Sydney Selwyn

Dr Stuart Semple

Dr Theodore Shennan

Professor Douglas Sleigh

Dr J. Smeall

C.J. Smith

James Smith

Dr Sheila Stewart

Sir Harold Stiles

Professor Ian Sutherland

James Sutherland

Dr R.H.A. Swain

Dr A. Telfer-Brunton

Professor Scott Thomson

Dr J. Tinne

Dr Ralph Tonkin

Dr Nina Tulloch

William Valentine

Professor C.E. Van Rooyen

Dr A. Wallace

Dr Brian Watt

William Webber

Robert Weir

Professor J. Wilkinson

George Wilson

Dr F. Winton

Dr Helen A. Wright

Dr Helen Zealley

POSTSCRIPT AND PROSPECT

by J. G. Collee

It is difficult to close the chapters of this account of a subject that has bourgeoned so remarkably and is yet again in another phase of exponential growth. As Charles Smith has recorded so carefully, Medical Microbiology in Edinburgh has been very well served by many dedicated and able people with much help from colleagues in various other disciplines. In the preceding pages, biographical notes of past members of staff of the University department and some important departmental associates are recorded. We had to draw a line somewhere, and we trust that present members of staff, and colleagues serving in other institutes, will forgive our leaving their historical record to another volume. The next account will surely note further significant contributions.

In Virology, there has been continuing success in elucidating the hepatitis B problem. Collaborative work at the University and at the Department of Molecular Biology with Professor Sir Kenneth Murray eventually led to the development of the Edinburgh University-Biogen link and the production of a successful vaccine. Work with the virus of AIDS (Human Immunodeficiency Virus, HIV) prospered with pioneering studies on a haemophiliac cohort and on drug-abusing groups. The Edinburgh research is contributing significantly to advances in the detection of HIV-antibody and antigen. Good work has been developed to elucidate mechanisms of ultraviolet activation of herpes simplex virus in the skin and to investigate the association of papillomaviruses with cancer. Studies on chlamydiae in relation to pelvic inflammatory disease and other infections have been rewarding.

In Bacteriology, the pseudomonas problems of cystic fibrosis patients yielded a rich seam of research of great biomedical interest. Studies of antibacterial drugs in various laboratories across the city have progressed, and key work on bacterial resistance mechanisms has been internationally acknowledged. The University department now accommodates the Scottish Antibiotic Reference Laboratory.

The Mycology Unit at the Central Microbiological Laboratories has done increasingly important work as yeast and fungal infections posed so many serious threats to compromised patients. Similarly, the City Hospital bacteriologists and virologists have been required to expand their expertise to cope with an extending spectrum of difficult clinical challenges. Rapid virological diagnosis is progressing. The establishment and development of the Scottish Mycobacteria Reference Laboratory at the City Hospital has been of major significance as the tubercle bacillus and related pathogens have posed worrying clinical problems.

Early work done in the past on scrapie in sheep by veterinary research workers at Moredun, Edinburgh, has assumed great importance with the advent of bovine spongiform encephalopathy (BSE) and the setting up of the joint AFRC-MRC Neuropathogenesis Laboratory. Other microbiological work by our veterinary colleagues has been of value in medical microbiology, with very useful studies on topics ranging from Johne's disease (paratuberculosis) to toxoplasmosis and from salmonellosis to ornithosis. Joint studies on leptospirosis produced work of special clinical value, and collaborative work on campylobacter infections and brucellosis and various other zoonoses has been most productive.

Traditional links with the Edinburgh Corporation Public Health Department (now Environmental Health) and the community medical and veterinary officers have greatly helped the cause of medical microbiology in Edinburgh. Links with the School of Dentistry have also been of great value, with collaborative contributions on periodontal infections and immunology and important advances in the characterisation and isolation of streptococci, anaerobic cocci and bacteroides organisms. Over the years, students of special calibre have been recruited to the Honours School in the University department from the ranks of the medical and dental classes and from Veterinary Medicine and the Science Faculty.

Within the department, the anaerobic bacteria continued to demand attention to elucidate the range of the infections in which they were involved and to isolate and identify the many species and subspecies concerned. Parallel work was done at the Bacteriology Laboratory at the City Hospital. We had to come to terms with pathogenic synergy in guiding the clinical management of many anaerobic and mixed infections. Edinburgh's contributions to the laboratory characterisation of pathogenic anaerobes have been gratifying, and our standardisation of anaerobic methodology was rewarding at a critical time in the development of the relevant technology. In common with other bacteriologists, we now look more positively at the defensive value of peroperative antimicrobial prophylaxis. Bacteriologists in the University department and at the Central Microbiological Laboratories worked along similar lines to develop effective strategies to protect our increasing numbers of neutropenic patients against opportunistic infections in the wards. And we helped to untangle the difficult web of antibiotic-associated diarrhoea and pseudomembranous colitis. Hospital infection control at last came into its own in our area and we began to catch up with the twentieth century in its last decade (though we have still so far to go). It is interesting that, in Edinburgh as elsewhere, we have been so slow to re-learn the infection-control teaching of Lister and Simpson and Pringle and Semmelweiss in our clinical and laboratory practice.

We have looked intensively at possible links between blood group secretor status and susceptibility to a range of diseases, and we have investigated possible microbial triggers of pathology in various conditions including diabetes, ankylosing spondylitis and thyrotoxicosis. Other collaborative studies on possible immunotherapeutic approaches to the treatment or prevention of septic shock in patients at risk have progressed. Our ability to diagnose, monitor and manage a range of sexually transmissible diseases has advanced considerably. We are now much better able to monitor the levels of some potentially toxic antibiotics in our patients, and we are very much better at blood culture methodology to detect bacteraemia at an early stage. The computerisation of our clinical bacteriological and virological laboratory services has been a huge and very successful undertaking.

The assessment and prediction of the relative value of a contribution in the vast field of medical microbiology and its related disciplines is almost impossible. The great importance of Duguid's work on the airborne transmission of respiratory pathogens could have been anticipated, but the special significance of his team's remarkable researches on bacterial fimbriae could not have been foreseen. Our exploitation of Nagler and Hayward's work on lecithinase-C was a rational progression. Our subsequent interest in the bacteroides organisms had a much greater clinical application than we could at first appreciate. Watt's preoccupation with the anaerobic cocci was thought to be another frustrating sideline until his group produced findings that led to his definitive paper on the characterisation of these underrated organisms (which the Newcastle workers had appreciated). Very painstaking work by Marmion and Norval set the record straight in the confusing field of rheumatoid arthritis, where so many misleading claims had been made by other workers who thought that they had established a microbial cause. Across the city, good microbiological links were strengthened, and we continued to send able colleagues to senior posts furth of Edinburgh and abroad. In turn, these ambassadors encouraged us by giving us opportunities for special training in their laboratories and by sending further recruits to our ranks.

In this context, Edinburgh's contributions to microbiological texts merit mention. Charles Smith has paid tribute to Mackie and McCartney's manual which is now being prepared for its 14th Edition, having generated a companion volume that has been well received. Many other microbiological and immunological textbooks have been produced from Edinburgh, and many of our microbiologists and microbial immunologists have been committed to the editing of a range of scientific journals which have a major impact on our disciplines. There is a continuing challenge to keep pace with developments while maintaining standards of precision and care.

The real challenge is to develop the technological and intellectual resources to appreciate and to respond to change and to meet the new demands of a subject that cannot stand still. Edinburgh's past history and present energies equip it well to carry its significant contributions into the new century.

BIBLIOGRAPHY

Anderson C.G. (1938) *An Introduction to Bacteriological Chemistry.* E&S Livingstone, Edinburgh.

Avery O.T., MacLeod C.M., McCarty M. (1944) Studies on the chemical nature of the substance inducing transformation of pneumococcal types. *J Exp Med* **79**: 137-158.

Bain D. (1987) Founders of Paediatric Pathology: Agnes Rose Macgregor. *Perspectives in Paediatric Pathology* **2**: 1-5.

Bell J. (1887) *Notes on Surgery for Nurses.* Oliver & Boyd, Edinburgh.

Bisset K.A. (1970) *The Cytology and Life History of Bacteria.* 2nd edn. E&S Livingstone, Edinburgh.

Boog Watson W.N. (1967) Sir John Murray – A chronic student. *Univ Edin J* **23**: 123-138.

Bourdillon R.B., Lidwell O.M., Thomas R.C. (1941) A slit sampler for collecting and counting airborne bacteria. *J Hyg* (Camb) **41**: 197-224.

Bowie J.H. (1955) Modern apparatus for sterilisation. *Pharm J* **174**: 473-489.

Bowie J.H. (1957) Surgical dressing steriliser of classical form: Suggestions for design, installation, maintenance and operation. *The Hospital Engineer* **11**: 74-98.

Bowie J.H. (1958) Requirements for an automatically controlled, high pre-vacuum steriliser. *Health Bulletin* (Edinburgh) **16**: 36-40.

Bowie J.H., Campbell I.D., Gillingham F.G., Gordon A.R. (1963) Hospital sterile supplies : Edinburgh pre-set tray system. *Br Med J* **2**: 1322.

Bowie J.H., Kelsey J.C., Thompson G.R. (1963) The Bowie and Dick autoclave tape test. *Lancet* **1**: 586 and 1215.

Campbell N. (1983) Earl of Suffolk and Berkshire (1906-1941). *Univ Edin J* Special Issue, June, **31** No. 1: 70-72.

Catford E.F. (1984) *The Royal Infirmary of Edinburgh:* 1929-1979. Scottish Academic Press, Edinburgh.

Chiene J. (1884) On the Desirability of Establishing Bacteriological Laboratories in Connection with Hospital Wards. (Paper read to Section of Physiology and Pathology at the 52nd Meeting of the British Medical Association, 1884). *Br Med J* **11**: 653.

Chiene J. (1908) Looking Back: 1907-1960. Reprinted from *The Student*, **1** 15 November, 1907, 53-60; **2**, 22 November, 1907, 101-108; **3**, 29 November, 1907, 149-161. Darien Press, Edinburgh.

Cheyne W. Watson (1889) Suppuration and Septic Diseases. Three lectures delivered at the Royal College of Surgeons of England, London, 1888. Young J. Pentland, Edinburgh and London.

Cheyne W. Watson (1925) Lister and his Achievement. First Lister Memorial Lecture delivered at the Royal College of Surgeons of England, London, 14 May, 1925. Longmans Green, London.

Comrie J.D. (1927) *History of Scottish Medicine to 1860.* 2 vols. Wellcome Historical Medical Museum, London. Bailliere, Tindall and Cox, London.

Cruickshank R. (1964) World Health Organization Edinburgh-Baroda Project in Medical Education. *Postgrad Med J* **40**: 311-312.

Cruickshank R. (1968) *Medical Microbiology.* E&S Livingstone, Edinburgh. (11th edition of Mackie and McCartney's: *A Handbook of Practical Bacteriology.*)

De Waal H.L. (1940) The serological types of haemolytic streptococci in relation to the epidemiology of scarlet fever and its complications. *J Hyg* (Camb) **40**: 172-203.

De Waal H.L. (1941) A study of the serological types of haemolytic streptococci in relation to the epidemiology of scarlatina and other infections due to these organisms. *J Hyg* (Camb) **41**: 65-99.

Dodzhansky T. (1941) *Genetics and the origin of species.* Columbia University Press, New York.

Duguid J.P. (1946a) The size and duration of air carriage of respiratory droplets and droplet-nuclei. *J Hyg* (Cam) **44**: 471-479.

Duguid J.P. (1946b) The sensitivity of bacteria to the action of penicillin. *Edin Med J* **53**: 401-412.

Duguid J.P., Gillies R.R. (1957) Fimbriae and adhesive properties in dysentery bacilli. *J Path Bact* **74**: 397-411.

Duguid J.P., Old D.C. (1980) Adhesive properties in Enterobacteriaceae. In: *Bacterial Adherence* vol 6. Ed. E.H. Beachey. Chapman and Hall, London; pp. 185-217.

Duguid J.P., Smith I.W., Dempster G., Edmunds P.N. (1955) Non-flagellar filamentous appendages ("fimbriae") and haemagglutinating activity in *Bacterium coli. J Path Bact* **70**: 335-348.

Duguid J.P., Wallace A.T. (1948) Air infection with dust liberated from clothing. *Lancet* **2**: 845-849.

Duvall E., Currie A.R. (1981) *Department of Pathology. The First Hundred Years: 1831-1931. To mark the 150th anniversary of the founding of the Chair of Pathology.* Printed by the University of Edinburgh.

Edinburgh Corporation Public Health Department, (1902, 1903, 1904, 1905, 1926, 1927 and 1948) *Annual Reports.*

Gibson H.J., Thomson W.A.R., Stewart D. (1933) Haemolytic streptococcus as a factor in causation of acute rheumatism. *Arch Dis Childhood* **8**: 57-72.

Gillies R.R. (1968) *Lecture Notes on Bacteriology.* Blackwell Scientific Publications, Oxford.

Gillies R.R., Dodds T.C. (1965) *Bacteriology Illustrated.* E&S Livingstone, Edinburgh.

Gordon M. (1937) Virus bodies. John Buist and the elementary bodies of vaccinia. *Edin Med J* **44**: 65-71.

Gortner R.A. (1938) Outlines of Biochemistry. Wiley, New York, 2nd edn.

Gould J.C. (1958) Environmental penicillin and penicillin-resistant *Staphylococcus aureus. Lancet* **1**: 489-493.

Gould J.C., Bowie J.H. (1952) The determination of bacterial sensitivity to antibiotics. *Edin Med J* **59**: 178-199.

Graham J. (1951) Sir John Fraser and his contributions to Surgery. *Edin Med J* **58**: 105-124.

Griffith F. (1928) The significance of pneumococcal types. *J Hyg* (Camb) **27**: 113-159.

Grant A. (1884) *The Story of the University of Edinburgh during its First Three Hundred Years.* 2 vols. Longmans Green, London.

Gray T.M. (1991) The Lister Institute site, Lauriston Place. The Lister Cooperative Ltd. Typescript of Notes by T.M. Gray, Architect, from the files of Gray Marshall and Associates, Edinburgh.

Green, C.A., Challinor S.W., Duguid J.P. (1945) Bacteriological investigation of air during an epidemic of haemolytic streptococcal throat infections. *Ann Rheumatic Dis* **5**: 36-48.

Guthrie D. (1960) *The Royal Edinburgh Hospital for Sick Children: 1860-1960.* Churchill Livingstone, Edinburgh.

Hackett C.J. (1963) On the Origin of the Human Treponematoses. *Bull Wld Hlth* **29**: 7-41.

Hershkey A.D., Chase M. (1953) Independent functions of viral protein and nucleic acid in growth of bacteriophage. *J Gen Physiol* **36**: 39-56.

Howard G. (1969) My Elizabethan Brother, the Earl of Suffolk. *Reader's Digest* November, **95**: 133-144.

Howie J.W. (1978) *Code of Practice for the Prevention of Infection in Clinical Laboratories and Post-mortem Rooms* (The Howie Code) HMSO, London.

Howie J.W. (1987) Public Health Microbiological Services (Scotland). In: *Improving the Common Weal: Aspects of Scottish Health Services 1900-1984.* Ed G. McLachlan. Nuffield Provident Hospital Fund in association with Edinburgh University Press, Edinburgh, pp. 443-456.

Howie J.W. (1988) Portraits from memory: Professor Robert Cruickshank. *Br Med J* **296**: 981-2.

Howie J.W., Timbury M.C. (1956) Laboratory tests of operating-theatre sterilisers. *Lancet* **2**: 669-673.

Keir D. (1951) *The Younger Centuries. The Story of William Younger and Co. Ltd., 1749-1949.* McLagan & Cumming, Edinburgh.

Lees R. (1961) The Lock Wards of Edinburgh Royal Infirmary. *Br J Venereal Dis* **37**: 187-189.

Linklater E. (1972) *The Voyage of the Challenger.* J Murray, London.

Lister J. (1909) *The Collected Papers of Joseph, Baron Lister.* 2 vols. The Clarendon Press, Oxford.

Low R.C., Dodds T.C. (1947) *Atlas of Bacteriology.* E&S Livingstone, Edinburgh.

Lund E. (1883) The Present Aspect of the Antiseptic Question. The Substance of the Oration for the year 1883 before the Medical Society of London. J.E. Cornish, London.

McAdam I.W.J. (1945) Penicillin treatment of acute haematogenous osteomyelitis. *Br J Surg* **33**: 167-172.

McAdam I.W.J., Duguid J.P., Challinor S.W. (1944) Systemic administration of penicillin. *Lancet* **2**: 336-338.

Mackie L.W. (1987a) May Hamilton Beattie. In: *Oriental Carpet and Textile Studies* **3**. Part I. Eds. R. Pinner, W. B. Denny. HALI Publications, London, pp. 6-11.

Mackie L.W. (1987b) A Bibliography of the Works of May H. Beattie. In: *Oriental Carpet and Textile Studies* **3**. Part I. Eds. Pinner R., Denny W.B., HALI Publications, London, pp. 12-14.

Mackie T.J. (1924a) Discussion on immunity with special reference to specificity and influence of non-specific factors. The specificity of acquired immunity and non-specific factors in immunisation. *Br Med J.* **2**: 1100-1102.

Mackie T.J. (1924a) Collaboration in laboratory methods. In: *Recent methods in the Diagnosis and Treatment of Syphilis.* Eds C. H. Browning, I. McKenzie, 2nd edn, London.

Mackie T.J. (1928) An inquiry into post-operative tetanus – a Report to the Scottish Board of Health. HMSO, Edinburgh.

Mackie T.J., McLachlan D.G.S., Anderson E.J.M. (1929) Certain factors that promote the development of the tetanus bacillus in the tissues, with special reference to post-operative tetanus – An experimental inquiry. A Report to the Department of Health for Scotland. HMSO, Edinburgh.

Mackie T.J. (1946) The basis of penicillin therapy. Honeyman Gillespie Lecture delivered in Edinburgh Royal Infirmary, 19 July 1945. *Edin Med J* **53**: 1-14.

Mackie T.J., van Rooyen C.E. (1937) John Brown Buist (1846-1915). An acknowledgment of his early contributions to the bacteriology of variola and vaccinia. *Edin Med J* **44**: 72-80.

Maclean U. (1975) *The Usher Institute and the Evolution of Community Medicine in Edinburgh*. Department of Community Medicine, Edinburgh.

Marquand D. (1977) *Ramsay MacDonald*. Jonathan Cape, London.

Muir R. *Muir's Bacteriological Atlas*. E&S Livingstone, Edinburgh 1927.

Muir R., Hamilton D.J. (1910-11) Pathology. In: *Encyclopaedia Britannica*. 11th edn. Cambridge University Press, Cambridge, pp 913-926.

Muir R., Ritchie J. (1897) *Manual of Bacteriology*. Oxford University Press, Oxford.

Neufeld F., Handel L. (1909) Ueber Herstellung und Prufung von Antipneumiokokkenserum und uber die Aussichten einer spezifischen Behandlung der Pneumonie. *Z. Immunitats Forsch* **3**: 159-171.

Neufeld F., Levinthal W. (1928) Beitrage zur Variabitat der Pneumokokken. *Z. Immunitats Forsch* **55**: 324-340.

Ritchie J. (1953) *History of the Laboratory of the Royal College of Physicians of Edinburgh*. Royal College of Physicians, Edinburgh.

Ross J.A. (1978) *The Edinburgh School of Surgery after Lister*. Churchill Livingstone, Edinburgh and New York.

Report (1885) *Records of the Tercentenary Festival of the University of Edinburgh, Celebrated in April 1884*. University of Edinburgh.

Report (1902) Bacteriological Examinations for the City by R.C.P. Laboratory. *Br Med J* **1**: 805-806.

Report (1938) Hawick Typhoid Epidemic. Account of discovery of carrier. *Glasgow Herald*, 26 May 1938.

Report (1939) *Annual Report, Department of Health for Scotland 1938*. HMSO, Edinburgh.

Report (1942) Smallpox. Edinburgh and District Outbreak 1942. In: *Edinburgh Corporation Public Health Department Annual Report, 1942*.

Report (1964) Medical Research Council Working Party's report on sterilisation by steam under increased pressure. *Lancet* **2**: 193-195.

Report (1964) *The Aberdeen Typhoid Outbreak. Report of the Departmental Committee of Enquiry*. Scottish Home and Health Department HMSO.

Selwyn S. (1965) Sir James Simpson and hospital cross-infection. *Med Hist* **9**: 214-248.

Selwyn S. (1966) Scottish Pioneers Against Hospital Cross-Infection. (Paper delivered to Scottish-Scandinavian Conference on Infectious Diseases, Edinburgh, 7 September 1965.) *Scot Med J* **11**: 21-24.

Selwyn S. (1991) Hospital Infection: the first 250 years. *J Hosp Inf* **18** (Suppl. A): 5-64.

Selwyn S., Wardlaw A.C. (1983) Microbiology, including Virology. Two Hundred Years of the Biological Sciences in Scotland. *Proc Roy Soc Edin* **84 B**: 267-293.

Smith C.J. (1978) *Historic South Edinburgh. Volume I.* Charles Skilton, Edinburgh and London.

Smith C.J. (1979) *Historic South Edinburgh. Volume II.* Charles Skilton, Edinburgh and London.

Smith C.J. (1986) *Historic South Edinburgh. Volume III. People.* Charles Skilton, Whittingeham House, East Lothian and Cheddar, Somerset.

Smith C.J. (1988) *Historic South Edinburgh. Volume IV. People.* Albyn Press. Whittingeham House, East Lothian.

Smith C.J. (1989a) *South Edinburgh in Pictures.* Albyn Press, Whittingeham House, East Lothian.

Smith C.J. (1989b) *Between the Streamlet and the Town. The History of the Astley Ainslie Hospital.* Polton House Press, Edinburgh.

Stewart C. (1973) *The Past Hundred Years: The Buildings of the University of Edinburgh.* Edinburgh University Press, Edinburgh.

Swain R.H.A. (1955) Electron microscopic studies of the morphology of pathogenic spirochaetes. *J Path Bact* **69**: 117.

Swain R.H.A. (1957) The electron-microscopical anatomy of *Leptospira canicola. J Path Bact* **73**: 397-411.

Tait H.P. (1974) *A Doctor and Two Policemen. The History of the Edinburgh Health Department, 1862-1974.* Edinburgh Corporation Public Health Department, Edinburgh. Turner A. Logan (1933) *History of the University of Edinburgh, 1883-1933.* Oliver & Boyd, Edinburgh.

Turner A. Logan (1937) *Story of a Great Hospital. The Royal Infirmary of Edinburgh: 1729-1929.* Oliver & Boyd, Edinburgh.

Van Rooyen C.E. (1937) Muir's Bacteriological Atlas. 2nd edn. E&S Livingstone, Edinburgh.

Van Rooyen C.E., Rhodes A.J. (1940) *Virus Diseases of Man.* Oxford University Press, Oxford. Williams T.I. (1984) *Howard Florey. Penicillin and After.* Oxford University Press, Oxford.

Wright H.A. (1950) Bacteriological Services: The First Fifty years. In: *Annual Report.* Edinburgh Corporation Public Health Department, Edinburgh. pp. 63-66.

ARS LONGA VITA BREVIS

Drawing of the quadrangle clock, Edinburgh Medical School,
by Tom Gray F.R.I.C.S., Architect, January 1993.